MODERN WAR STUDIES

North American Spies

New Revisionist Essays

edited by
Rhodri Jeffreys-Jones
and
Andrew Lownie

UNIVERSITY PRESS OF KANSAS

© The Contributors, 1991

Published by the University Press of Kansas (Lawrence, Kansas 66049), which was organized by the Kansas Board of Regents and is operated and funded by Emporia State University, Fort Hays State University, Kansas State University, Pittsburg State University, the University of Kansas, and Wichita State University.

Library of Congress Cataloging-in-Publication Data
North American spies : new revisionist essays / edited by Rhodri
  Jeffreys-Jones and Andrew Lownie.
    p.   cm.—(Modern war studies)
  Includes bibliographical references and index.
  ISBN 0 7006 0525 8 (hardcover)
    1. United States—History. Military—20th century. 2. Spies—
United States—History—20th century. 3. Spanish-American War—
Secret service—United States. 4. World War, 1939–1945—Secret
service—United States. 5. United States. Central Intelligence
Agency—History. 6. United States. Defense Intelligence Agency—
History. I. Jeffreys-Jones, Rhodri. II. Lownie, Andrew.
III. Series.
E745.N67 1991
327.1273'09—dc20   91–36303

Printed in Great Britain

ISBN 0 7006 0525 8

Contents

Acknowledgements   vi

About the contributors   vii

Foreword   x

1 Introduction: the stirrings of a new revisionism?
   Rhodri Jeffreys-Jones   1

2 The secret operations of Spanish consular officials
within Canada during the Spanish–American war
   Graeme S. Mount   31

3 Tyler Kent: isolationist or spy?
   Andrew Lownie   49

4 Democracy goes to war: politics, intelligence and
decision making in the United States in 1942
   David Walker   79

5 The OSS and the Burma Road 1942–45
   Richard B. Laidlaw   102

6 The Missouri Gang and the CIA
   Danny D. Jansen and Rhodri Jeffreys-Jones   123

7 British McCarthyism
   Karen Potter   143

8 The birth of the Defense Intelligence Agency
   Patrick Mescall   158

9 The Bold Easterners revisited: the myth of the CIA
élite
   Robert E. Spears, Jr   202

10 Sense and sensationalism in American spy fiction
   Katy Fletcher   218

A guide to further study   241

Index   254

Acknowledgements

The authors and editors thank a number of individuals for their help in preparing this book for publication. Several scholars and novelists and one former United States Secretary of Defense gave advice on various points or read and constructively criticised one or more chapters. They include Harry C. Allen (emeritus, University of East Anglia), Daniel Calhoun (University of California, Davis), John Costello, Philip J. Davies (University of Manchester), Alan Furst, S.J. Hamrick, Norman A. Graebner (emeritus, University of Virginia), David Ignatius, Loch K. Johnson (University of Georgia), Warren F. Kimball (Rutgers University, Newark), C. Roland Marchand (University of California, Davis), Peter D. Marshall (emeritus, University of Manchester), Angus MacKay (University of Edinburgh), Robert S. McNamara, Paul Preston (Queen Mary and Westfield College, University of London), Faith Pullin (University of Edinburgh), Victor H. Rothwell (University of Edinburgh), Jill Stephenson (University of Edinburgh), Lord Thomas of Swynnerton, John A. Thompson (University of Cambridge), George A. ('Sam') Shepperson (emeritus, University of Edinburgh), Wesley K. Wark (University of Toronto) and D. Cameron Watt (London School of Economics).

Martin Spencer, who achieved so much for scholarly publishing as director, successively, of the university presses at Manchester and Edinburgh, encouraged our project in a positive manner. Following his untimely death, Maureen Prior gave unstinting support on behalf of Edinburgh University Press. Michael Briggs of the University of Kansas Press was most helpful editorially, and expeditious in arranging American publication. The editors further would like to thank Toby and Linda Morris, whose word-processing skills helped to make the editing of this book a pleasurable task.

About the contributors

RHODRI JEFFREYS-JONES is a Reader in the Department of History at the University of Edinburgh, where he set up and still teaches 'American espionage, 1898–1981', a one-year postgraduate course leading to the degree of M.Sc. in History (hereinafter, M.Sc./American Espionage). At the University College of Wales, Aberystwyth, he won the Alun Lewis Memorial Prize in History. After obtaining his doctorate from Cambridge University he was a Charles Warren Fellow at Harvard University. His latest book, *The CIA and American Democracy* (New Haven: Yale Univ. Press, 1989), met with widespread critical acclaim. He is currently the general editor of Perspectives in Intelligence History, a new series of books being launched by Edinburgh University Press.

ANDREW LOWNIE attended Fettes College, Edinburgh, whence he won an English Speaking Union Scholarship to North Carolina. He received his MA from the University of Cambridge, where he specialised in American history, took the Dunster History Prize and served as President of the Union. He subsequently graduated from Edinburgh, M.Sc./American Espionage. As a London and Edinburgh literary agent he represents authors from locations as diverse as Australia and Number 10, Downing Street. He writes regularly for the London *Times* on intelligence matters and is the author of *A Literary Guide to Edinburgh* (Edinburgh: Canongate, 1992).

KATY FLETCHER graduated MA from the University of Edinburgh, and, thereafter, M.Sc./American Espionage. She writes widely on spy fiction and recently published, with Donald McCormick, *Spy Fiction: A connoisseur's guide* (Oxford: Facts On File, 1990).

DANNY D. JANSEN was one of the last contingent to be drafted into the United States Army at the time of the Vietnam War. In Vietnam, he was a jungle fighter with the Rangers, and refused to participate in the Phoenix assassination programme. He dropped out of the University of Kansas on his return home, to serve with the Hazardous Materials Team for Kansas City fire department. After a chemical-poisoning work accident, he resumed his education and interest in intelligence matters, took a history BA from Avila College and travelled to Edinburgh to graduate M.Sc./American Espionage.

RICHARD B. LAIDLAW retired at the rank of Lieutenant-Colonel from the British Army. After some years in general medical practice, he graduated from Edinburgh, M.Sc./American Espionage.

GRAEME S. MOUNT is Professor of History at the Laurentian University, Sudbury, Ontario. His most recent book is, with Edelgard E. Mahant, *An Introduction to Canadian–American Relations* (2nd ed: Toronto: Nelson, 1989). His chapter is based on the paper with which he inaugurated the 1989–90 seminar series of the University of Edinburgh North American Studies Programme.

PATRICK MESCALL is a graduate of Fordham University who won a St Andrews Society of New York scholarship to study in Edinburgh, where he graduated M.Sc./American Espionage in 1990. He is the only history graduate student in any field to have obtained the M.Sc. degree 'with distinction' since the inauguration of the programme in 1983.

KAREN POTTER attended the University of Edinburgh on a Rotary International fellowship for post-graduate study in 1982–83. She is a graduate of Southern Methodist University in Dallas, Texas. She works in Austin, Texas, as the capitol bureau chief for the *Fort Worth Star-Telegram* newspaper, reporting on and overseeing coverage of Texas government and politics.

ROBERT E. SPEARS JR, studied at Wake Forest University, North Carolina, where he became Junior Varsity National Champion in the competition held annually by the American Debate Association. Spending his junior year at the University of Edinburgh, he became in 1990 the first non-British student to carry off the class medal in American history.

DAVID WALKER took his MA at the University of Edinburgh before graduating from the same institution M.Sc./American Espionage. He then won a St Andrews Society scholarship to study at the University of California, Davis. He has published several items on intelligence problems in the Second World War, and is currently completing a doctoral dissertation titled 'United States intelligence, 1941–45: evaluation and influence'.

Foreword

This collection of essays appears in a new series of books called *Perspectives in Intelligence History*. Some volumes in the series will trace the history of foreign intelligence in particular countries over a number of decades. Others, like the essays in this volume, offer new perspectives on special aspects of intelligence history. Every book in the series will be based to the fullest possible extent on verifiable evidence.

Until quite recently, most historians of international relations took little or no account of the role of secret intelligence. They were deterred both by the problems of source material, most of which was either banned or unusually difficult to track down, and by the books on espionage garishly displayed at airport bookstalls which seemed to suggest that intelligence was no subject for serious scholars. This volume is the work of a new and adventurous generation of intelligence historians, associated with the pioneering MSc course on American espionage at Edinburgh University, who are rightly convinced that any history of international relations which neglects intelligence is at best incomplete and at worst distorted.

Many obstacles still confront the intelligence historian – not least in Britain, where the government continues to regard some intelligence files for the period before the First World War as too sensitive to release even in a hundred years' time. But there are also many new opportunities, such as those offered by the new material on the operations of the Stasi and other Eastern European intelligence services which has gradually been surfacing since the disintegration of the Soviet Bloc. This exciting new series is well-placed to profit from such opportunities.

Christopher Andrew
Cambridge, June 1991

1

Introduction:
the stirrings of a new revisionism?

RHODRI JEFFREYS-JONES

'Disinformation' is a telling word in espionage jargon. The disinformation technique is aimed at a nation's real, potential or imaginary foes, yet others, too, may be deceived. The disinformation phenomenon suggests that scholarly historians of secret intelligence should put themselves in a more than usually sceptical frame of mind. Their scepticism needs to embrace the contemporary records left by actors in the intelligence drama. It must also be directed at much of the historical writing about hitherto secret events in the past, for intelligence veterans have written numerous memoirs and history books, and those who professionally mislead their contemporaries may practice an equally expert deception on future generations.

The essays in this book challenge the prevailing wisdom on several of the main aspects of North American intelligence history since 1898.[1] They oppose the professional scepticism of the historian to the demands on public credulity made by official accounts. In that sense, the essays have an affinity to the US 'revisionist' school of writing that flourished in the 1930s and 1960s. Like the old revisionists, this book's essayists ask challenging new questions and offer divergent hypotheses. Like the old revisionists, they cover some unexplored ground – notably, this book contains the first history of the US Defense Intelligence Agency. Yet, there are differences between the old challenges and the new. Inevitably, new generations arrive; the freshness of approach in this book's essays and the youth of some of the contributors hint at the emergence of scholars who will be helping to set the scholarly agenda for the next century. Their concerns herald changing emphases in the intelligence history field – including an appetite for methodological challenge, and an implicit belief in what promises to become an addition to the rights demanded by the modern citizen, the right to know.

The significance of the essays in this book, as of scholarly work now being published elsewhere, may be explained in the context of an overview of the historiography of US[2] secret intelligence. However, that historiography is still relatively immature, so there is no standard framework within which one can discuss trends in the writing of intelligence history.[3] For this reason, we shall need to open this book by constructing a framework of our own.

We shall start by seeking a model outside the intelligence history field. But the model has to be a specific one, for there is no standard model for the development of all types of historiography. Writers about particular subjects have addressed the distinctive features of their fields. For example, the history of black slavery has engaged the minds of some brilliant scholars, but the theories which animate their research are not especially helpful to writers on intelligence. Happily, this particularity does not rule out cross-fertilization. The historiographies of different subjects do share some characteristics: for example, the tendency of every historian to be a child of his or her age, and to interpret the past in the light of present-day concerns.

The historiographies of some subjects have special affinities to one another. Such a special affinity surely exists between the historiographies of, respectively, secret intelligence and diplomacy. The affinity is not quite as obvious as one might imagine, it is true. The adoption of the historiography of foreign policy as our model excludes consideration of important subject matter. Excluded, for example, is the history of domestic intelligence (counter-espionage, the exploits of the Federal Bureau of Investigation, the Drugs Enforcement Agency, the Royal Canadian Mounted Police and other government organisations with clandestine dimensions); excluded also is the history of private espionage (industrial spying and the efforts of detective agencies such as the Pinkerton organisation); excluded, finally, might be the literary history of intelligence – though, as Katy Fletcher shows in her essay, spy fiction is not so divorced from 'reality' as one might imagine. In spite of these exclusions, however, diplomatic historiography is the closest available fit. There is a significant overlap of subject matter and problems, especially where foreign intelligence is concerned, and with respect to the problems of official secrecy and official history.

To ensure an even closer fit, we shall confine our model to the wars and cold war of the past hundred years, the period in which intelligence historiography has emerged, and on which the essays in this book concentrate. This territory is very familiar to students of diplomatic historiography. It is customary and sensible for such historians to explain the historiography of foreign policy as a procession of viewpoints, following each other in roughly chronological order, and reflecting the changing concerns of successive generations.[4] The first viewpoint to appear on any event is likely to be an official version, such as a government publication, a politician's memoir or a selection of policy documents. The official version may well be a useful and authoritative source of information, but it is different from most other schools of interpretation in that it is uncritical, and is invariably an apology for the conduct of an official or group of officials. Soon after the First World War, for example, officials of the Woodrow Wilson administration published versions of events which simply elaborated on American wartime propaganda and peace aims.[5] In 1952 William Langer published an official history of American entry into the Second World War, and soon thereafter former President Harry Truman supplied, in his memoirs, his perspective on the development of the cold war under his aegis.[6] Both accounts justified the policies of administration officials.

Next, it is the turn of that characteristically American breed, the 'revisionists'. Athan Theoharis notes that there have been both 'Right' revisionists and 'Left' revisionists. He offers the following definitions of the revisionist school of thought:

> The common themes of 'revisionist' historiography are those of executive irresponsibility, the mendaciousness or secretiveness by which policymakers develop public support for particular decisions, and . . . criticism of the principal ideas and priorities that determine official policy. . . . The 'revisionists' share a set of assumptions that the foreign policy decisions that led to both world wars and to the Cold War were not the result of public demand, but the converse, and were shaped by the interests and priorities of policymakers, as opposed to international events or the requirements of the national interest.[7]

The revisionist Charles C. Tansill in one book drew attention to the role of President Wilson's pro-British advisers in explaining American entry into the First World War. In another, he argued

that President Franklin D. Roosevelt manoeuvred the Japanese
into attacking at Pearl Harbor, thus securing the entry of the United
States into the Second World War.[8] The greatest revisionist of all
was one of the towering geniuses of the American historical profession. According to Charles A. Beard, US officials not only conspired to secure American entry into the Second World War, but
contrived, through their official accounts of events, to distort the
historical record and ensure that 'the people . . . were to bear the
blame at the bar of history'.[9]

America's post-1945 superpower status and the appalling potential dangers of nuclear warfare made foreign policy a desperately
important matter. Its history became hotly debated, and one school
of thought followed another at an accelerated rate. The official
apologists and the revisionists were barely warming to the fray
when the 'realists', among whom Hans Morgenthau, Walter
Lippmann and George Kennan were originally to the fore, began
to make a formidable contribution: Kennan argued that, in the
sense that America could not have defeated Nazi and communist
totalitarianism simultaneously, the Second World War had been
'not fully winnable'; a realist could only practise the art of the
possible, meaning, in the context of the cold war, the patient but
firm 'containment' of Soviet expansionism.[10]

'New Left' historians acknowledged a debt to the earlier school
of revisionists, especially Beard. William Appleman Williams, the
New Left standard-bearer, argued that United States foreign policy
furthered the economic self-interest of a small élite. His 1959 book,
The Tragedy of American Diplomacy, affected a generation of historians.[11] 'New Left' thinking became bound up with the 1960s
protest movement against the Vietnam War, and inevitably produced a conservative reaction. This new conservatism, or neo conservatism, became an important intellectual component of the
movement that, in 1981, put Ronald Reagan into the White House.
Guenter Lewy was a historian who exemplified the new spirit. In
his book *America in Vietnam* (1978), he sought to restore national
pride, and to present United States policy in Vietnam in a better
moral light.[12]

None of the foregoing schools of thought has played a dominant
role. The same could be said of the 'corporatist' interpretation of
foreign policy. This approach seeks to identify coalitions, within and
between elements in government bureaucracy, business, organised
labour and agriculture, which proved influential in determining
foreign policy in certain periods. It aims at synthetic, rather than

confrontational, interpretation, and is perhaps a reaction against the battles of the 1960s and 1970s that raged both in domestic politics and in the historical profession. The corporatist approach sometimes achieves interpretative synthesis, but it has also attracted its own set of critics, and must be rated one of several conflicting currents within the diplomatic history profession.[13] In sum, foreign policy historiography is characterised by considerable diversity.

When one turns to intelligence history, one finds a similar diversity. But the balance-through-variety which exists within foreign policy historiography is absent from the historiography of secret intelligence. Official versions of intelligence history have had an influence far heavier than that achieved by official histories in other spheres of the historical discipline.

One reason for the heavy influence of official versions of intelligence history is that there is a link between the historical and intelligence professions. In the Second World War, no fewer than forty professional historians worked in the Research and Analysis branch of America's Office of Strategic Services (OSS) – of whom seven were to serve terms, in future years, as president of the American Historical Association.[14] In 1981 a historian working for the Central Intelligence Agency (CIA) noted that the agency had 'closer ties with the academic community, including the historical profession, than most other federal agencies'.[15] As Robert Spears indicates in his contribution to this volume, the composition of the CIA remains a controversial and intractable problem. Yet there can be little doubt about the services that historians have rendered to intelligence organisations in several countries.[16]

Of the two main reasons for the prominence of historians in the intelligence profession, the first may not be entirely creditworthy: out of a desire for self-preservation, historians have sought desk jobs in times of war. At such times, intelligence functions were expanding, so these historians were often successful in their quests. This was the case in Britain in the First World War, and both the British and the Americans seem to have followed the precedent after 1939.[17]

The second reason for the prominence of historians in the intelligence profession is that historians have pertinent skills to offer. They are trained in the analysis and presentation of raw political and international data. Furthermore, as Robin Winks and others have shown, they are versed in the 'science' of detection.[18] These skills are adaptable to the investigative and analytical aspects of intelligence work. Additionally, historians are notoriously familiar with the techniques of propaganda. This means they can expose abuses of the truth by others, as Pieter Geyl demonstrated in his 1955 book, *Use and Abuse of History*. But, equally, they can manipulate information for reasons of state – as did Geyl himself when working for Dutch intelligence.[19]

Trained historians who have worked in intelligence naturally enjoy an advantage when it comes to writing intelligence history. They can combine an authoritative 'feel' for the subject matter with the skills of the scholar. Some of them have had privileged access to secret documentation. It is therefore not surprising that their writings form an important part of the foundation of our understanding of past episodes in intelligence history. In Britain, Sir Harry Hinsley, who worked at the British Code and Cypher School throughout the Second World War and then became a history professor at Cambridge University, played the leading role in producing the official, multi-volume *British Intelligence in the Second World War*.[20] In America, the Harvard historian William Langer, author of the previously mentioned official account of American entry into the war, was the man who set up the intelligence analysis divisions of both the OSS and the CIA. His official history set the framework of assumptions for a good number of subsequent interpretations of US intelligence history.[21]

The official history of American intelligence has had a relatively heavy influence for a further reason, its fecundity. The official accounts have been numerous. They have also been – as befits a pluralistic democracy – far from monolithic, and for this reason they have left a growing legacy of debating points. This is especially evident when one turns to that subjective component of official history, the public servant's memoir. Former White House officials have rounded on the CIA especially, claiming that it has been incompetent, unresponsive to presidential needs and given to unauthorised initiatives. Not so, say the intelligence veterans in their own memoirs. According to these veterans, the CIA has done a good job on the whole, but its director has too often been the 'fall guy' for an incompetent president.[22]

Within the intelligence community, there are further differences of opinion which have helped to set the agenda for debate, and which further swell the importance of the official contribution to intelligence history. Like other government agencies, the CIA has a historical office.[23] And, quite distinct from the scholars working on the historical dimensions of such problems as the policies of the Organization of Petroleum Exporting Countries, there is a group working on the history of the agency itself.[24] A proportion of its past work is still secret. However, it has contributed to the agency's historical self-awareness, and recent declassification has revealed a healthy measure of internal debate.

The weight of the official history legacy is illustrated in what we now know about the secret work of the CIA's historical office. In 1951, just four years after the CIA was set up, the agency approached Arthur Darling, a minor historian then in the twilight of his career. Darling agreed to work for the agency. Between 1952 and 1954 he did research that culminated in a twelve-volume typescript, 'The Central Intelligence Agency: An instrument of government, to 1950'[25] Two of Darling's colleagues then produced a sequel on the period 1950–1953, a sequel that ran to ten volumes in spite of the omission of any discussion of the clandestine services.[26] These works, however, were not to the taste of some officials. Ludwell Lee Montague, a former member of the CIA's Board of National Estimates who had joined the agency's historical staff, was one such official.[27] Though he took pride in his descent from the Lees of Virginia, Montague evidently basked in his record of service to the *federal* government. In the 1960s he worked on what became a five-volume study, 'General Walter Bedell Smith as Director of Central Intelligence, October 1950–February 1953'.[28] He took special pride in this opus, which he described as his 'final service before retirement'.[29]

The disdainful Montague claimed that Darling 'had little experience in Government and he sometimes failed to comprehend the full significance of the material that he had collected'.[30] He noted that former OSS chief William Donovan had 'laughed' when he read Darling's introductory chapter. Darling, Montague continued, had overpraised General Smith's two immediate predecessors as directors of central intelligence, Hoyt S. Vandenburg and Roscoe C. Hillenkoetter.[31]

But it should be borne in mind that Montague had served Smith in war and peace. His loyalties were evident. His claim that it was Smith who had created 'for the first time, a really effective United States Intelligence Community', merely contributed to a growing debate that inevitably escaped the confines of the CIA. Indeed, within a short space, CIA historian Thomas F. Troy had produced a further secret work, entitled 'Donovan and the CIA: A history of the establishment of the Central Intelligence Agency'.[32] The title of the first chapter, 'A question of paternity', summed up an important historical debate about who really founded the CIA, and with what intention.

The intellectual life of the American intelligence community reflects the pluralism of the United States itself, and is sometimes at variance with thinking in the White House and other branches of government. This means it is wrong to refer to a *unitary* official version of intelligence history. But internal debate has had the effect of strengthening, not weakening, official renderings of intelligence history.

In contrast, non-official historians are only just beginning to warm to their task. One reason is that American intelligence history is a relatively recent phenomenon. As Graeme Mount shows in his essay, counter-intelligence in the shape of the Secret Service was vigorous in the USA and Canada in 1898. However, it was not entirely effective, and large-scale central intelligence operations are an even more recent phenomenon. But the disentangling of intelligence history has been frustrated not only by its confusing proximity to the present, but also by the exceptionally patchy nature of the evidence. While secrecy pervades many types of governmental activity, it affects all secret intelligence by definition. Delays in the declassification of official histories have meant that academic historians were first deprived of helpful information, then flooded with facts in unexpected doses (a sudden public intimation of the scholarly treasure-trove in store came in a 1975 congressionally commissioned document based on 'approximately seventy-five volumes from the series of internal CIA histories' which the author claimed were 'a unique institutional memory').[33] Non-official scholars have been starved of the historian's life-blood, documentary evidence. Where secret intelligence is concerned, the public has been left, to a disproportionate degree, at the mercy of official versions of history.

The official domination of intelligence history has had some harmful effects. One of these effects has been a tendency to treat as axiomatic the importance of intelligence work. But for British intelligence achievements, Hinsley asserts, Germany would not have been defeated until 1949, and the four years' delay 'is probably a conservative estimate'.[34] Because of his intelligence background and obvious sympathy for his wartime colleagues, Hinsley's judgement is open to question. But at least he makes a coherent case for his view. Those who for political reasons wish to emphasise the potential value of intelligence have sometimes heedlessly exaggerated its historical value.

Even more serious than the exaggeration of the role of intelligence agencies is, of course, the misrepresentation of that role, and of its benefits to a particular nation. Even independent scholars find it tempting to succumb to the official line, however dubious: J.A. Hobson once complained that professors 'are not so much the intellectual mercenaries of the vested interests as their volunteers'.[35] The bias of those who are serving or have served government is, naturally, more pronounced. The same bias potentially exists, in the United States, in a wider circle: the phenomenon of the 'revolving door', whereby scholars step in and out of government, opens up the danger of endless apologia, all apparently in the name of academic objectivity, for endless policy errors.[36]

Yet another harmful effect of official domination of the record, and especially of the monopolisation of archival material, has been the emergence of a mini-industry of sensational literature. Sensational writers have invented the history that professional scholars have been unable to write. While some journalists undoubtedly perform a vital task, others have a weakness for pointless and unsubstantiated revelation. Espionage history has proved irresistibly seductive to a substantial body of popular writers, offering as it does the subliminal attractions of the hidden, its biographical element, its moral ambivalences, and its relationship to the dramatic theme of national security and survival in a nuclear age.[37] The sensationalists have joined the official historians in exaggerating the importance of intelligence, especially of certain dramatic incidents. In a scholarly manifestation of Gresham's law, they have helped to exclude reputable scholars from the field – partly by giving intelligence history a bad name, and partly by saturating the markets with their bad books. The popular literature has been so flawed that it has had the further deleterious effect of conferring on official history what it does not deserve, a relative degree of respectability.

While official history is just one phase in the development of the historiography of foreign policy, it threatens to become more of a stumbling block than a building block in intelligence studies. Yet, it has not entirely stifled the development of an intelligence historiography. By comparison with the historiography of foreign policy, intelligence historiography's progression through phases – official, revisionist, realist, New Left, neo-conservative, corporatist – is erratic, to say the least. But it is still helpful to look at the different schools of thought through the progression prism, if only to show how muddled the interpretative conventions are, and how acute is the need to break with them.

Though, as we have seen, official histories were *written* at an early stage, they usually did not *appear* until much later. Perhaps testifying to modern America's increasingly ardent belief in the right to know, the first official history of the CIA in fact appeared at an earlier point in the agency's life than the first official account of the Office of Naval Intelligence (which took thirty eight years) or the OSS (thirty four years). But it still took twenty eight years.[38] Furthermore, prior to the great intelligence debate of the 1970s, neither presidents nor their advisers commented extensively on intelligence matters. In one sense, these delays and omissions wreak havoc with 'normal' historiographical progression.

In another sense, the delays and omissions make surprisingly little difference to historiographical development. This is because official historians' beliefs had an impact in spite of publication delays. These beliefs were already evident to contemporaries from public policy statements and from government propaganda, and the official viewpoint on intelligence history could be further appreciated from what official historians wrote on other topics.

Langer's official account of the entry of the United States into the Second World War is a case in point. Here, it is plainly his view that, while President Roosevelt and his cabinet expected war, America was surprised at Pearl Harbor because of the shortcomings of the intelligence community.[39] Langer thus, by implication, justified his own efforts, at both the OSS and the CIA, to put the intelligence preparedness of the nation on a better footing. It became an article of faith among CIA memoirists that United States intelligence had been inadequate in the 1930s, that this had led to intelligence disaster in 1941, and that the way to stop such unpleasant surprises in the future was to have a well-developed, centralised, peacetime intelligence capability. This view influenced professional historians outside the CIA too. Roberta Wohlstetter, in her classic 1962 study of Pearl Harbor, saw the 1930s problem as poor co-ordination. David Kahn, a leading authority of cryptology history, took issue with Wohlstetter in an essay he published in 1984. Kahn pointed to racial prejudice against the Japanese and to uneven collection of data as the leading factors in 1930s intelligence weakness. But, like Wohlstetter, he reflected the official view that Pearl Harbor was an intelligence disaster.[40]

Well before the appearance of Langer's book, political opponents of the Roosevelt and Truman Democratic administrations took up the cudgels. Walter Trohan of the *Chicago Tribune* championed the right-wing Republican assault on the New Deal and its postwar successor, the Fair Deal. Heralding a 1950 book by the conservative historian John T. Flynn, Trohan said the war was the result of Democratic incompetence, and an attempt to distract the nation from its continuing economic problems. The CIA was not merely unnecessary, it was a New Deal plot to subvert American values. He fumed at the fact that Langer, an apologist for official policy, was to be given privileged and exclusive access to the foreign policy documents many years in advance of potential critics of government policy.[41] Charles Beard, though not a conservative in the Trohan/-Flynn mould, addressed the same theme. In his 1948 book *President Roosevelt and the Coming of the War*, written without the assistance of secret documents, but based largely on the extensive congressional hearings into the Pearl Harbor attack, he argued that Roosevelt had plotted American entry into the war, while deceiving the American people about his true intentions.[42] Beard had made the revisionist case while the official historians were still resting in their starting blocks.

The noise of the battle between the official and revisionist points of view continued with such intensity that it tended to drown out other voices. George Kennan, the leading 'realist', had been one of the main advocates of the CIA. But when the Eisenhower administration declined to stand up to McCarthyism, he refused to give further assistance to the CIA or to any other branch of government, and he concentrated on writing about Western relations with Russia.[43] Another leading realist, Norman Graebner, believes that the CIA was, at best, an irrelevance to American history.[44] The CIA did, in due course, become the ogre of the international left instead of the American right, and a target ripe for attack by New Left historians in the United States.[45] Ronald Radosh obliged, in 1970, with a book that attacked the CIA's involvement with organised labour.[46] Yet, perhaps because of the reported opposition of both the CIA and military intelligence to United States participation in the Vietnam War, to the ending of which the New Left too was passionately committed, serious New Left scholars generally neglected intelligence history.

Nor did the neo-conservatives contribute substantially to the history of intelligence. Potentially, neo-conservative intellectuals had something to say. Following attacks on the intelligence community in the mid-1970s, they lined up to support former governor Ronald Reagan's bid to become President and endorsed his promise to revive the CIA. Neo-conservatives are supposed to be disillusioned 1950s neo-liberals, and one reading of CIA history would be that it moved from 1950s liberalism to 1980s conservatism. General histories of the Agency by intelligence veteran Ray Cline and by the Irish journalist John Ranelagh uphold the cold war values they feel have animated American intelligence history.[47] But the neo-conservatives have a problem with consistency, as they uphold the war in Vietnam which so worried intelligence analysts, and as they uphold the principles of minimal government with low taxation, yet high government spending on intelligence and on defence matters generally. Like the realist and New Left schools, the neo-conservative school withered on the vine.

In contrast, the revisionists, those who by Theoharris's definition deplored 'executive irresponsibility, the mendaciousness or secretiveness by which policymakers develop public support for particular decisions', showed signs of a revival in health. The first well-received critique of the intelligence community appeared in 1964, the work of two journalists, and bore the unmistakably revisionist title, *The Invisible Government*.[48] In the 1970s, journalists had a field day at the expense of the White House and the intelligence community. Through their exposure of the Watergate affair with its rogues' gallery of White House officials and of picturesque, if low-ranking, former employees of the CIA and FBI, Bob Woodward and Carl Bernstein seemed to make revisionists of most Americans, and of many citizens of foreign countries, where 'gate' became a suffix charged with political contempt.[49]

Revisionists began to thrive in the aftermath of the Watergate affair and of the great intelligence debates that followed. They drew strength from the writings of disillusioned intelligence officers, whose memoirs at times combined semi-official history with virulent revisionism. Revisionist historians drew further sustenance from the declassification of intelligence documents. This declassification was frustratingly slow by comparison with the opening of other US government archival material, and serious scholars still fume at the degree of obstruction they encounter, especially when it seems pointless, or more to do with saving someone's reputation than with the protection of national security. But declassification in the United States was rapid by comparison with what happened in other countries. In 1982 James Bamford published the first study of the National Security Agency, exposing its abuses of civil liberties. In 1983 a book by Bradley F. Smith questioned the mythology behind the OSS's achievements. Both these revisionist studies were heavily and authoritatively documented.[50]

While all this is a healthy antidote to the official versions of intelligence history, it is perhaps time to ask: is there life beyond orthodox revisionism? The ever-increasing availability of document-ation on the Second World War and the cold war does open up new possibilities. New journals have assisted the scholar. Notably, *Intelligence and National Security* publishes well-documented arti-cles on the intelligence history of several countries, the United States included.[51] The intelligence-history field, moreover, abounds with reference books and bibliographies.[52] Drawing on the mount-ing abundance of sources, some exceptionally able non-revisionist scholars have now written books on American intelligence history. Lawrence Freedman tackled the subject of the Soviet estimate in 1977; Walter Laqueur analysed the work of the 1950s analysts in a work he published in 1985; Ernest May edited a book of well-researched essays in the same year. The list of contributors to May's book borrows from the roll-call of leading contemporary historians, including such names as Stone, Kennedy, Watt and Erickson. What-ever the state of its historiography, intelligence history is coming of age.[53] It is notable that the Freedman, Laqueur and May books are all concerned with the history of analytical intelligence, and not with covert operations and political scandal. This distinguishes them from earlier writers, and brings intelligence history into one of its better homes, the study of international relations.

What is especially encouraging is the diversification in intelli-gence history methodology. One recalls the flowering, in the 1960s, of the 'new social history', which freed the study of ordinary people from its formerly constricting mode, the institutional study of labour unions. Historians like Gutman broadened the scope of social his-tory; others like Fogel enlivened it by borrowing from other disci-plines.[54] Similarly, historians are bringing to the study of intelli-gence history methods which, though tried and proven in other fields, are new in the intelligence context. Laqueur and May, for example, used the techniques of comparative history. Robin Winks has combined two disciplines, literary criticism and history, in his writings, and in his 1987 book *Cloak and Gown,* he has innovated in another way: the book is a study of scholars in the OSS and early CIA, and falls into the category of prosopographical or 'collective biography' studies.[55] Winks and company have introduced new standards of professionalism into the writing of intelligence history. As a result of this, historians are poised to move beyond the Mani-chean oppositions of official and revisionist historiography.

The essays in this volume are diverse in character, and it would be wrong to try to force them into a descriptive straitjacket. Yet, they display some common characteristics. Most of them exhibit the dominant trait of the old revisionism – they challenge various types of official history, and, in general, may be said to be sceptical of the reasoning of officialdom. To varying degrees, though, the essays have moved beyond the traditional revisionist boundaries. They exploit, in a scholarly fashion, the documentary resources that are now available. They apply new methodologies to intelligence history. They stop short of the polemics which marred some of the earlier revisionist writing, and do not court the idea that there have been active conspiracies against the public interest. They allow for external factors affecting intelligence policy, and explore nuances in internal pressures, instead of dismissing those pressures as being of little account. In lieu of railling quixotically against élitist targets, they prefer to demystify the windmills, rejecting, in the process, any fatalistic acceptance of governmental secrecy, and taking for granted the right to know.

Let us now review the essays with these points in mind. They provide a commentary on some of the main aspects of the development of the modern American intelligence community. They do not cover every major espionage agency – for example, there is no contribution on the National Security Agency, the secret bureaucracy set up in 1952 to run high-technology signals eavesdropping. But they do tackle some of the main problems in the histories of the Secret Service, the Office of Strategic Services (OSS), which operated as a wartime intelligence agency in 1942–45, the Central Intelligence Agency (CIA), founded in 1947, and the Defense Intelligence Agency (DIA), established in 1961 and, like the CIA, still operating today.

The essays are arranged chronologically. The imposition of a thematic framework would have been a laboured exercise inconducive to the development of individual viewpoints. Furthermore, chronological progression is always a help to the non-specialist reader. Such a reader will be further assisted by the fact that the internal organisation of most of the essays is likewise chronological.

The opening essay, by Graeme Mount, is about the role of the US Secret Service in the war of 1898, but is at the same time a contribution to the history of Canadian counter-intelligence. This is, therefore, an appropriate point at which to ask whether Canadian espionage historiography can ever be revisionist in quite the same sense as its American counterpart. The agonies of US historians perhaps arise from America's late entry into the two world wars, which gave occasion for bitter recrimination at the time and much debate thereafter; Canada, like the warring nations of Europe, was spared the intensity of American-style self-doubt on foreign policy matters.[56]

On the other hand, your approach as a historian may be just as much influenced by the country you are looking at as by the country you happen to inhabit – and Mount is looking at Spain and the United States as well as Canada. His essay bears the 'new' revisionist stamp interpretatively and methodologically. It deals with the Secret Service's attempts to counter the efforts of a Spanish spy network in Canada. It revises the sanguine version of the agency's exploits given by Secret Service chief John E. Wilkie and since accepted too uncritically by a number of historians, including me.[57] Combining in an unusual way the methodologies of the local and international historian, Mount has used Spanish consular reports and foreign ministry archives to show that, contrary to Wilkie's claims, Iberian intelligence activities in Canada survived the attentions of the US Secret Service. In the course of his investigation he not only corrects US official bias, but raises new questions – about the future of Canadian secret intelligence, and about US–Canadian intelligence relations.

The next essay, by my fellow-editor Andrew Lownie, is set in Grosvenor Square, London, in 1940. It is about a cypher clerk at the American embassy, Tyler Kent. America had not yet entered the war, and the USA had neither established the OSS nor stepped up counter-intelligence measures. Kent obtained copies of secret transmissions between Prime Minister Churchill and President Roosevelt, but before he could pass them on he was arrested and imprisoned for the remainder of the war. Lownie's why-did-he-do-it treatment of this episode is clearly a variant of the whodunnit detective story and of its kissing cousin, the historical investigation. It is, however, a whodunnit with footnotes and, more than this, with footnotes that reflect a commitment to the right to know – Lownie used the Freedom of Information Act to obtain Federal Bureau of Investigation (FBI) documents pertinent to his case.

Lownie thus exhibits a characteristic trait of the new revisionists. But, like others in the newer generation of historians, he also reacts to official accounts with a scepticism that was typical of the traditional revisionists. Previous accounts of Kent's motivation held that he was a naïve opponent of American entry into the war, acting alone in the hope of alerting and helping isolationist senators, or that he was a Nazi spy, or that he was an isolationist dubbed a Nazi for the sake of convenience. The idea that opponents of Roosevelt's pro-British policy were naïve or soft on Nazism is consistent with the Langer/official version of history. In arguing that the evidence is just as consistent with Kent's having been a Soviet as any other kind of agent, Lownie frees the case from the prison of orthodoxy.

The Japanese attack at Pearl Harbor in 1941 brought America into the war. At the same time, it convinced leading policy makers that US intelligence had been caught napping. The administration's response was to create, in 1942, the OSS, under the leadership of the charismatic William J. 'Wild Bill' Donovan. The notions that the OSS was a great success and that it was the true parent of the later peacetime organisation, the CIA, are at the heart of the official versions of the genesis of modern American secret intelligence. In successive chapters, David Walker, Richard Laidlaw and Danny Jansen set out to revise, in their different ways, this official version of history.

In July 1942 the British and Americans decided to take the offensive against the Nazis by launching an invasion of North Africa in the autumn. They codenamed the invasion Operation Torch. The OSS had the tasks of providing intelligence, and secretly recruiting local help from the anti-fascist French. On 8 November, Allied troops, accompanied by OSS control officers who had slipped out of Casablanca and Oran, landed in force on the African beaches. Just a few days earlier, far to the east in Egypt, the British had triumphed against General Rommel's army at the second battle of El Alamein. At last, the Russians, who had been fighting hard on the eastern front, could be reassured that help was arriving in the 'west'. As one might expect, OSS officers recorded their participation in Operation Torch as one of the triumphs in the history of their organisation.

David Walker questions the official view of the OSS's role in Operation Torch. The organisation's efforts had mixed results, both in intelligence and in operational terms. Donovan and others inflated the OSS's achievements as part of a propaganda campaign designed to entrench the OSS in Washington's wartime bureaucracy, and, ultimately, in the capital's peacetime bureaucracy as well. In this revisionist interpretation, Walker confirms suspicions voiced, in wartime and since, by Donovan's many critics. He goes beyond the traditional critique, however, in attempting a synthesis of intelligence history, military history and political history. He argues that Torch was strategically misconceived. He suggests, not only that strategic intelligence was as faulty as tactical intelligence, but that the nub of the matter was President Roosevelt's weak political leadership. This weakness made him oversensitive to the fickle moods of domestic opinion, and too eager to embrace operations that might increase his popularity at home. By utilising interdisciplinary perspectives, Walker introduces a new dimension to revisionism.

The Allies tried to use the multi-front strategy to extend and weaken the Japanese, as well as the Germans. This aim helps to explain the story of the notorious Burma Road. The goal was to reinforce Chinese resistance to Japanese occupation by driving a communications and transport link from the British bastion, India, through Burma, the British colony conquered by Japanese forces in 1942. The OSS established a special unit, Detachment 101, to conduct guerrilla operations inside Burma which would be of assistance to advancing British and American forces. The OSS recruited local support from the Kachin tribesmen. In the renewed but ill-fated campaign to open the Burma Road in 1944, the OSS and Kachins fought bravely. Because of British–American rivalry, there are conflicting official views of the Burma campaign, but OSS historians could point to Detachment 101's role as having been an honourable episode that established a valuable precedent for undercover US contacts with South-East Asian independence movements and anti-communist factions.

Laidlaw regards the Burma Road campaign as having been ill-conceived strategically. British ambitions to re-impose imperial control helped to account for the irrational decision to take on the Japanese in jungle warfare with uncertain local support. But Laidlaw directs attention, too, to the lack of British–American co-ordination stemming from US opposition to British imperialism, and from incipient American ambitions to replace British influence with their own. He argues that the OSS utilisation of the Kachins left an unfortunate legacy to the future CIA. One might portray Laidlaw, critical as he is of both British and American policy, as being doubly revisionist. Equally, one might describe him as a Scotsman whose natural distrust of things emanating from London were nurtured by his experiences as an army officer serving in various outposts of the dwindling British Empire.

Locality and military service have also affected the outlook of the next contributor – showing just how misleading it can be to label people *too* precisely. Danny Jansen's essay is about the events leading up to President Truman's establishment of the CIA in 1947. While it is conventional for intelligence officials to forswear any right to speak on behalf of their agency, the CIA has nevertheless developed what one might describe as a crypto-official view of an important aspect of its own genesis. According to this view, Truman was wrong to dismantle the OSS in 1945, was weak and vacillating in his approach to intelligence matters in 1945 and 1946, but came to his senses in 1947, establishing the CIA and then authorising its development into the effective organisation it had become in the 1950s.

But Truman later claimed that the agency had developed, in the 1950s, into a different kind of beast from the one he originally had in mind. In her 1988 novel, *Murder in the CIA*, his dutiful daughter Margaret fervently upheld this view. Commenting on the view of history being inculcated into new trainees, she wrote – plainly not meaning it to be fiction – 'it was obvious that the Truman hand in creating the CIA in 1947 was being deliberately glossed over', and that the 1950s agency had become 'autonomous from virtually all control'.[58] Danny Jansen is thus confronted with two, contending versions of official history.

Jansen defends both President Truman's record and his version of events. Using newly released evidence from the post-presidential files at the Truman library, he resurrects the significance of a forgotten man, and of a forgotten institution. In 1946, he argues, Admiral Sidney Souers and the Central Intelligence Group played a more constructive role than has hitherto been realised. Donovan was too rash to run a peacetime intelligence service, and Truman was right in dispensing with his services. In advancing these views, Jansen's Midwestern origin is evident – to him, Truman was a neighbour with a familiar and commendable outlook. Jansen's military outlook is also relevant. He served with the Rangers in jungle combat and reconnaissance missions in the war in Vietnam – where he witnessed an atrocity in connection with intelligence operations. He is sceptical of Donovan's wartime role, and – like Laidlaw – unforgiving of the OSS chief's rashness in exposing himself to the risk of capture by the enemy.[59]

Jansen's scepticism of one official version of history means he must defend another, yet he clearly has more than a toe in the revisionist camp. Furthermore, his reliance on scholarly methods is a hallmark of the new wave of intelligence historians. So is his resort to proto-prosopographical methodology – he assumes that the people behind the CIG and CIA were motivated by personal interests and prejudices like everyone else, and were not just automatons responding antiseptically to national needs.

In contrast to the military experiences of Laidlaw and Jansen, Karen Potter's schooling is as a professional journalist with an academic background. She typifies the American journalist's belief in the right to know about matters of public concern. That belief characterises the newer generation of historians too – yet, the investigative spirit has not burned quite so brightly on the British, as distinct from American, side of the Atlantic. Potter asks an American's question about an aspect of British history concerning which the British themselves have been instinctively cryptic: was there a British version of McCarthyism, and, if there was, how should it be compared with its American counterpart?

Potter finds that, whereas American McCarthyism not only employed spying techniques but was also a product of spy scares, its British equivalent was relatively restrained, and predominantly a response to events in Eastern Europe. She dispels the polite fiction that McCarthyism never existed in Britain, a finding that raises questions about the histories of both countries – McCarthyism evidently did not have an exclusively American set of causes. At the same time, there were clearly differences in scale and intensity. And it is evident that panic responses to treason can occur in inverse proportion to actual treason in the intelligence services or elsewhere. While Potter's approach is not a corrective to official history, it supplies a stimulating perspective because, in deploying the comparative approach, it is yet another example of methodological variety.

Although American McCarthyism was so closely bound to the Alger Hiss trials and other spy cases, and although the FBI was implicated in some of Senator McCarthy's more dubious exploits, the CIA remained free of taint. Allen Dulles opposed Senator McCarthy's excesses, and the foreign intelligence community continued its development in spite of the suspicions of some powerful members of the United States Senate. The formation of the National Security Agency in 1952 boosted America's ability to spy on potential enemies, and the CIA enhanced its co-ordination of estimates and its expertise in new areas such as the measurement of Soviet economic progress. At the same time, though, there developed within the latter organisation an emphasis on covert operations which, while not directly deleterious to the agency's intelligence function, tended to fix the CIA's image in a way which a number of intelligence supporters subsequently came to regret.

Although intelligence veterans sometimes look back on the 1950s as the golden age of the CIA, it was clear by 1961 that the intelli-

gence community had run into serious problems. One problem is
summed up in the phrase 'missile gap'. The three separate branches
of the armed services competed with each other for resources.
In support of their demands for appropriations, their respective
intelligence branches exaggerated the strength of the Soviet opposition. One result was the coining of the fallacy that Russia had
more nuclear-tipped missiles than America, a misconception that
aggravated the arms race and came to light in the early 1960s. A
second major problem was the CIA's over-commitment to covert
operations, a policy that culminated, in 1961, in an unsuccessful
attempt to rid Cuba of Castro – the embarrassing Bay of Pigs
disaster. In light of these problems, it is tempting to regard the
Kennedy administration's establishment of the Defense Intelligence
Agency in 1961 as a reactive and retributive reform, designed to
eliminate competitive military estimates, and to curb the excesses
of the CIA.

Patrick Mescall's essay is the first history of the origins of the
DIA. As there is no published official version of the history of the
DIA, it cannot be said to be revisionist, there being nothing to
revise. The essay is nevertheless critical in tone, particularly in its
treatment of Secretary of Defense Robert S. McNamara. Mescall
argues that the creation of the DIA was a response to long-standing
tensions within the services, rather than a measure designed to
eliminate the incompetence exposed by the Bay of Pigs fiasco. With
an eye on the continuation of inflated military estimates and on the
DIA's disagreements in the 1970s with the civilian CIA, Mescall
asks why the DIA failed in its intended task. He suggests there
was a failure in leadership. There is more than a hint of revisionism,
then, in this essay which is necessarily a pioneering work in institutional history.

The last two essays are characterised by methodologies which
are far removed from the armoury of the official historian. Robert
Spears examines a much discussed but seldom analysed aspect of
CIA history, the composition of its élite. In the 1950s 'Golden Age',
or so the story goes, the agency was blessed (or cursed) with an
adventurous leadership with an Ivy League background and experience in the OSS. Then the Bay of Pigs pricked the bubble of
infallibility. A new leadership generation sought to democratise
CIA recruitment, seeking talent outside the Ivy League and looking
with sympathy at applications from members of 'minority' groups,
blacks and women.

Spears considers the virtues of prosopographical analysis – one of the methods favoured by the revisionist Beard. At the same time, in attempting to use the Freedom of Information Act, he shows that he shares the right-to-know values of other contributors to this volume. The obstruction he has encountered in prosecuting his FOIA enquiries is conspicuous. Though America is more open than Britain, US bureaucrats do guard a great number of secrets. So, in spite of their purely academic character, some of Spears' FOIA questions remained unanswered. It is therefore fortunate for Spears that he is no cliometric determinist – his essay does furnish enough evidence to throw doubt on recruitment liberalisation, but it is chiefly of interest because it indicates how the debate about élitism was just as important as the statistics of the subject. What people believed about the CIA was sometimes just as influential as what people within the agency thought or did.

If the Bay of Pigs failed to provoke a convincing reform of the intelligence community, it did at least stimulate attempts to improve its image. One such attempt was a series of spy novels written pseudonymously by E. Howard Hunt, the minor CIA functionary who later acquired global notoriety through his role in the Watergate scandal. Hunt tried to create, in Peter Ward, an American spy hero. Would Hunt have succeeded in reglamourising the CIA, but for his disgrace and incarceration under the Nixon administration? Perhaps not, for he was out of tune with the concerns of his time, not least the 1960s revival in feminism – while others reinterpreted penis envy with Betty Friedan, Hunt wrote a novel called *The Venus Probe*.[10]

Like Pat Mescall, Katy Fletcher is a pioneer in her field. For, while American detective fiction and British spy fiction have each received critical attention, American spy fiction has not – a remarkable omission, in light of its prolificacy. Fletcher takes a sceptical look at the spy hero. In the sense that such a hero's values reflect official orthodoxies (even if his actions are anti-bureaucratic and maverick), she is exhibiting a revisionist tendency. But there is a problem, of course, in assuming that fiction is linked to 'real' propaganda, or to 'reality' at all. Fletcher addresses this problem with an attempt to define terms. In so doing, she brings a fresh approach to the study of American espionage history.

If, as an aid to appreciating the collective viewpoint, one were to take a collective look at the contributors to this volume, one characteristic stands out. This is not the fact that they all at some stage studied or contributed to the study of the history of American espionage at the University of Edinburgh – the fact that half of them are British and half North American reduces locality to a point of interest affecting individuals only. Rather, the point of interest is the low age of the contributors, the arithmetic average being (as of 1991) just over 34, and six of the contributors falling into the 21–31 age band. Though a few of the contributors have published extensively, the main contributions of most of them lie in the future.

To our previously mentioned characteristics of the 'new' revisionism (scepticism of official history, methodological variety and commitment to the right to know) we can, then, add the youth of at least some of its practitioners. Methodologically, the new revisionism in intelligence history is perhaps no more than the belated arrival of historiographical sophistication in a field numbed by the weight of official history. Once the official histories have been laid to rest, it is possible that revisionism will become a less-prominent feature of intelligence history writing. But, in the meantime, it seems likely that the continuing stream of official intelligence narratives will receive, at the hands of a rising generation of historians, a reception that is healthily sceptical, and, on current evidence, increasingly scholarly and sophisticated in tone.

Notes

1. In this introductory essay, the term 'North American' means the United States and Canada. The term 'American' means the United States alone.
2. Graeme Mount's chapter is a contribution to the history of secret intelligence in Spain and Canada, as well as the United States. Little is known about the history, let alone the historiography, of espionage in modern Spain. As we shall see below, more is known about Canadian secret intelligence. But the differences between Canadian and American historiography are significant (indeed, instructively so), and it would be a mistake to attempt a fusion here, interwoven though the histories of the North American neighbours may be. On Canadian intelligence historiography, see Wesley Wark, 'The evolution of military intelligence in Canada', *Armed Forces and Society*, 16 (fall 1989), 77–98. Stuart Farson devotes nine pages to the literature on Canada in his article, 'Schools of thought: national perceptions of intelligence', *Conflict Quarterly*, 9 (1989), 52–104.
3. The journal *Diplomatic History* has commissioned from Wesley K. Wark of the Univ. of Toronto an article which will be 'a historical review of the literature on the CIA and the US intelligence community since 1945' (Wark letter to RJ-J, received November 1990). Although there is a shortage of work on the structure of intelligence historiography, a number of authors have written articles with a historiographical dimension: Edward Bennett, 'Intelligence and history from the other side of the hill', *Journal of Modern History*, 60 (June 1988), 312–37;

Harry Howe Ransom, 'Being intelligent about secret intelligence agencies', *American Political Science Review*, 74 (March 1980), 141–8, and Kenneth G. Robertson, 'The study of intelligence in the United States', in Roy Godson, ed., *Comparing Foreign Intelligence*, (New York: Pergammon-Brassey, 1988), 7–42.

4. See Jerald A. Combs, *American Diplomatic History: Two centuries of changing interpretations* (Berkeley, Calif.: Univ. of California Press, 1983). The chronological approach characterises most of the works listed in Joseph A. Fry, 'United States diplomacy: a bibliography of historiographical works', *The Society for Historians of American Foreign Relations Newsletter*, 20 (Sept. 1989), 17–35.

5. See, for example, Robert Lansing, *The Peace Negotiations: A personal narrative* (Boston, Mass. Houghton-Mifflin, 1921), as well as the posthumously published *War Memoirs of Robert Lansing, Secretary of State* (Indianapolis, Ind.: Bobbs-Merrill, 1935) and the collection of essays by former government appointees edited by Wilson's former personal adviser: Edward M. House, *What Really Happened at Paris? The story of the peace conference* (New York: Scribner, 1921). A sick man by the end of his presidency, Wilson died in 1924 without writing his own account of events between 1914 and 1919 (though the journalist Ray Stannard Baker edited the six-volume *Public Papers of Woodrow Wilson* in 1925–7 (New York: Harper). Had he lived to write his memoir, Wilson would have left a version of events different from that of Lansing, whom he dismissed from his cabinet in February 1920. United States official history can be far from monolithic – as we shall see below, in our review of the historiography of the CIA.

6. William L. Langer and S. Everett Gleason, *The Challenge to Isolation: The world crisis of 1937–1940 and American foreign policy*, 2 vols. (New York: Harper & Row, 1952) and Harry S. Truman, *Memoirs* (Garden City, N Y: Doubleday, 1955–6). For a slightly earlier account by the official who served as American ambassador to the Soviet Union and claimed to have witnessed the outbreak of the cold war at first hand, see Walter Bedell Smith, *My Three Years in Moscow* (New York: Lippincott, 1950). Smith later encouraged the writing of official CIA history – see below.

7. Athan G. Theoharris, 'Revisionism', in Alexander DeConde, ed., *Encyclopedia of American Foreign Policy*, 3 vols. (New York: Scribner, 1978), p. 901.

8. Charles C. Tansill, *America Goes to War* (Boston, Mass.: Little, Brown, 1938) and *Back Door to War: The Roosevelt foreign policy, 1933–1941* (Chicago, Ill.: Regnery, 1952). An earlier revisionist who does not quite fit Theoharris's mould was Harry Elmer Barnes, who challenged the notion that 'war guilt' for the 1914–18 tragedy attached to the Germans exclusively: *The Genesis of the World War: An introduction to the problem of war guilt* (New York: Knopf, 1926).

9. Charles A. Beard, *President Roosevelt and the Coming of the War 1941: A study in appearances and realities* (New Haven, Conn. Yale Univ. Press. 1948), p. 229.

10. George F. Kennan, *American Diplomacy 1900–1950* (New York: Mentor, 1964 (Univ. of Chicago Press, 1951)), pp. 66, 99. The realist critique, particularly that of Hans J. Morgenthau, was to inspire the work of the prolific historian, Norman Graebner – see his *America as a World Power: A realist appraisal from Wilson to Reagan* (Wilming-

ton, Del.: Scholarly Resources, 1984), which, at pp. 293–8, contains a
bibliography of his articles and essays since 1951.

11. William A. Williams, *The Tragedy of American Diplomacy*, rev. edn.
    (New York: Dell, 1972).
12. Guenter Lewy, *America in Vietnam* (Oxford: Oxford Univ. Press,
    1978), p. vii.
13. For a corporatist plea, see Thomas J. McCormick, 'Drift or mastery?
    A corporatist synthesis for American diplomatic history', *Reviews in
    American History*, 10 (Dec. 1982), 318–30, and John Lewis Gaddis,
    'The corporatist synthesis: a skeptical view', *Diplomatic History*, 10
    (fall 1986), 357–62; for an example of the corporatist approach, see
    Michael J. Hogan, *The Marshall Plan: America, Britain, and the recon-
    struction of Western Europe, 1947–1952* (Cambridge: Cambridge
    Univ. Press, 1987).
    The 'internationalist' approach might also be considered for
    inclusion in our overview. The exponents of this approach correctly
    hold that the foreign (and no doubt intelligence) history of any one
    country can be understood fully only in its proper international con-
    text. Enthusiasts for this approach offer not so much a special view-
    point, as a broadening of vision.
14. Barry M. Katz, *Foreign Intelligence: Research and analysis in the
    Office of Strategic Services, 1942–1945* (Cambridge, Mass.: Harvard
    Univ. Press, 1989), p. xii.
15. Sumner Benson, 'The historian as foreign policy analyst: the challenge
    of the CIA', *The Public Historian*, 3 (1981), 16.
16. For a discussion of historians in intelligence and of the relationship
    between intelligence and history, see Edward W. Bennett's review
    article, cited above, n. 3.
17. For lists of British historians serving in intelligence organisations in
    1914–18, see 'Appendix 5: academics in wartime Whitehall', in Stuart
    Wallace, *War and the Image of Germany: British academics
    1914–1918* (Edinburgh: John Donald, 1988), pp. 237–40. The appendix
    shows that historians predominated among the academics in Admir-
    alty, War Office and War Trade intelligence, followed by classicists
    and philosophers. Chapter 10 in Wallace's book details the active role
    of Britain's leading historians in wartime propaganda.
18. Robin Winks, ed., *The Historian as Detective: Essays on evidence*
    (New York: Harper, 1970). See Winks' introduction, pp.xiii-xxiv, and,
    on Holmes, Poirot and 'scientific history', the extract from R. G.
    Collingwood's *The Idea of History* (New York: Oxford Univ. Press,
    1956), pp.39–60 at page 59.
19. Geyl was a partisan of the Great Netherlands theory of history, envisa-
    ging an organic unity between the Flemish parts of Belgium and the
    Dutch provinces. He was unable or unwilling to eliminate ambivalence
    from the final sentence in his *Use and Abuse of History* (New Haven,
    Conn.: Yale Univ. Press, 1955), a brilliant and respected book in which
    he said (p.89) that historians should 'promote legitimate [sic] use and
    . . . check the abuse of history'. When Geyl was London correspondent
    for the *Nieuwe Rotterdamsche Courant* (1913–19) and then a professor
    of Dutch studies (1919–24) and Dutch history and institutions
    (1924–35) at the Univ. of London, he worked for a secretly funded
    agency that promoted the Dutch viewpoint in the foreign press,
    especially concerning territorial disputes with the Belgians: Bob de

Graaf, 'De voorlichting over Nederland en Indië aan de buitenlandse pers, 1900–1935. van particulier initiatief naar overheidstaak'. *Jamabatan: Tijdschrift voor de geschiedenis van Indonesië*, 3, ii (1984–5), 28.

20. *British Intelligence in the Second World War*, 4 vols. (London: HMSO): . . . *Its Influence on Strategy and Operations*, I (1979), II (1981), III Part 1 (1984), III Part 2 (1988); . . . *Security and Counterintelligence*, IV (1990).

21. Langer, *The Challenge to Isolation*, 2 vols.: II *The Undeclared War 1940–1941*, pp. 935–6.

22. Notably at variance were the accounts given of intelligence affairs in the Jimmy Carter administration by national security affairs assistant Zbigniew Brzezinski and CIA director Stansfield Turner: Brzezinski, *Power and Principle: Memoirs of the National Security Advisor, 1977–81* (New York: Farrar, Straus & Giroux, 1983), pp. 64, 72–3; Turner, *Secrecy and Democracy: The CIA in transition* (Boston, Mass.: Houghton-Mifflin, 1985), pp. 88, 119. The retired senior CIA official Harry Rositzke (a prominent campaigner on the intelligence community's behalf in the politically troubled 1970s) observed that 'it is a part of the CIA director's job to be the fall guy for the President': Rositzke, *The CIA's Secret Operations: Espionage, counterespionage, and covert action* (New York: Reader's Digest Press, 1977), p. 239.

23. For example, the US Nuclear Regulatory Commission, established in 1975, employed George T. Mazuzan and J. Samuel Walker as official historians. With privileged access to primary materials, they wrote a history of nuclear regulation from the inception of the Atomic Energy Commission to the privatisation of the atomic energy industry: *Controlling the Atom: The beginnings of nuclear regulation 1946–1962* (London: Univ. of California Press, 1984). The Peace Corps is another organization that sponsored an official history: Gerard T. Rice, *Twenty Years of Peace Corps* (Washington, D.C.: Peace Corps, 1981).

24. For an account of the work of CIA historians on OPEC, see Benson, 'The historian as foreign policy analyst: the challenge of the CIA'.

25. The Darling work is now declassified and has recently been published: Arthur B. Darling, *The Central Intelligence Agency: An instrument of government* (University Park, Pa.: Penn State Press, 1990). Darling was born in Kansas in 1892 and died in Paris in 1971. He was educated at élitist East Coast institutions, the Phillips Academy, Andover (where he also taught after junior appointments at Yale), Yale (AB, 1916) and Harvard (Ph.D., 1922). His liberal-expansionist views further associated him with the stereotypical 1950s image of a CIA officer (discussed by Robert Spears in Chapter 9): his two main books were *Political Change in Massachusetts, 1824–1848: A study of liberal movements in politics* (New Haven, Conn.: Yale Univ. Press, 1925) and *Our Rising Empire, 1763–1803* (New Haven, Conn., and Oxford: Yale Univ. Press and Oxford Univ. Press, 1940).

26. George Jackson and Martin Claussen, 'Organizational history of the Central Intelligence Agency, 1950–1953', mentioned in Ludwell Lee Montague, 'General Walter Bedell Smith as Director of Central Intelligence, October 1950–February 1953', The DCI Historical Series, 5 vols. (Washington, DC: Historical Staff, Central Intelligence Agency, 1971): I 'The Essential Background', vi.

27 Arthur S. Hulnick, 'CIA's relations with academia: symbiosis not

psychosis', *International Journal of Intelligence and Counterintelligence*, 1 (winter 1987), 42.

28. Montague worked for two Directors of Central Intelligence, Admiral Sidney W. Souers and General Walter Bedell Smith. He received his Ph.D. from Duke Univ. in North Carolina, where in 1940 it appeared under the imprint of the univ. press: *Haiti and the United States, 1714–1938* (reprinted; New York: Russell & Russell, 1966). He was both a Lee buff and a Civil War buff. In 1955 (according to the Library of Congress catalogue), the Society of the Lees of Virginia presented to the Library of Congress a copy of his article, 'Richard Lee, the emigrant, 1613(?)–1664', *Virginia Magazine of History and Biography*, 62 (Jan. 1954). While still working on his CIA history project, Montague moved from Arlington, Virginia to settle in Gloucester County, Virginia. He had already published a 97-page study, *Gloucester County in the Civil War* (Gloucester, Va.: DeHardit 1965). The Montague–Souers correspondence is an important source for Chapter 5 in this book. Like Darling's history, Montague's is now largely declassified and is available to a wider public: *General Walter Bedell Smith as Director of Central Intelligence, October 1950–February 1953* (University Park, Pa: Penn State Press, 1991).

29. Letter, Montague to Sidney Souers, 24 Oct. 1969, Montague folder, Box 2, Papers of Sidney W. Souers, Harry S. Truman Library, Independence, Missouri.

30. Montague, 'Smith', I, vii.

31. *ibid.*

32. This remained a classified document for a few years after its completion in 1975. In 1981, after declassification, it was published by Univ. Publications of America (Frederick, Md). This was not the first time that the CIA's version (or versions) of its own history had appeared. The Church Committee, set up by the Senate in 1975 to investigate intelligence matters, commissioned the young historian Anne Karalekas to produce an official history of the agency. Karalekas had access to the CIA's own official histories, as well as to supplementary documentation, and produced a work that clarified the historical development of the agency's Byzantine bureaucratic structures. Her work was close to CIA self-perception, even if she avoided the partisanship so characteristic of writers like Montague and Troy: 'History of the Central Intelligence Agency' in 'Supplementary detailed staff reports on foreign and military intelligence' (Final Report of the Select Committee to Study Governmental Operations with Respect to Intelligence Activities, 5 books, book 4), *Senate Report*, 94 Cong., 2 sess., no. 94–755 (23 April 1976).

33. Karalekas, 'History', p. 1, n. 1. The appearance, in 1990–1, of the Darling and Montague official histories (cited above), is not a surprise in light of Karalekas's earlier intimation of the existence of such volumes, but it will invite some hasty reappraisals.

34. F.H. Hinsley, 'British intelligence in the Second World War: an overview', *Cryptologia*, 16 (Jan. 1990), 10.

35. J.A. Hobson, *Free Thought in the Social Sciences* (1926), quoted in Wallace, *War and the Image of Germany*, p. 199.

36. Though the revolving door increases the risk of hagiography, it probably has a beneficial effect on government because it exposes the civil service to a wider pool of talent, and to fresh ideas.

37. The attractions of espionage to sensational writers, to spy novelists and to their readers, may be partly understandable in terms of the universal child's experience, remembered in adulthood, of secrets within the family, of the power which those secrets confer, and of the desire to share in them. I owe this notion to my late godmother, Lily Pincus, co-founder of the Tavistock Institute for Marital Studies in London, and author, with Christopher Dare, of *Secrets in the Family* (London: Faber & Faber, 1978). See pp. 9–10.

38. The ONI was founded in 1882, and A.P. Niblack's *The History and Aims of the Office of Naval Intelligence* (Washington, DC: GPO) appeared in 1920. The OSS having been established in 1942 (and terminated in 1945), the *War Report of the OSS*, edited by Kermit Roosevelt (New York: Walker), appeared in 1976.

39. 'In view of the critical developments in Japanese–American relations from the summer of 1941 to December 7, not to mention the specific warnings and alerts, it remains inexplicable that responsible American military authorities should have been taken so completely by surprise': Langer, *The Undeclared War 1940–1941*, p. 936.

40. Roberta Wohlstetter, *Pearl Harbor: Warning and decision* (Stanford, Calif.: Stanford Univ. Press, 1962), p.399; David Kahn, 'United States Views of Germany and Japan in 1941', in Ernest R. May, ed., *Knowing One's Enemies: Intelligence assessment before the two world wars* (Princeton, NJ: Princeton Univ. Press, 1984), pp. 476–7, 500–1. For examples of CIA officials' deprecating views on 1930s intelligence, see Allen W. Dulles, *The Craft of Intelligence* (London: Weidenfeld & Nicolson, 1963), pp. 35, 47 and Ray S. Cline, *The CIA under Reagan, Bush and Casey: The evolution of the agency from Roosevelt to Reagan* (Washington, DC: Acropolis, 1981), pp. 26, 27. Dulles was a former director of the CIA, and Cline a former deputy director for intelligence.

41. See Langer's account, *In and Out of the Ivory Tower: The autobiography of William L. Langer* (New York: Watson Academic Publications, 1977), pp. 210, 212 and John T. Flynn, *The Roosevelt Myth* (New York: Devin-Adair, 1950). Trohan's views appeared in the *Chicago Tribune* in the 1940s, and he repeated them in an oral history interview conducted on behalf of the Harry S. Truman Library by Jerry N. Hess, 7 Oct. 1970.

42. Beard, *Roosevelt and the Coming of the War*, pp. ii, 227–9.

43. George F. Kennan, *Memoirs 1950–1963* (London: Hutchinson, 1972), p. 177.

44. Conversations at the author's home in Edinburgh, 6–8 May, 1990. In his book of essays, *America as a World Power: A realist appraisal from Wilson to Reagan* (Wilmington: Scholarly Resources, 1984), Graebner does not mention the CIA or the OSS at all.

45. See Rhodri Jeffreys-Jones, 'The CIA and the demise of anti-anti-Americanism: some evidence and reflections', in Rob Kroes and Maarten van Rossem, eds., *Anti-Americanism in Europe*, European Contributions to American Studies, vol. 11 (Amsterdam: Free Univ. Press, 1986), pp. 121–36.

46. Ronald Radosh, *American Labor and United States Foreign Policy: The cold war in the unions from Gompers to Lovestone* (New York: Vintage Books, 1970).

47. Cline, *CIA*; John Ranelagh, *The Agency: The rise and decline of the*

CIA–from Wild Bill Donovan to William Casey (New York: Simon & Schuster, 1986).

48. David Wise and Thomas B. Ross, *The Invisible Government* (London: Jonathan Cape, 1964).

49. The Bob Woodward and Carl Bernstein exposure of the White House cover-up of the Watergate scandal appeared in the contemporary press and is conveniently summarised in their book, *All the President's Men* (New York: Simon & Schuster, 1974).

50. For an example of the semi-official revisionist genre, see Ralph W. McGehee, *Deadly Deceits: My 25 years in the CIA* (New York: Sheridan Square Publications, 1983). I am grateful to the historian Wesley K. Wark for showing me his work in progress called 'Struggle in the spy house: memoirs of US intelligence'. In a letter to me dated 16 Feb. 1991. Dr Wark remarked that in being 'highly politicised and frequently constructed as a contribution to an on-going debate on public policy', intelligence literature could be 'marked out from diplomatic history'.

James Bamford's book is *The Puzzle Palace: A report on America's most secret agency and its special relationship with Britain's GCHQ* (London: Sidgwick & Jackson, 1983); Bradley F. Smith's *The Shadow Warriors: OSS and the origins of the CIA* (London: Andrè Deutsch, 1983).

51. This London-based journal with an international advisory board started publication in January 1986. *Lobster* is another British periodical publication specialising in intelligence matters. Published in Hull, it is of slightly greater antiquity than the *INS* journal; its articles are well researched and cover a wide range of intelligence agencies all over the world, but they are iconoclastic rather than academic. Another British publication is the *Study Group On Intelligence Newsletter*, the first issue of which appeared in July 1989. This has commentary, on archives and on recent publications, which will undoubtedly help future historians. The British Study Group has its counterparts in other countries: for example, in Canada where a flourishing society for intelligence studies produces the Canadian Association for Security and Intelligence Studies *Newsletter*. In the United States, there has appeared, since Feb. 1982, a publication called *Foreign Intelligence Literary Scene: A bimonthly newsletter/book review*. Though edited and heavily influenced by intelligence veterans, it is helpful bibliographically and as a repository of autobiographical fragments. The Feb. 1985 issue of *FILS* ran a lead article on other new and forthcoming intelligence journals. Of these, the most helpful to historians is the *International Journal of Intelligence and Counterintelligence*. This has appeared quarterly since the autumn of 1985, and contains articles of both current and historical interest. *Cryptologia*, published quarterly in Terre Haute, Indiana, is devoted to all aspects of cryptology, including its history. Backfiles of other journals may also prove helpful to future historians: *Intelligence Report* (since 1979, this American Bar Association monthly has discussed court cases and legislation bearing on intelligence matters), *American Intelligence Journal* (National Military Intelligence Association) and *Periscope* (the Association of Former Intelligence Officers' quarterly). Mention should finally be made of a helpful, commercially produced, bibliographic periodical guide, the

National Intelligence Book Center's *Surveillant*, which started publication in 1990.

52. The slick titles of the first two items in the following selection should not be allowed to detract from their utility as reference books: Richard Deacon (pseud. Donald McCormick), ed., *Spyclopedia: The comprehensive handbook of espionage* (London: Macdonald, 1988); Donald McCormick and Katy Fletcher, *Spy Fiction: A connoisseur's guide* (Oxford: Facts on File, 1990); Paul W. Blackstock and Frank L. Schaf, Jr, eds., *Intelligence, Espionage, Counterespionage, and Covert Operations: A guide to information services* (Detroit, Mich.: Gale, 1978); George C. Constantinides, *Intelligence and Espionage: An analytical bibliography* (Boulder, Colo.: Westview, 1983); Robert Goehlert and Elizabeth R. Hoffmeister, eds., *The CIA: A bibliography* (Monticello, Ill.: Vance Bibliographies, 1980); Myron J. Smith, Jr, ed., *The Secret Wars: A guide to sources in English*, 3 vols. (Santa Barbara, Calif.: ABC-Clio): I *Intelligence, Propaganda and Psychological Warfare, Resistance Movements and Secret Operations, 1939–1945*, 1980; II *Intelligence, Propaganda and Psychological Warfare, Covert Operations, 1945–1980*, 1981; III *International Terrorism 1968–1980*, 1980; Walter Pforzheimer, ed., *Bibliography of Intelligence Literature*, 8th edn (Washington, DC: Defense Intelligence College, 1985). Referring especially to holdings in Georgetown Univ. and containing several works not listed elsewhere is Marjorie W. Cline *et al.*, eds., *Scholar's Guide to Intelligence Literature: Bibliography of the Russell J. Bowen Collection* (Frederick, Md: Univ. Publications of America, 1983). Sanders A. Laubenthal's *Survey of Resources for Intelligence Research* (Washington, DC: Defense Intelligence College, 1986) is a review of archival resources in or near the capital.

53. Lawrence Freedman, *US Intelligence and the Soviet Strategic Threat* (London: Macmillan, 1977); Walter Laqueur, *A World of Secrets: The uses and limits of intelligence* (New York: Basic Books, 1985), pp. 110–70; May, *Knowing One's Enemies: Intelligence assessment before the two world wars* (Princeton, NJ: Princeton Univ. Press, 1984), pp. 37–61 (Stone), 172–204 (Kennedy), 237–70 (Watt) and 375–423 (Erickson). Among the major works by Norman Stone is *The Eastern Front 1914–1917* (London: Hodder & Stoughton, 1975), by Paul M. Kennedy, *The Rise and Fall of the Great Powers: Economic change and military conflict from 1500 to 2000* (London: Unwin Hyman, 1988), by Donald Cameron Watt, who is chairman of the British Intelligence Study Group, *How the War Came: The immediate origins of the Second World War, 1938–1939* (London: Heinemann, 1989); and by John Erickson, *The Road to Stalingrad* (London: Weidenfeld & Nicolson, 1983 (1975)).

54. Both these historians were publishing in the 1960s, but the full maturity of their scholarship is perhaps best represented by two works in the following decade: Herbert G. Gutman, *Work, Culture and Society in Industrializing America* (Oxford: Basil Blackwell, 1977) and Robert W. Fogel and Stanley L. Engerman, *Time on the Cross* (Boston, Mass. Little, Brown, 1974).

55. See Robin Winks, *Modus Operandi: An excursion into detective fiction* (Boston, Mass.: David R. Godine, 1982), in which chapter 5 (pp. 45–79) is on spy fiction, and *Cloak and Gown: Scholars in the secret war, 1939–1961* (New York: Morrow, 1987).

56. Not surprisingly, one authority on Canadian intelligence historiography seeks to identify 'national' viewpoints instead of discussing revisionism: Farson, 'National Perceptions'.
57. John E. Wilkie, 'The Secret Service in the War', in *The Spanish–American War: A history by the war leaders* (Norwich, Conn.: Chas. C. Haskell, 1899), pp. 422–36. In my study, I did challenge Wilkie's account, and noted that 'it is by no means clear that the discrediting of Carranza put a stop to all Spanish espionage centered in Montreal', but I neither followed the story through, nor realised the need to explore the records of Spanish consulates throughout Canada: Rhodri Jeffreys-Jones, *American Espionage: From Secret Service to CIA* (New York: Free Press, 1977), p. 33.
58. Margaret Truman, *Murder in the CIA* (New York: Ballantine, 1988), p. 112.
59. Laidlaw, a military veteran like Jansen, is indignant at Donovan's risky overflights of the Burma war zone: conversation in the author's Edinburgh home, 23 Aug. 1990.
60. Betty Friedan, *The Feminine Mystique* (New York: Dell, 1983 (1963)), pp. 82, 114 ff; David St John (pseud. E. Howard Hunt), *The Venus Probe* (New York: Signet, 1966).

2

The secret operations of Spanish consular officials within Canada during the Spanish–American War

GRAEME S. MOUNT

Spain's Montreal spy ring of 1898 deserves another look. The episode surrounding its operations demonstrates that Canada was already and almost inadvertently developing its own foreign policy – one of close co-operation, within limits, with both the United Kingdom and the United States – a policy which would be a hallmark of Canadian foreign relations throughout the twentieth century. It demonstrates that as long ago as 1898, friendly nations were spying inside Canada.[1] It demonstrates that, at a time when Canada lacked a Department of External Affairs and the United Kingdom looked after Canadian interests in other countries, Canada was so important to at least two nations that they were prepared to operate inside Canada without reference to Canadian law or legal niceties. It demonstrates the role of consulates in that disregard for Canadian law, a problem still of concern to the Canadian Security and Intelligence Service (CSIS).[2] It is more difficult, however, to demonstrate that intelligence gathering seriously affected the outcome of the Spanish–American War. Also, while the experiences of 1898 may have affected subsequent intelligence gathering in the United States, there is little evidence that it did so in Canada or in Spain.

Contrary to what others have written, this article demonstrates that clever American counter-intelligence did not smash the Montreal spy ring of 1898.[3] Rhodri Jeffreys-Jones and Norman Penlington had to write without benefit of Spanish sources, without which it was not possible to make the links between the Spanish spies expelled early in July and the rest of Spain's intelligence network.[4] Patricia Sherrin, faced with the same handicap, exaggerated the importance of Spain's spy in Victoria and failed to realise his subordination to superiors in Montreal.[5] As late as 1989, Nathan Miller was to write, 'The breakup of the Montreal spy ring was the most effective piece of American counter-intelligence of the war'.[6] Previous comments by the present writer have explained the context of the spy ring and dealt briefly with its operations, but not in the detail now available.[7]

As Rhodri Jeffreys-Jones has already reported, the United States spy system had two branches – foreign and domestic. In the realm of foreign intelligence, the US Navy had its own spies abroad. A correspondent of the *New York World* watched as Spanish Admiral Pascual Cervera y Topete sailed with his fleet from the Portuguese-owned Cape Verde Islands towards the Caribbean.[8] The United States had a spy at Cadiz itself, base of the Spanish Navy.[9] Since 1895 the Coast Guard had been on the lookout for filibusters offering illegal assistance to Cuban rebels. It was relatively simple to switch sides, and to adapt Coast Guard procedures and conditions to war time conditions. Nor was American foreign intelligence limited to naval matters. American agents travelled behind Spanish lines in Cuba.[10] The United States even had a spy, Domingo Villaverde, right in the palace of the Spanish Captain-General of Cuba; he operated the Havana end of the cable which linked Havana with Key West.[11]

The Spanish government was just as active in the realm of foreign intelligence. The problems addressed in this chapter stemmed from its relocation of officers from its Washington legation to Canada, where they worked alongside officials of the Spanish consulate-general in Montreal. At the outbreak of the war, moreover, Spain upgraded its consular posts in Halifax and Quebec City, key east coast Canadian ports, with the appointments of Joaquin Torroja and Pedro Arias y Solis, previously consuls at Philadelphia and Tampa respectively. Spain also sent a young man, Angel Cabrejo, to Victoria, where he pretended to chaperone his sister who pretended to be studying there. From Victoria he could easily monitor traffic through the Strait of Juan de Fuca, through which ships headed to and from the naval base at Puget Sound would have to pass.

Thus it came to pass that Canada came to be the scene of the cut and thrust of espionage and counter-espionage between a former and a future world power. The State Department in Washington instructed consulates to be on the alert for anything unusual, and US consulates in Halifax, Montreal, Vancouver and Victoria sent numerous reports about suspicious people and events. For example, the United States consul in Victoria, Abraham Smith, quickly became aware of Cabrejo's presence and notified Washington accordingly.[12]

It will already be apparent that consulates were important in a number of ways. For reasons we shall examine below, they were crucial to Spain's intelligence offensive. But they were also important to the United States. US consulates were active on the intelligence front world-wide. From Gibraltar the US consulate could monitor Spanish naval traffic headed in the direction of the Philippines,[13] and in Hong Kong, Americans and Spaniards – including people connected with their respective consulates – maintained a wary eye upon each other.[14] US consulates from St. Thomas in the Danish Virgin Islands[15] to Veracruz in Mexico,[16] as well as in Kingston, Ontario[17] and Montreal[18] fed information to the US Secret Service.

For it was the Secret Service that had assumed responsibility, during the Spanish–American War, for US 'domestic' surveillance. The Secret Service had thirty years of experience watching for smugglers of forged money. It received assistance from the Post Office, which intercepted suspicious correspondence,[19] and from interested military personnel and private citizens. With their help, the Secret Service maintained surveillance over Spain and Spain's friends. To US counter-intelligence ways of thought, Montreal and Toronto fell into the 'domestic' category.

The Secret Service, headed by businessman/journalist John Elbert Wilkie (1860–1914), reported to the Treasury Department, the body directly concerned about counterfeit money. The Coast Guard also reported to the Treasury. There were legitimate concerns that information from Spanish spies would facilitate naval attacks on American cities and provide information about the United States Army, its capacity and its intentions, to Spanish officers. One New York detective agency warned Wilkie to 'be on the lookout for Spanish spies disguised as priests'.[20] Mrs. Cora Hemer of Pittsburgh warned President McKinley, who forwarded the message to the Secret Service, about 'Spaniards who are passing themselves as French and Italians'.[21] R.E. Logan, a military officer at Kansas City, Missouri, advised that Enrique Guerra, Spanish vice-consul in that city until the outbreak of war, had not gone to his reported destination in Mexico for the duration of the conflict, but to Tampa – point of embarkation for Cuba-bound US troops.[22] Some of the Secret Service discoveries were rather important – above all, a letter from a Spaniard in Houston to General Ramon Blanco, Spain's commander in Havana, offering to poison the water supply 'and get two or three thousand of these despicable Americans out of the way in one night'.[23]

While these were matters for legitimate concern, other Secret Service activities were potentially a source of diplomatic embarrassment. For example, Wilkie received a warning from a Post Office official in Washington to keep one Mrs George B. Bacon of Montreal under close surveillance,[24] and the Secret Service intercepted Spanish consular mail from Jamaica[25] and the Bahamas[26] – yet there is no evidence that anyone approached the neutral governments concerned in order to request permission for these activities.

Canada as a whole proved attractive to the Spaniards for a variety of reasons. First, Canada offered direct cable service to Europe. Most cables south of the United States led to that country, the inviolability of whose cable system Luis Polo y Bernabe, the Spanish Minister in the United States at the outbreak of hostilities, reportedly did not trust.[27] Forced to leave Washington, Polo and his colleagues took an express train to Buffalo and crossed the border at Niagara Falls. Toronto's *Mail and Empire* reported that as soon as he found himself on Canadian soil, Count Polo 'received and sent a large number of cable and telegraphic messages'.[28] One of Polo's concerns while in Ontario was the safety of Spanish subjects working in the cigar industry at Tampa, Florida.[29] From Toronto, Polo advised Pio Guillon, the Minister of State or Foreign Minister, that communications were possible with Spanish authorities in Cuba through the Spanish consulate in Kingston, Jamaica. He had made arrangements, reported Polo, for schooners to run from the north coast of Jamaica to Santiago de Cuba.[30]

Also helpful was the fact that Canada appeared to have only minimal counter-intelligence to monitor the Spaniards and their activities. Interference from the host government seemed unlikely in Canada.[31] Until crises arising out of the First World War forced a reassessment of the arrangement, Canada did not control its own foreign relations but left such matters to the United Kingdom. The British Empire was to speak with one voice, and if the United Kingdom went to war, all parts of the Empire found themselves automatically at war against the common enemy. If the government at Westminster proclaimed neutrality, as Lord Salisbury's government did in 1898, the entire Empire would be neutral. Foreign embassies and legations were across the Atlantic in London, and Canada had neither a diplomatic corps of its own nor a body to watch the diplomats, officials and spies of others.

Foreign governments which wanted to send a message to the

Canadian government in Ottawa were supposed to contact the Foreign Office in London, which then related the contents to the Colonial Office, which in turn told the Governor-General in Ottawa, *de jure* an appointee of the Crown but *de facto* an appointee of the British government. Foreign countries, did, however, have consular posts on Canadian soil, and they could report to their respective embassies in London or directly to their own Foreign Offices. Spain had opened consular posts in Quebec City in 1865, Halifax in 1867, and Montreal in 1870, where officials could assist merchants with Spanish goods or sailors in distress. The presence of these posts meant that there was an infrastructure into which Polo and members of the legation staff could blend.

Montreal offered particular advantages. By 1898 Spain had a consulate-general in that city, led by Consul-General Eusebio Bonilla Martel. Toronto, by contrast, had only a Spanish vice-consulate headed by an Anglo-Canadian, and the staff from the Washington legation would have been highly conspicuous beside him. Besides, Montreal was the hub of Canada's rail transportation network. Trains to New York, Halifax and the Pacific coast radiated from what was then Canada's largest and most strategically located city. Also, from Montreal, observers could monitor the movement of ships between the Great Lakes and the Atlantic Ocean, and in that city Spanish officials could establish and make contact with decision-makers at several Canadian head offices. If Canada was the country from which to operate, Montreal had to be the centre of any Canadian operations.

On 6 May the legation staff – including First Secretary Juan Dubosc and Naval Attaché Ramon Carranza – took a train to Montreal. Once there, the legation staff occupied rooms 126 and 128 at the Windsor Hotel on Dominion Square,[32] and proceeded to work in conjunction with Bonilla's Spanish consulate-general. From Montreal, Polo sent an agent to Washington to uncover what he could about a possible US invasion of Cuba.[33] On 20 May, his last full day in Montreal, Polo assigned specific intelligence (*vigilancia*) duties to members of his staff and provided a monthly budget for that purpose.[34] Polo evidently made no attempt to establish contact directly with any of Spain's Canadian consuls. Similarly, he avoided contact with both Canadian and British Columbia authorities. Consul-General Bonilla, however, was in touch with Angel Cabrejo in Victoria[35] – as well as with Joaquin Torroja, the Spanish consul in Halifax.[36]

On 21 May, the day Polo left Montreal, Bonilla received an additional £2,000 for intelligence and telegrams.[37] Two days later, he and Dubosc began to send cable after cable to the Minister of State. Their ciphered cables reported on the movements of US warships in the Pacific and in the Caribbean, on US troop movements, and on US war plans. For example, on 26 May Bonilla reported rumours that the United States would not attack Havana before destroying the Spanish fleet.[38] As early as 4 June, Dubosc was able to identify Puerto Rico as a target for invasion.[39] Not a single cable bore Carranza's name, although he recruited spies who funnelled data to him. Aware of their high profile, the transplants from Washington hired spies whose background was not Spanish and whose surnames ended in consonants. One was George Downing, a former officer of the United States Navy. The name J. Henry Balfour appeared on a letter mailed to Carranza from Wyncote, Pennsylvania, which the Secret Service managed to intercept. Anxious for people with military experience to join the United States Army at Tampa and at San Francisco, Carranza managed to find Frank Arthur Mellor of Kingston, Ontario, who in turn recruited others. Carranza also hired Englishmen, presumably because they would not be as obvious as Spanish spies. These individuals enjoyed varying degrees of success.

The Secret Service was well aware of what Dubosc and Carranza were doing. While Carranza talked to Downing at the Windsor Hotel, a Secret Service agent in the next room listened and took notes. Downing was arrested in Washington and was found dead in his jail cell a few days later.[40] The Secret Service intercepted a letter from a Spanish official in Madrid to Dubosc while Dubosc was still in Toronto.[41] On 28 May one W.A. Wallace of Denver, Colorado, informed George D. Meikeljohn, the Assistant Secretary of War, that he had overheard a conversation in which Dubosc's name was mentioned.[42] Secret Service files include even a 21 May newspaper report under a Montreal dateline that, although Polo was leaving for Spain, Dubosc was remaining to 'direct Spain's spy system in America'.

On 6 June Canada's major newspapers carried banner headlines about these activities. An American had entered the house at 42 Tupper Street into which Dubosc and Carranza had moved, stolen a letter which Carranza had written to a cousin in Spain but had not yet mailed, and passed it along to his superiors in Washington. The letter purportedly contained a description of Carranza's espionage activities, details of US naval disposition, and a recommendation that the time was now ripe for the Cadiz squadron to bombard Boston, Portland and Long Island.[43] Washington officials translated

Carranza's letter into English and released it to the newspapers, according to Carranza embellishing its contents in the process.[44] Sir Julian Pauncefote, British Ambassador in Washington, saw what he thought was the original letter in the company of an embassy official well versed in Spanish, and he guaranteed the authenticity of the translation. Whether the published letter was a translation of the authentic original, however, remains in some doubt.[45]

Repercussions of this exposé rebounded in Madrid, London, Washington, and Ottawa, but Dubosc, the anchorman at the communications desk, stalled for time. He hired a Montreal lawyer, H.C. St Pierre, to argue his case with Canadian authorities.[46] At a press conference on 9 June, Dubosc denied any wrongdoing at all. It was perfectly all right, he said, to provide 'Spain with news and general information . . . published openly here in the newspapers'. Of course, given the nature of Carranza's activities, Dubosc was not being entirely honest. Nevertheless, Dubosc threatened that any deportations of Spaniards arising from the incident would seriously damage British neutrality.[47]

Despite Dubosc's warning, the Canadian government of Sir Wilfrid Laurier ordered both him and Carranza to leave Canada, but Dubosc remained in Montreal until 9 July. In the month that remained to him, he continued to inundate Madrid with cables. On 8 June, for example, he reported the American army's logistical problems in Tampa, the rallying point for troops prior to departure in Cuba, where soldiers were suffering heat prostration and mules were dying. The next day, while notifying Madrid of the plans of Admiral William T. Sampson and the 'deplorable' state of the US Army, he said he was certain that the Canadian government 'would expel us'. 'We are surrounded by American spies,' commented Dubosc before returning to the subject of ship movements. Over the next month, Dubosc and Bonilla sent dozens of additional cables about US ship and troop movements, the state of the US Army, and US war plans.

By 21 June Dubosc had also established contacts within Montreal's business community to find ships that would take food and other necessities to Spanish forces in Cuba and Puerto Rico.[48] The very day of his departure, Dubosc was still active, advising Madrid about attempts to send food from Halifax to Spanish soldiers in Cuba and Puerto Rico, announcing the annexation of Hawaii by the United States and speculating about the Philippines.[49] Furthermore, he made sure that Spanish clandestine operations would continue after his departure. They became the responsibility of the consul-general at Montreal and of the consuls at Halifax and Quebec City.[50] Spain's men in these last two cities who would be assisting Bonilla were, as already noted, men of experience.

One can argue, of course, that the American agent who entered the Tupper Street household and stole the Carranza letter were more deserving of expulsion than the Spanish officials, who had broken no Canadian law. However, British policy at the time was to cultivate good relations with the United States, and the Laurier government was not inclined to rock the boat. Thus, despite Spanish protests, Colonial Secretary Joseph Chamberlain instructed Laurier to expel Carranza and Dubosc, and it would have been contrary to both British policy and Laurier's own sentiments to prosecute any Americans. In British eyes, Dubosc 'was using Canadian territory for the purpose of operations of a belligerent nature against the United States government'.[51] Rejecting the charge, Spanish authorities continued to protest the expulsions long after the war had ended.[52]

Spanish operations in Montreal could nevertheless, could continue because, unlike Carranza and Dubosc, Consul-General Bonilla had a legitimate reason for being in Canada. Thanks to a 'patriotic' employee of the Western Union Telegraph Company, the U S Secret Service managed to intercept ciphered telegrams which Bonilla had sent to Spain's agents in Vancouver and Victoria, Frank Mellor and Angel Cabrejo respectively. In the absence of the key, the telegrams were not useful to the American interceptors, who discussed Bonilla's role among themselves but decided not to raise the matter with the Canadian government.[53] So Bonilla continued, without impediment, to cable Madrid about US war plans and ship movements, and with news from the war zone as reported by American newspapers and other sources.[54]

Within the confines of the possibilities open to it, the Spanish government made use of the intelligence it received from Montreal. Despite the fact that Canada still lacked the legal right to deal directly with foreign countries, Bonilla took it upon himself to protest to Ottawa over permission which Canadian authorities had given the American cruiser, the *Gresham*, to sail out of Lake Ontario, through Canadian waters on the St Lawrence River, towards the Atlantic Ocean. Spain's new Minister of State, the Duke of Almodovar del Rio, approved Bonilla's initiative , and instructed Spain's ambassador in London, the Count of Rascon, to do what he could to stop the *Gresham* from reaching international waters.

Rascon protested that the *Gresham*'s passage would constitute 'a clear violation of [Canadian] neutrality'.[55]

Alerted by the British consulate in Chicago that the *Gresham* and three sister ships were setting sail, Lord Salisbury had time to prepare for a confrontation with Spain. Salisbury told Spanish authorities that, before the outbreak of war, the government of Canada had promised the *Gresham*'s commander that she would be allowed to set sail. Although the war had subsequently started, Canadian authorities believed that they should keep their promise. When Rascon persisted, Salisbury assured him that he had telegraphed Montreal but 'had not yet received a categorical reply'. Rascon finally had to settle for a request that Salisbury insist that the Canadian government act 'in strict compliance with neutrality'.[56] Despite the outcome, the time and energy that the Duke of Almodovar del Rio and the Count of Rascon gave to the *Gresham* affair provide impressive testimony to the effects of consular intelligence reports and initiatives.

Throughout the spring and summer, Bonilla continued to receive sums of money from Madrid with which to pay for *vigilancias*.[57] The Spanish Foreign Office stated that the moneys were coming 'to improve the situation of this Consulate General in the present circumstances' on the advice of the Spanish Minister in Washington (Polo), who, of course, was no longer there.[58] Bonilla sent news of ship movements[59] as well as of matters of public record, such as the contents of the Governor-General's Speech from the Throne at the end of the 1898 parliamentary session. (In that speech, Lord Aberdeen – the Governor-General – expressed his hearty approval at the improvement in relations between Canada and the United States.)[60] In Polo's absence, Bonilla supervised Spain's consular employees across Canada, in Bermuda and throughout the West Indies. In addition, he continued with normal consular duties, such as the repatriation of Spanish prisoners of war, and looked after the requirements of Spanish subjects throughout North America, with Austrian help where necessary.[62] Once the fighting stopped, moreover, Bonilla fed Madrid rumours of US plans for the peace talks.[63]

On balance, it appears that the departures of Polo, Carranza, and Dubosc added stress to Bonilla's life, but that he managed to cover the gaps rather well. The same cannot be said of Dubosc and Carranza. Energetic, patriotic and competent, they had to cope with too many American counter-spies in Montreal. The advantages of Montreal's accessibility to the United States, which were partially responsible for attracting the Spaniards to that city, could also work

in the Americans' favour, and given the greater proximity of the
United States than of Spain to Montreal and the bias of the British
and Canadian governments, the Spaniards could not win, no matter
how accurate the information they managed to retrieve.

Yet, although it made sense to know what the enemy was doing
and thinking, all the intelligence in the world could not have helped
Spain to defeat the United States in 1898. Spain's was a lost cause,
and its leaders knew it. Indeed, one can argue that the Spanish—
American War, bloody and unpleasant for those who participated,
was also a charade whose roots lay in the Spanish political situation.
Spain's Liberal Prime Minister, Praxedes Sagasta, had assumed
office on 4 October 1897 after the assassination of his Conservative
predecessor, Antonio Canovas del Castillo. For a generation the
two men had headed coalitions which took turns in and out of
government. One of Sagasta's first steps upon regaining office in
1897 was the dismissal of General Valeriano Weyler y Nicolau,
Captain General of Cuba. As Captain-General, Weyler had directed
the war against the Cuban insurgents, and his determined measures
proved grist for the mill of anti-Spanish propagandists inside the
United States.

Spaniards who wanted Spain to keep its Empire regarded Weyler
as a hero, and on his return to the Spanish peninsula they gave
him a hero's welcome. Sagasta's grant of autonomy (internal self-
government) to Cuba and Puerto Rico early in 1898 reinforced the
Prime Minister's soft image in the eyes of Weyler and among his
supporters, and Weyler was not reluctant to make speeches. Given
the chauvinistic mood Weyler helped to engender, Sagasta had
little choice but to fight the United States. Defeat at the hands
of the North American giant after a gallant fight would be more
honourable than Spanish withdrawal without an international war.
Such 'honour' might well allow the Sagasta government and the
fragile monarchy to survive; Spanish withdrawal from Cuba without
a war against the United States would probably be fatal to the
Sagasta government and the dynasty.[64] And Spaniards did fight
gallantly – on land, at sea, and in the intelligence war. Lose they
did, but the dynasty survived.

The competence of some Spanish intelligence officials cannot
disguise the overall hopelessness of Spain's cause in 1898. To a
certain extent, it is true that Madrid contributed to its own defeat.
For example, it was in vain that Admiral Patricio Montojo y Pasaron
pleaded with his home government for equipment necessary to the
defence of the Philippines. Segismundo Bermejo, the Minister of

the Marine, told him to compensate for lack of weaponry with additional enthusiasm, but enthusiasm alone was no match for the US fleet of Admiral George Dewey.[65] Admiral Cervera, too, found fault with high officialdom – he was appalled at the lack of planning on Bermejo's part before he had to set sail for the Caribbean on a voyage which he considered utterly quixotic.[66]

More seriously, though, geography, natural resources and people were on the side of the United States. For the Americans, Cuba was close to home, and their ships arrived in the battle zone ready for action. For the Spaniards, Cuba was a distant place, and their ships arrived in need of refurbishing.[67] Coal – the source of fuel for both navies – was readily available to the Americans but not to the Spaniards. The engines of two of Cervera's ships, the *Maria Teresa* and the *Cristobal Colon*, were in such need of fine tuning that they burned excessive quantities of coal – 900 tons of it between Cadiz and the Cape Verde Islands alone. In the Cape Verdes it proved to be impossible to buy more than 700 tons, for the prescient United States consul there had bought most of the available coal himself.[68] Informed by Bermejo that there were quantities of coal on the Dutch West Indian island of Curaçao, Cervera headed there but managed to get only 400 tons.[69] With his ships undermaintained and underfuelled, Cervera's ability to manoeuvre was limited, so he took shelter in the harbour of Santiago, Cuba. When a British vessel attempted to deliver coal to his fleet at that port, the US Navy captured her.[70] Even had mobility not been a problem, the Spanish admiral would have found most Cuban harbours in the hands of insurgents and friendly to the Americans.[71] Without effective naval power, Spain could not be a viable adversary against the United States.[72]

Prime Minister Laurier was probably wise to expel Dubosc and Carranza, although it was quite partial of him to do so while the American burglars remained at large. Whatever the merits (or otherwise) of Spanish goals in the Spanish–American War – and the desirability of continued Spanish rule in Cuba was, at best, arguable – Spain could not win. There was no advantage to Canada in an association with the loser, especially when the adversary was the adjacent and powerful United States. Canadians had paid a price a couple of generations earlier when, at the end of the Civil War, the United States government had inflicted penalties as reprisals for alleged British North American sympathies for the Confederacy, and when, with US popular support, the Fenians were able to launch raids across the international border.[73] Between

1899 and 1902, by contrast, when the British Empire found itself at war in South Africa, Canada did not experience Irish-American terrorism comparable to that of the 1860s and 1870s. Following the Spanish–American War, American public opinion was more friendly to Canada than it had been on the earlier occasion.

Probably because the war was militarily one-sided, decided by two quick US naval victories off the Philippines and Cuba, neither Canada nor Spain absorbed serious lessons about intelligence gathering. Canada's knowledge of the art was to remain rudimentary for a long time. Decades later, the Canadian government still had to depend upon British and American sources to screen foreign diplomats or refugees entering Canada. In 1942, for example, the Spanish government of Generalissimo Francisco Franco nominated Fernando de Kobbe-Chinchilla as that country's consul to Vancouver. Before the Canadian government accepted him as *persona grata*, it asked the British and American governments whether to do so. Only after he had been several months at his post did Ottawa discover that he might be a Japanese spy.[74] When Soviet cipher clerk Igor Gouzenko defected from his legation in September 1945 with extensive documentation on an international spy ring, the Canadian government did not know what to do and had to seek advice from the British and Americans.[75] As refugee claimants left Europe for Canada on the eve of the Second World War, Canadian authorities depended on the FBI and British security agencies to distinguish between genuine refugees and communist, Nazi and fascist infiltrators.[76] Because of this continuing Canadian dependence at the end of the Second World War, British and American intelligence agencies were able to debrief Nazi agents and then 'approve' them as immigrants fit for residence in Canada.[77]

The results were different in the United States. According to Jeffreys-Jones, the war was more important for intelligence than intelligence was for the war. That might not have been the case had the Spanish Navy arranged an adequate coal supply. The five armoured Spanish cruisers which were available might have harassed United States shipping, as had the *Alabama* and her sister ships during the Civil War, while Spain's professional army held America's badly organised amateurs to a draw in Cuba.[78] This is, however, one of the might-have-beens of history.

On the other hand, the Secret Service developed considerable expertise during the 1898 war, expertise that was to prove useful in tracking down German spies during the First World War. The Secret Service provided the federal Bureau of Investigation with personnel when the administration of Theodore Roosevelt established that fledgling national police force in 1908, and later J. Edgar Hoover directed the bureau by methods which the Secret Service had used. Even the private sector was to feel the impact of the Spanish–American War, for William J. Burns, founder of Burns Security, was a Secret Service veteran of 1898.[79] In turn Burns became director of the Bureau of Investigation (later known as the FBI) from 1921 to 1924.[80]

Rhodri Jeffreys-Jones and Nathan Miller see more sinister repercussions arising from the events of 1898. In the context of the Watergate scandal, Jeffreys-Jones commented: 'abuses can occur when surveillance is instituted in the name of national security . . . Continuous, central surveillance was . . . begun by the United States during the Spanish–American War of 1898, when the Treasury Department's Secret Service organised an "emergency force" for counter-intelligence work'.[81] By its performance in Montreal, Nathan Miller commented:

> the Secret Service established guideposts for the future. American officials violated Canadian neutrality, committed burglary, stole a private communication, and jailed a suspect for the duration of the war without charge. Obviously, in the burgeoning world of intelligence professionalism, legal niceties were not to be allowed to get in the way of a job well done.[82]

Information on Spain's intelligence service is not as readily available,[83] but Spain's failure in 1898 was a political/military one, not a matter of faulty intelligence. Since 1898, Spain has been involved in two external conflicts. The one in Morocco went so badly that King Alfonso XIII turned away from civilian politicians and called upon Miguel Primo de Rivera to restore stability. (Primo's dictatorship lasted from 1923 to 1930.) During the Second World War, Franco sent his Blue Division to join German forces in their self-destructive adventure on the Soviet front. Good intelligence could not have produced victories in either Morocco or the Soviet Union; the military difficulties, as in 1898, were too overwhelming. Perhaps amid the losses of the Spanish–American War, the historian can learn the most important lesson of all: good intelligence by itself cannot ensure victory.

Notes

1. *Globe and Mail*, 14 Oct. 1989.
2. *Globe and Mail*, 22 Feb. 1986.
3. Rhodri Jeffreys-Jones, *American Espionage: From Secret Service to CIA* (New York: Free Press, 1977); Miller Lowenthal, *US Intelligence: Evolution and Anatomy* (New York: Praeger, 1989); see also 'Catching Spain's Spies', *Boston Sunday Herald*, 2 Oct. 1898; and J.E. Wilkie, 'The Secret Service in the war,' in *The American–Spanish War: A history by the war leaders* (Norwich, Conn.: Chas. C. Haskell, 1899).
4. Norman Penlington, *Canada and Imperialism, 1896–1899* (Toronto: Univ. of Toronto Press, 1965), pp. 101–8. G.J.A. O'Toole's otherwise excellent book, *The Spanish War: An American Epic* (New York: W.W. Norton, 1984), which discusses the gathering of Spanish and American intelligence around the world, fails even to mention Montreal in its index.
5. P.M. Sherrin, 'Spanish spies in Victoria,' *BC Studies*, XXXVI (winter 1977–78), 23–33.
6. Nathan Miller, *Spying for America: The hidden history of US intelligence* (New York: Paragon House, 1989), p. 171.
7. Edelgard E. Mahant and Graeme S. Mount, *An Introduction to Canadian–American Relations*, 2nd ed (Toronto: Nelson, 1989), pp. 78–80; Graeme S. Mount, 'Friendly liberator or predatory aggressor? Some Canadian impressions of the United States during the Spanish–American War,' *North/South: Canadian Journal of Caribbean and Latin American Studies*, XI, 22 (1986), 59–76.
8. O'Toole, *Spanish War*, p. 194
9. *ibid.*, p. 228.
10. William R. Corson, *The Armies of Ignorance: The rise of the American intelligence empire* (New York: Dial 1967), p. 595.
11. O'Toole, *Spanish War*, pp. 19, 32–3, 208 and elsewhere.
12. Abraham E. Smith, Victoria, to A.A. Adee, Assistant Secretary of State, Washington, 18 June 1898, Despatch 64, US Department of State, Records of the US Consulate in Victoria, microfilm T-130–12, National Archives of the USA, Washington, DC.
13. David F. Trask, *The War with Spain in 1898* (New York: Macmillan, 1981), p. 374.
14. *ibid.*, pp. 68, 97, 375.
15. William R. Day, Secretary of State, Washington, DC, to the Secretary of the Treasury, Washington, DC, 25 June: Records of the Secret Service, Correspondence 1863–1950 (Re Spy Suspects during the Spanish–American War), National Records Center, Suitland, Md. Cited hereafter as RSS.
16. Thomas W. Cridler, Third Assistant Secretary of State, Washington, DC, to the Secretary of the Treasury, Washington, 28 May; RSS.
17. Cridler, Washington to the Secretary of the Treasury, Washington, 24 May RSS.
18. John Bassett Moore, Assistant Secretary of State, Washington, to the Secretary of the Treasury, Washington, 1 July, RSS. Moore forwarded a telegram from John L. Bittinger, US consul-general in Montreal. See also Cridler, Washington, to the Secretary of the Treasury, Washington, 18, June; RSS. Cridler advised about the activities of Spain's agent in Victoria who was sending ciphered telegrams to Montreal.

19. E.g. Agnes Harrison, Santa Cruz, California, to Prime Minister Praxedes Sagasta, Madrid, 20 April RSS.
20. John W. Kimball, Kimball's Detective Agency, New York, to John E. Wilkie, Washington, 1 July, RSS.
21. Mrs Cora Hemer, Pittsburgh, to President William McKinley, Washington, 6 July, RSS.
22. R. E. Longan, Kansas City, to Adjutant-General, US Army, Washington, DC, 17 June, RSS.
23. Lena Huhn me Agguirra, Houston, to General Ramon Blanco, Havana, 29 May, RSS.
24. G.B. Hamlet, Chief Inspector, Post Office Department, Washington, to John E. Wilkie, Washington, 27 May, RSS.
25. Jose Buigar de Delmar, Kingston, Jamaica, to Pedro Solis, Quebec City, 2 Aug., RSS.
26. The Spanish Consul in Nassau to the Spanish Consul-General in Montreal, 21 May, RSS.
27. *The Globe*, 22 April.
28. *The Mail and Empire*, 22 April.
29. Polo, Toronto, to the Minister of State, Madrid, 27 April, Document #118, Legajo #H1481, Archives of the *Spanish Foreign Office*, Madrid. Cited hereafter as Spanish Archives.
30. Polo, Toronto, to the Minister of State, Madrid, 28 April, in *Spanish Diplomatic Correspondence and Documents, 1896–1900: Presented to the Cortes by the Minister of State* (translation) (Washington: Government Printing Office, 1905), p. 180.
31. This was a reasonable assumption, though there was a Canadian Secret Service in 1898, quite distinct from the Dominion Police, and it did assist the Americans in Halifax.
32. *The Montreal Star*, 17 May.
33. Polo, Toronto, to the Minister of State, Madrid, 13 May, Legajo #H2420, subfile Aprovisionamientos en el Canada, Spanish Archives, Document 13.
34. Bonilla, Montreal, to the Minister of State, Madrid, 3 June, Legajo #H1973, Spanish Archives.
35. The author has checked the 1898 records of both the premier and the lieutenant-governor of British Columbia at the Provincial Archives of British Columbia, Victoria. For evidence of Bonilla's contacts with Cabrejo, see Bonilla, Montreal, to the Minister of State, Madrid, 15 May, Legajo #H1973, Despatch #22, Spanish Archives; also, the Minister of State, Madrid, to Bonilla, Montreal, summary of despatch #34 (11 July), July summary, Legajo #H1973, Spanish Archives.
36. E.g., Minister of State, Madrid, to Bonilla, Montreal, 15 April, Legajo #H1973, Despatch #10, Spanish Archives.
37. Minister of State, Madrid, to Bonilla, Montreal, summary of despatch #13 (21 May), May summary, Legajo #H2420, Spanish Archives.
38. Between 23 May and 31 May, Dubosc and Bonilla sent sixteen cables to the Ministry of State, Legajo #H2420, Spanish Archives.
39. Dubosc, Montreal, to the Minister of State, Madrid, 4 June, Legajo #H2420, subfile Aprovisionamientos en el Canada, Spanish Archives, Document 12.
40. Jeffreys-Jones, *American Espionage*, p. 31.
41. Marques Puente de Loma, Madrid, to Juan Dubosc, Toronto, late April, RSS.

42. W.A. Wallace, Denver, to George d. Meikeljohn, Washington, 28 May; RSS.

43. This summary is taken from a version of the letter, Ramon de Carranza to José Gomez Ymay, 26 May, published in Wilkie, 'Secret Service in the War', pp. 433–6.

44. *La Presse* and *The Montreal Star*, 6 June. See also *The Globe* and *The Mail and Empire* of the same date.

45. Jeffreys-Jones, American Espionage, p. 41.

46. Jeffreys-Jones, 'The Montreal spy ring of 1898 and the origins of "domestic" surveillance in the United States,' *Canadian Review of American Studies*, V, 2 (Fall, 1974), pp. 125–127. There are several letters between the Canadian Prime Minister, Sir Wilfrid Laurier, and St Pierre in Volume 79 of the Laurier Papers, National Archives of Canada, Ottawa. See also a letter from Sir Julian Pauncefote, Washington, to Lord Aberdeen (Governor-General of Canada), Ottawa, 9 June, Laurier Papers, Volume 750, #215006. See also the Colonial Office memo of 12 June, CO 42/862, p. 493.

47. *The Montreal Star*, 10 June.

48. Dubosc, Montreal, to the Minister of State, Madrid, 21 June, Cable #35, Legajo #H2420, Spanish Archives.

49. Dubosc, Montreal, to the Minister of State, Madrid, 3 June, Legajo #H1973, Spanish Archives.

50. Dubosc, Montreal, to the Minister of State, Madrid, 6 July, Cable #51, Legajo #H2420, Spanish Archives.

51. Colonial Office memo of 28 July, CO 42/859, pp. 237–8. See also letter from the Foreign Office to the Colonial Office, 27 Oct., CO 42/864, p. 209.

52. The expulsions attracted attention in both the Spanish Cortes and the Madrid press. A Cuban deputy, Rafael Maria de Labra, raised the matter on the floor of the Cortes, 19 June; Valentin Gomparre to the Minister of State, 21 June, Document E29, Legajo #H2420, subfile Discusion Parlamentaria. There were front page stories in the Madrid newspaper, *El Liberal*, 12 and 13 June and 12 Aug. *see also* El Tiempo (Madrid), 8 June.

53. Bonilla, Montreal, to Mellor, Vancouver, 13 and 15 July; Bonilla, Montreal, to Cabrejo, Victoria, 15 July; A.W. Greely, Chief Signal Officer, Washington, to the Assistant Secretary of War, 16 July; all in RSS.

54. Bonilla, Montreal, to the Minister of State, Madrid, Cables #55–66, Legajo #H2420, Spanish Archives.

55. Minister of State, Madrid to Bonilla, Montreal, summary of despatch #18, 13 June, June summary, Legajo #H1973, Spanish Archives.

56. Count of Rascon, London, to the Minister of State, Madrid, 27 June 1898, Legajo #H2420, Spanish Archives. See also the letter of Pauncefote, Washington, to Lord Aberdeen, Ottawa, 26 April, Laurier Papers, Volume 750, #214945.

57. E.g. Minster of State, Madrid, to Bonilla, Montreal: money for Angel J. Cabrejo, Victoria, #22, 15 May; £2,000, #27, 29 May; May summaries. £150 to be paid monthly for a special commission to Manuel Martinez Aquiar for responsibilities in Canada and the United States, 2 July; 1,800, #42, 15 July; July summaries; Legajo #H1973, Spanish Archives.

58. Minister of State, Madrid, to Bonilla, Montreal, #22, 30 June, June summary, Legajo #H1973, Spanish Archives.
59. Bonilla, Montreal, to the Minister of State, Madrid, #54, 8 August, Aug. summary, Legajo #H1973, Spanish Archives.
60. Canada, House of Commons, *Debates*, 13 June, p. 7890. Bonilla, Montreal, to the Minister of State, Madrid, #18, 13 June; Bonilla, Montreal, to the Minister of State, Madrid, #27, 15 June; June summary. Minister of State, Madrid, to Bonilla, Montreal, #23, 11 July, July summary; Legajo #H1973, Spanish Archives.
61. E.g. Bonilla, Montreal, to the Minister of State, Madrid, #40, 14 July, July summary, Legajo #H1973, Spanish Archives.
62. E.g. Minister of State, Madrid, to Bonilla, Montreal, #10, 11 June, June summary; Bonilla, Montreal, to the Minister of State, Madrid, #43, 8 August, August summary; Legajo #H1973, Spanish Archives.
63. Bonilla, Montreal, to the Minister of State, Madrid, 14 Sept. (Cable #69) and 21 Sept. (Cable #70), Legajo #H2420, Spanish Archives.
64. Trask, *War with Spain*, p. 59; O'Toole, *Spanish War*, pp. 65–6, 109, 121, 379.
65. O'Toole, *Spanish War*, p. 179.
66. *ibid.*, pp. 141, 167, 168.
67. *ibid.*, pp. 97–98, 216.
68. *ibid.* p. 170.
69. *ibid.* p. 211.
70. *ibid.* pp. 214–18.
71. Havana was one important exception: *ibid.*, p. 121.
72. This is certainly O'Toole's opinion: *ibid*, p. 357.
73. Mahant and Mount, *Canadian–American Relations*, pp. 52–4.
74. Canada, Department of External Affairs, *Documents on Canadian External Relations*, pp. 1867–72. Above all, see the Memorandum from the Under-Secretary of State for External Affairs to the Prime Minister, 11 Sept. 1943, p. 1867.
75. Denis Smith, *Diplomacy of Fear: Canada and the cold war, 1941–1948* (Toronto: Univ. of Toronto Press, 1988), pp. 94–109.
76. Donald Avery, 'Canada's response to European refugees, 1939–1945: the security dimension', in Norman Hillmer, Bogdan Kordan and Lubomyr Luciuk, eds., *On Guard for Thee: War, ethnicity, and the Canadian state, 1939–1945* (Hull, PQ: Canada, Minister of Supply and Services, 1988), p. 182.
77. The findings of the researcher Alti Rodal on this point created considerable media consternation in Canada late in 1987. See, for example, Sol Littman, 'Strong vibes from a quiet source', *Canadian Dimension*, XXI, 7 (Nov. Dec. 1987), 24–7.
78. Interview with Rhodri Jeffreys-Jones, Edinburgh, 18 Oct. 1989. For further evidence that this was a possibility, see O'Toole, *Spanish War*, p. 381.
79. Interview with Rhodri Jeffreys-Jones, Edinburgh, 18 Oct. 1989.
80. Jeffreys-Jones, *American Espionage*, p. 22.
81. Rhodri Jeffreys-Jones, 'The Montreal spy ring p. 119.
82. Miller, *Spying*, pp. 171–2.
83. Even Ernest R. May does not mention it: May, *Knowing One's Enemies: Intelligence assessment before the two world wars* (Princeton: Princeton Univ, NJ. Press, 1986). Hugh Thomas, Angus MacKay and Paul Preston, three authorities, have written to the author to say that

they are unaware of any connection between the Spanish–American War and any subsequent development of Spanish intelligence. They also say that they are unaware of any literature on the subject: Hugh Thomas to the author, 1 Nov. 1989; Angus MacKay to the author, 26 Oct. 1989; Paul Preston to the author, 14 Feb. 1990.

The author wishes to express his gratitude to the Social Science and Research Council of Canada for financial assistance with the research of this chapter.

3

Tyler Kent: isolationist or spy?

The name Tyler Kent is occasionally to be found in the footnotes of books dealing with the outbreak of the Second World War. Rarely does he merit more than a few lines, and his copying of the then-secret correspondence between President Franklin D. Roosevelt and the future Prime Minister Winston L.S. Churchill, for which he was arrested in May 1940, is largely dismissed as the action of an unimportant code clerk. Tyler Kent is now a largely forgotten and discredited figure overshadowed by the men with whom he was so closely involved.

And yet history for them and us could so easily have been quite different. This is the case even if one accepts the theory that I shall challenge in this chapter, namely that Kent was an isolationist, who believed that his country, America, should not enter the Second World War. In the course of his job he became aware that, in the critical months of 1940, Roosevelt was secretly in touch with Churchill. He was determined that Roosevelt's behaviour should be brought to public notice and decided to steal the correspondence and show it to isolationists like Charles A. Lindbergh, the famous American aviator then settled in England.

If Kent had been successful in publicising the contents of their correspondence, the political careers of both Roosevelt and Churchill might well have been curtailed. Roosevelt could not have afforded, with a strong isolationist mood in America and a presidential election in prospect in November, being seen to be in secret communication with the British and infringing America's publicly proclaimed stance of neutrality. Kent's actions therefore threatened Roosevelt's chances of defeating his Republican opponent Wendell Wilkie and winning an unprecedented third presidential term.

American aid might have been less generous and Britain would have been forced to continue facing Hitler alone. The result might have been that Churchill, perceived to be operating behind the back of Chamberlain, would have been replaced as prime minister by a British cabinet prepared, in the absence of American aid, to sue for a negotiated peace with Hitler.[1]

Kent was potentially an important participant in the debate about Britain's attempts to enlist American support immediately before and after the fall of France. He was aware of the extent of the Churchill–Roosevelt correspondence, something which is still hotly debated to this day, and his actions had a significance and ramifications that continue even now. Kent's story has been called 'the greatest spy story' of the war[2] and 'unquestionably one of the strangest episodes in US diplomatic history'.[3]

There have always been doubts about Kent's story. Recent evidence has come to light from the files of the State Department and Federal Bureau of Investigation (FBI) suggesting that Kent was not simply a code clerk who felt he needed to expose American foreign policy to Congress. The intelligence writer Nigel West has suggested that Kent was recruited as a Soviet agent while serving in Moscow, and that he was part of a Russian spy ring that operated close to the centre of Anglo-American policy making during the crucial opening months of the Second World War.[4] While conclusive evidence that this is the case has not yet been found, certainly the story of the American code clerk is even stranger and more complicated that it has hitherto appeared.

Tyler Gatewood Kent was born on 24 March 1911 in Newchang, Manchuria where his father, William Patton Kent, was the United States consul. The young Kent followed his father to postings in Leipzig, Switzerland, Bermuda and Belfast and after three years at St Albans School, Washington, he entered Princeton University in 1929. Given his aptitude for languages, it was perhaps not surprising that he should on graduation in 1931 spend the next two years developing these at the universities of Paris and Madrid. Finally, setting his heart on a diplomatic career, he entered the Foreign Service School, Georgetown University, for the academic year 1933–4.

There is still some mystery over how Kent entered the State Department, and in particular how he came to be posted so quickly to Moscow. Writing to Walter Winchell of the New York *Daily Mirror* on 8 March 1944, his mother vaguely claimed that 'enthusiastic about Russia, he was selected in 1933 by Ambassador William Bullitt for the staff to open the American Embassy in Moscow.'[5] According to an FBI minute of Kent's own account when interviewed in 1951, he met a man in 1933.

> name not recalled, in Washington DC who had been in Moscow, Russia, and who told him that the State Department was in need of US personnel accomplished in the Russian language for assignment in Russia. Inasmuch as subject was accomplished in the Russian language, he applied for a position in the diplomatic service of the State Department and after receiving such an appointment as a Clerk in the State Department's diplomatic service, he was assigned to the American Embassy in Moscow, Russia, arriving at the Embassy March 2, 1934.[6]

Kent's references included Harry Bird, the Senator for Virginia, his mother's home state. Interviewed by the FBI in the 1950s, Bullitt claimed that 'Cordell Hull, Secretary of State, had personally recommended Tyler Kent to him for employment', much against Bullitt's own wishes.[7]

America had only just officially recognised the post-revolutionary government and the new posting was a challenging one. Kent's responsibility at the embassy, he later claimed, was 'to read various Russian newspapers and periodicals, translate them, and prepare dispatches from them . . . to contact various Russian agencies and business houses to obtain information of an economic nature . . . to act as courier for the State Department.'[8] After a bad start, in which he was almost fired for laziness, Kent impressed his superiors. Ambassador Bullitt wrote to Assistant Secretary of State Walton Moore in June 1934 that 'young Kent seems to have turned over a new leaf'.[9]

Yet Kent seems to have led an extravagant lifestyle in Moscow, living beyond his apparent means. He had no declared income beyond his diplomatic pay of $2,500 a year, and colleagues later claimed they were surprised to observe that he was able to run a car, live in private rented accommodation and maintain a mistress – Tatania Alexandrovna Ilovaiskaya was the daughter of a Russian professor. But his lifestyle appears to be unconnected with his transfer, in the fateful month of September 1939, to the American embassy in London. Kent later claimed that 'this was a routine transfer and was not initiated by himself nor were there any extenuating circumstances.'[10] Intriguingly, however, an FBI memorandum of 25 May 1944 quotes an undated internal memorandum which suggests 'Kent was transferred from the American Embassy in Moscow, Russia, to the American Embassy in London, England, because he had become persona non grata in Moscow due to his openly critical attitude of Russia.'[11]

For whatever reason, Kent's new posting brought him into the nerve centre of American foreign policy at a critical juncture of the war. All important European diplomatic traffic, including that from Bullitt, now ambassador in Paris, came through London. Kent, as one of the code clerks, saw everything. He was therefore well informed about the secret peace manoeuvres that took place throughout the first six months of the war, in particular the mission of Sumner Welles in the spring of 1940.[12]

It was however the secret correspondence between Roosevelt and Churchill, then First Lord of the Admiralty, that most interested Kent. The young code clerk had become convinced that Roosevelt was operating behind the back of Congress and in direct contradiction of his stated public position of not committing America to the war. Kent soon began making copies of various telegrams, which he later claimed he intended to show to leading isolationists in America and thereby scupper Roosevelt's chances of re-election.[13]

Kent was unaware, however, that he had come under British surveillance on the day he arrived in London, 5 October 1939. His return journey was via Stockholm, and it was there he met a naturalised Swede, Ludwig Matthias. They travelled together to Bergen and Newcastle, and in London had dinner together at the Cumberland Hotel. The British security service, MI5, had been tipped off that Matthias was a Gestapo agent, and he was kept under surveillance. On leaving the Cumberland Hotel, Kent was seen to be carrying a bulky envelope.[14]

He again came to the notice of MI5 at the end of February 1940 when he was observed as being a member of the Right Club, an anti-semitic and anti-communist organisation run by the Member of Parliament for Peebles, Archibald Maule Ramsay.[15] The activities of the Right Club were based around the Russian Tea Rooms in South Kensington, run by a former imperial naval attaché to London called Nikolai Wolkoff. Kent soon came under the spell of the admiral's daughter, Anna, then aged thirty-eight and the club's secretary.[16]

Like Ramsay and Wolkoff, Kent claimed to believe that 'the Nazi menace was the lesser of the two evils as compared to the Communist menace'.[17] He was not alone in this belief. The Right Club had some five hundred members, many of them holding influential positions in the City, government and the armed forces. The Club's chairman was the fifth Duke of Wellington. Another early member was William Joyce, subsequently derisively known as Lord Haw-Haw after he took German citizenship and broadcast Nazi propaganda in English. There were scores of other pro-German groups such as the Link and Anglo-German Fellowship[18] in Britain between 1933 and 1940. Equally, there were many American businessmen who subscribed to the view that a strong Germany could act as a bulwark against Russia.[19]

The Right Club had been penetrated by a young MI5 agent, Joan Miller, who had previously worked for the cosmetics firm, Elizabeth Arden.[20] Miller, who, with her case officer Maxwell Knight, became one of the best-known MI5 agents of the Second World War, had masqueraded, with another MI5 agent Marjorie Mackie, as a fellow-sympathiser in order to determine the full membership of the Right Club and thereby round up all of them at once. Her infiltration of the Right Club paid an unexpected dividend when she was able to pass back to MI5 the fact that Wolkoff was in close touch not just with 'fifth-columnists' but also with the Italian military attaché – and with a clerk at the American embassy. [21]

MI5 for the moment continued to monitor Kent and say nothing. There is no indication that the American authorities were informed of the code clerk's activities, which is surprising given that MI5 quickly discovered that Kent was copying highly secret cables. It may have been that the British needed to collect evidence against Kent, or that MI5 did not feel they could pass on their 'intelligence' without the risk of it being compromised.[22]

It is quite clear from Foreign Office files at the Public Record Office that the British did not trust Kent's ambassador. This was Joseph P. Kennedy, the father of the future president of the United States. Kennedy had expressed defeatist views on the likelihood of British survival in the face of a Nazi onslaught, and cautioned Washington against pinning its faith on a sinking ship. The British authorities monitored the suspect ambassador's every move.[23] Relations were better, however, better, if not entirely candid, between MI5 counter-intelligence chief Guy Liddell and the man responsible for security matters at the American embassy, the chargé d'affaires Herschel Johnson. There is no reason why Johnson should not have been informed without Kennedy knowing, and indeed this may have been the case.

At this point, however, we must note a further twist to the story of US embassy security lapses. On 7 February 1940 Liddell wrote to Johnson:

> I have heard from an informant whose statements have in other respects proved to be accurate, that at any rate just prior to the war and possibly still, the German Secret Service had been receiving from an American Embassy, reports at times two a day, which contained practically everything from Ambassador Kennedy's despatches to President Roosevelt including reports of his interviews with British statesmen and officials. The source from which the German Secret Service got these documents is not definitely known, but is someone who is referred to as 'Doctor', and our informant who is in a position to know is of the opinion that the 'Doctor' is employed in the American Embassy in Berlin.[24]

The next day Johnson wrote a letter marked 'personal and strictly confidential' to Jimmy Dunn at the State Department about this 'disturbing information' enclosing a copy of Liddell's letter.[25] Six days later, after a meeting with 'a man of Liddell's organization', Johnson was able to fill out the background:

> Shortly before the outbreak of the war, a British informant, a German operating in Berlin, conveyed to the British Secret Service certain information of a very important character. Incidental to this transaction it was brought out that the German Secret Service was in possession of very full reports of confidential despatches and telegrams to the Department from this Embassy in which were reported interviews with British statesmen etc. . . . It seems that the informant is actually also in the German Secret Service and in touch with a man named Jankhe, who is in the Abteilung Pfeffer of [Hitler's deputy Rudolph] Hess's office.[26]

The British had had the information for three months, but claimed they needed to check its accuracy before informing the Americans. Johnson grimly noted in the letter 'I personally am not quite sure that the British have told United States all they know.'[27]

It seemed apparent that the leaks were coming from the American embassy in London or the State Department because none of the other American embassies had been privy to the leaked information. The search began to find out the identity of 'the Doctor'. Progress was slow. Assistant Secretary of State Breckinridge Long noted in his diary on 4 April:

> It has developed that certain information has been leaking. Just where the leak is nobody knows. How recently there has been leakage is not known. We do not know that there has been any leakage since the actual outbreak of the war. The reason we do know there was a leakage prior to that time is that we have now been confidentially informed from British sources that certain American news is known at Berlin. It must have got to Berlin out of London through some form of secret communication. How it was obtained in the first instance for transmission to Germany is not known. On the theory that it may have been a leakage from somewhere over here I called a secret conference consisting of [Adolph A.] Berle [the assistant secretary of state notionally in charge of intelligence co-ordination from 1940], Dunn, Fitch, Berle's Assistant Warren and Mr Frank, my Assistant. We decided to make a thorough check of the whole line of communication, physical and otherwise, from the time it leaves the desk until it leaves the boundaries of the United States on the wires. Also it will be a two-way check and will cover the wires of incoming messages and the whole distribution system within the Department. No one else is to know about it.[28]

The leak could not have come from Kent who only joined the embassy staff after the supposed leak began. Was there another spy in the embassy passing material to the Germans, or could there be another explanation? One veteran of the US Central Intelligence Agency (CIA) has put forward an interesting theory:

> Is it conceivable that the Liddell visit to Johnson was a 'valentine' suggesting that US commo was penetrated and that the Germans (if not the British) were regularly reading JPK's output? Was it an effusively polite way of telling Kennedy that his zipper was down? The names Hess and Janke thrown in to tickle the Americans. (Everyone knew Rudy and Jankhe had previously been a hot ticket in Mexico). Was this the first punch at JPK by the services?[29]

Perhaps 'the Doctor' never existed and the British were merely subtly telling the Americans that they should tighten up their security.[30] If 'the Doctor' did exist, the British may have been trying to neutralise him by warning him that he was known. The most likely explanation may be that MI5 was firing a warning shot across Kennedy's bows. There was great concern about some of his contacts and about whether or not he was actually leaking information.[31] Indeed Kent claimed, when interviewed by the historian John Costello, that Kennedy was himself keeping copies of the secret correspondence between Churchill and Roosevelt for his own purposes.[32]

MI5 continued to keep Kent under surveillance and indeed decided that the time was ripe to draw in the net. During the first week of May another member of the Right Club, most probably Christabel Nicholson, the wife of an admiral and later a defendant with Kent, had her home searched. This alarmed Anna Wolkoff, who entrusted her 'most incriminating papers' to Kent.[33] Ramsay had already given the code clerk the membership list of the Right Club in the belief that the American would be protected by diplomatic immunity.[34]

At lunchtime on 18 Saturday May Liddell telephoned Johnson to ask if one of his assistants could see Johnson that afternoon at 3 p.m. The assistant, Captain Maxwell Knight, explained how Kent had been under surveillance since his arrival and gave a detailed account of Kent's meeting with Anna Wolkoff. Knight informed Johnson that MI5 intended to arrest Wolkoff, who was a naturalised British citizen, on the following Monday, and asked permission to search Kent's lodgings at the same time.[35]

Kent's now imminent arrest needs to be seen in the context of British political developments that month. Churchill had become Prime Minister on 10 May, the day the Germans invaded the Low Countries. Britain's situation in those last two weeks of May appeared desperate as the British Expeditionary Force withdrew on Dunkirk. There was considerable concern about fifth columnists, and the cabinet decided that there should be a series of arrests under the Defence of the Realm Regulations. Among those picked up were Sir Oswald Mosley (the founder of the British Union of Fascists, who was duly interned for the war) and Archibald Ramsay. Churchill was also determined to act with a flourish against fifth columnists, and to exert his authority by firing a warning shot across the bows of those who might be tempted to sue for a negotiated peace.[36]

There was a fever of activity that weekend (17–19 May)which included Johnson paying a visit to the King's country residence at Windsor, where Kennedy was staying, to seek permission to waive Kent's diplomatic immunity. This the ambassador did immediately, only confirming the fact later with the American Secretary of State. That evening Johnson returned from Windsor at about the same time as Kent began his night shift in the code room. Little did the young foreign service official know it would be his last in government service.

Just after 11 a.m. on Monday, 20 May, Johnson, Franklin Gowen (a second secretary at the American embassy), Knight and three officers from Scotland Yard drew up outside Kent's lodgings at 47 Gloucester Place. They had already picked up Anna Wolkoff earlier that morning. Pushing past the maid who answered the door, they rushed upstairs to find Kent in bed with a woman.

Kent was taken to the embassy for questioning, while the woman, Irene Danischewski, was allowed to go home. There is considerable speculation about Danischewski and why she was not questioned. In his memorandum Gowen noted Knight's logic 'that anyhow the telephone at her house is tapped and she is under constant observation'.[37] Gowen was struck by the fact that 'Kent's alleged mistress', as he described her in a fit of caution, 'took the police raid calmly – indeed, one might assume that she knew what was coming. From the way she behaved and looked at the police officers she made me think that she had been "planted" on Kent by Scotland Yard'.[38]

In Kent's flat were found some 1,500 documents grouped in files with headings like 'Churchill', 'Halifax' (Lord Halifax was Foreign Secretary), 'Germany' a number of telegrams between Churchill and Roosevelt, duplicate keys to the index bureau and code room, letters from Ramsay, the membership book of the Right Club and photographic plates.[39]

Kent was confronted at the embassy by Kennedy. The ambassador's fury may be imagined – his campaign for American neutrality had been tarnished, fatally as it transpired, by his employee's disloyalty. Kent maintained, and stuck to his story, that he had taken the documents to pass to isolationists in America, and thereby alert them to the perceived conspiracy to bring America into the war.[40] Whether out of genuine belief or for reasons of propaganda or disinformation, however, the British and American authorities treated the case as one of German espionage. Yet Kennedy, it should be noted, kept his options open regarding the source of the initiative behind Kent's disloyalty. He cabled the State Department that night:

> Following the receipt on Saturday of information that Tyler Kent associated with a gang of spies working in the interests of Germany *and Russia*, I today caused his private quarters to be searched. . . . In view of the urgency and importance of this matter I have indicated to the police that I waive any immunity for Kent regarding such proceedings as may be necessary to develop the facts.[41]

Cordell Hull replied, asking if the strip cipher system had been compromised and formally dismissing Kent from government service. He also suggested 'that a careful check be made of all your code clerks and of their associates and activities outside of the Embassy'.[42]

On 22 May Kennedy cabled Hull:

> The British authorities are primarily concerned with the possible communication to the enemy through Tyler Kent of highly confidential information concerning the safety and security of this country, which the authorities naturally know that we possess. The investigating authorities inform me that it would greatly assist them if I could assure the Foreign Office that there would be no objection on the part of the United States Government to the placing of formal charges against Kent involving violation of British laws.[43]

Long replied, on behalf of Hull: 'There is no objection on the part of this Government to formally charging the offender with violations of British law. Publicity in connection with such charges might not be helpful under the circumstances.'[44]

The matter was indeed to be handled with discretion. It was not until 1 June that the Home Office made a statement naming Kent and explaining that he had been 'interned by an order of the Home Secretary under the defense regulations'.[45] The State Department refused to comment 'for the protection of this Government'.[46] Kent's widowed mother, who lived in Washington, finally obtained an interview with Assistant Secretary of State Breckinridge Long. She later recalled that he said he could give her no further information about her son. He kept repeating: 'Nothing like this has ever happened in American history'.[47]

Over the next few weeks there was a flurry of telegrams between Washington and London attempting to discover exactly what Kent had had access, to and whether or not the stolen documents could be produced in court. Investigations into Kent's activities and contacts continued for several weeks.[48] Then, on 1 August, Kent was charged with five violations of the Official Secrets Act of 1911 and two counts of larceny. Two paragraphs to this effect appeared in the *New York Times* the next day. It was the first public report of the case. On the 8 August the accused appeared before magistrates at Bow Street, where an adjournment was granted to enable witnesses to attend a further hearing on Monday 19 August.

Kent's trial opened at the Old Bailey on Wednesday, 23 October before Mr. Justice Tucker. The Solicitor-General, Sir William Jowitt, prosecuted, with Mr Maurice Healey KC acting for Kent, who had to pay his own defence costs. The trial was held *in camera* in order to preserve the confidentiality of the MI5 officers giving evidence and also of the contents of the telegrams Kent had stolen.

Kent admitted meeting Anna Wolkoff 'at the end of January or the beginning of February 1940' and Ramsay 'about the beginning of March'.[49] Under questioning he justified his actions on the ground of a higher loyalty to the American people, and confessed to having taken documents within ten days of arriving in Britain.[50] Many of them came from other American embassies in Europe and the thefts went back to 1937.[51]

Two of the documents produced in court were copies of telegrams between First Lord of the Admiralty Churchill and President Roosevelt. In the first dated 29 January 1940, Churchill had written:'I gave orders last night that no American ship should in any circumstances be diverted into the combat zone round the British Isles declared by you. I trust this will be satisfactory'.[52] The second, of 28 February 1940, confirmed that despite 'the difficulties of discriminating between various countries . . . the order still stands and no American ship has been brought by the Navy into the danger zone'. [53] The importance of the telegrams was that it showed that the British, worried about antagonising American commercial interests, gave them preferential treatment. Should this discrimination in favour of one neutral have become public, it would have been politically embarrassing for both Roosevelt and Churchill. It was a case of some neutrals being less equal than others.

Much was made of the fact that Kent had tried to obtain a transfer in February 1940 to Berlin. Mr Justice Tucker pointed out that 'that would be a very convenient way of taking to the enemy such documents as he had acquired from the embassy in London'.[54] Much too was made of Anna Wolkoff's attempts to communicate with the Italian military attaché and Lord Haw-Haw, William Joyce. The Official Secrets Act of 1920 provided that, if it could be shown that the person accused had 'been in communication with or attempted to communicate with a foreign agent', then that was evidence that they acted 'for a purpose prejudicial to the safety or interests of the State'. Kent claimed not to know that Wolkoff had been in touch with Joyce, but the jury were unconvinced.[55]

Journalists, among them Malcolm Muggeridge, were only permitted for the sentencing, when Kent received seven year imprisonment and Wolkoff ten.[56] This was on 7 November. Roosevelt had been safely re-elected two days earlier. After sentence had been pronounced, Kent asked to make a statement:

> I have been tried on the basis of documents selected for the purposes of the Prosecution, taken from a group of over 500 other documents which were in my possession . . . The jury has been asked to determine so subjective a thing as my intent with regard to those four documents, and they have had no opportunity of seeing the four documents in their proper light, namely against the background of the total sum of documents which are in my possession . . . My Counsel has been denied free access, again by the American Embassy, to a file of my personal correspondence, which contained papers essential to my defence . . . Your Lordship, I submit that I have not committed a felony, because I had no felonious intent. I have committed a gross indiscretion, possibly a misdemeanour, but I submit that felonious intent is a prerequisite to the commission of a felony.[57]

An appeal worded, possibly in the interest of economy, by Kent himself, was rejected on 5 February 1941. The Director of Public Prosecutions remarked that 'points on his appeal were so involved that no one really understood what he was trying to get at. From a law point of view his arguments were quite useless.'[58] Shortly afterwards, Kent went on a two-week hunger strike and was reported to have had a nervous breakdown. He was transferred to Cape Hill on the Isle of Wight, 'an internment camp for political prisoners built around an old monastery', where he spent the rest of the war.[59]

Even with Kent in prison the case continued to smoulder. In the summer of 1941 Ramsay brought a libel action against the *New York Times*. He had taken exception to the suggestion that 'he had sent to the German legation in Dublin treasonable information given him by Tyler Kent'. He was awarded a farthing in damages.[60] Kent's supporters now made much of the fact that Kent had been refused a libel application while Ramsay had been allowed to proceed with his. But it seemed that everyone in officialdom wanted to forget the lowly code clerk. Kent's mother, however, continued the struggle to find out what had happened to her son. Denied a passport to visit Britain in person, in July 1941 she sent Otis T. Wingo, a former classmate of Kent's at Princeton, to find out what had happened to her son. Wingo was to be the first of several emissaries during the war.

The controversial nature of the case came to public notice late in the same year. On 11 November, Richard Stokes, the MP for Ipswich and well known for his views espousing a negotiated peace, asked a number of questions in the House of Commons about the mysterious Roosevelt–Churchill correspondence. In particular he wanted to know 'whether any of these cablegrams or messages were sent by the Prime Minister [Winston Churchill] behind the back of the then Prime Minister [Neville Chamberlain]? Home Secretary Herbert Morrison could only reply, No information can properly be given out about confidential documents which were extracted from the American Embassy.'[61]

The *Washington Times-Herald* ran a story in an early edition the next day giving the background to the Kent case. This, according to historian James Leutze, was 'the first public reference to the unprecedented contact between an American president and the head of a warring nation's naval establishment'.[62] The *Times-Herald* story stressed that 'Disclosure of the text of the cablegrams would establish whether Mr Churchill invited, or Mr Roosevelt made, any commitments of the United States Government to a policy of aiding Britain that was not contemplated by existing United States law.'[63]

The entry of the United States into the war in December 1941 made such questions temporarily redundant, and Mrs Kent's campaign more difficult. With Still denied a passport to visit Britain, she arranged for a journalist, Ian Ross Macfarlane, to make a further trip on her behalf. His instructions were to see Kent's solicitor and if possible visit Kent on the Isle of Wight. Macfarlane arrived in England by Atlantic clipper in March 1942 and accomplished his objectives.

In September he returned, bringing with him John Bryan Owen, a grandson of the former pacifist Secretary of State William Jennings Bryan and son of a former United States Minister to Denmark, Ruth Bryan Rhodes. John Bryan Owen had been openly critical of the British and American governments' handling of the Kent case. But his potential usefulness to the Kents' cause ended on 3 January 1943, when he was found dead in mysterious circumstances in his room in Greenwich Village.[64]

The Kent case surfaced again on the 16 June 1944 when the House of Commons debated the continued imprisonment of Ramsay.[65] This was followed on the 19th by debates in the United States Senate and House of Representatives.[66] The approach of another presidential election, with Roosevelt running for a fourth term, may have engendered some of the heat. But the Earl of Halifax, the former Foreign Secretary who was now ambassador to Washington, could not dismiss the furore as mere electioneering. He cabled the Foreign Office on 25 June:

> If any fact about Kent–Ramsay case could be made public without prejudice to security it would do much to clear the air. Otherwise there is considerable danger that issue of alleged collusion between President and Mr Churchill behind backs of the United States Congress and people to make American entrance into war inescapable will be injected into election issue to our detriment and continue to cloud pages of journalists and historians long after.[67]

A month later, questions were asked at the Democratic National Convention touched off by questions in the House of Commons from Tom Driberg.[68] The *Washington Times-Herald* fanned renewed speculation with an article captioned 'Mysterious death of Owen linked to Tyler Kent jailing'.[69] The publicity forced the State Department to issue, on 2 September, a defence of their handing over of Kent to the British authorities.[70]

There was at least some support for the tough line on the Kent case. Three days after the State Department release, the Associated Press solicited a comment from Joseph Kennedy. The former champion of neutrality had been relieved of his diplomatic post in 1940, but he still obliged. Perhaps he was moved to do so by the death, just three weeks earlier, of his oldest son – Joseph P. Kennedy, Jr, had been killed on a cross-Channel bombing raid against German flying-bomb emplacements. In his telephone interview, the bereaved father said: 'If we had been at war, I wouldn't have favoured turning Kent over to Scotland Yard or have sanctioned his imprisonment in England. I would have recommended that he be brought back to the United States and shot.'[71]

Yet the campaign on behalf of Kent continued. On 26 September the *Washington Times-Herald* carried the headline 'British free Ramsay, Tyler Kent's friend'. Gerald L.K. Smith published a pamphlet shortly afterwards drawing public attention to the Kent case. He asked, 'Why should an American citizen whose forebears fought in every American war be imprisoned abroad in outright denial of his diplomatic rights, when even his parliamentary friend has been released?'[72] As a former associate of the 'Radio priest' Father Charles E. Coughlin, Smith was well known for his unsavoury racism as well as for his isolationism, and his privately published pamphlet may not have been the most helpful contribution to the campaign for Kent's freedom.

With the war drawing to a close in Europe, Kent's lawyer Graham Maw approached the Home Office in an attempt to secure an early release but was unsuccessful. On May the Home Secretary revealed, that all but one political prisoner of the war had been released but Kent, because convicted in a civil court, was still detained.[73]

With the election of the Labour Party leader Clement Attlee as Prime Minister, Mrs Kent redoubled her efforts to secure the release of her son, now several months over his allotted time, given deductions for good behaviour. At last, her hopes if not her efforts were to be rewarded. A letter from the Under-Secretary of State at the Home Office dated 23 August 1945 informed her that

> Your son is subject to a Deportation Order made by the Secretary of State on the 23rd May 1940, and it is proposed to enforce this Order by sending him back to the United States of America as soon as possible after he becomes eligible for release on licence on his sentence of penal servitude.[74]

It was now becoming clear that, while the British had originally only intended to deport Kent, they had for some reason then decided to try him under British law. It was evident, too, that the

American authorities had been anxious to keep him out of circulation until after the November 1940 elections.

On 30 August a meeting took place in Sir Frank Newsam's office at the Home Office to discuss the public release of the Kent trial transcript. Among those present, according to the Foreign Office minute, were two members of the Security Service (MI5), Lt.-Col. E.J.P. Cussen and Brigadier O.A. Harker.[75] It was agreed

> that the Home Office should consult the Lord Chief Justice on the proposal to give a conditional exemption from Court Orders and that as soon as his concurrence had been obtained the Home Office, in collaboration with MI5, should draft a statement for inclusion in the letter which the Chief Press Censor would issue to editors when the Press Censorship came to an end.   [76]

Finally, on 21 November 1945, Kent was escorted aboard the British freighter *Silver Oak* on the first stage of his journey home. The sailing had been postponed four times. Tyler Kent arrived in America on 4 December. He had been in prison for five and a half years.[77]

Kent immersed himself in civilian life. On 6 July 1946 he married Clara Hyatt, an heir to the Carters Little Liver Pills fortune, a woman thirteen years older than him and whose first marriage to a consular official had ended in divorce nine years before. [78] He became in turn a farmer and newspaper proprietor, and might easily have vanished into obscurity.

But this he was not allowed. In Britain, the MP Richard Stokes continued his campaign, asking the Attorney-General in May 1948 for the documents relating to the Kent trial to be made public. In America the case was reopened two years later when an amendment to the Foreign Agents Registration Act of 1933 under the Internal Security Act of 1950 resulted in a request to Kent that he register. This he refused to do 'on the ground he had never acted on behalf of any foreign individual group, political party or country'.[79]

This brought him to the attention of the Justice Department and an investigation was begun. Many of his former colleagues were questioned. Among them was William Bullitt, his former ambassador in Moscow. It was during an interview on 2 June 1950 that Bullitt told the FBI that Kent, whom he regarded as 'brilliant but neurotic', had been pressed on him by Cordell Hull. He claimed to have noted at the time that the pushing of Kent was 'indicative of the manner in which Communist and Russian sympathisers could be employed by the Department of State'.[80]

On 7 September 1951 FBI agents interviewed Kent at Annapolis. They thought he 'was quite cooperative and appeared to be sincere and straight-forward in his answers'.[81] Six weeks later Kent was told 'registration with this Department under the terms of the Act is not required'.[82] The case against Kent was formally closed in March 1952.

Yet, as late as 1966, the FBI file remained open. Interviews with former colleagues of Kent suggested 'that the true facts concerning the Kent plot had not been completely revealed', especially the role of 'Anna Volkova'.[83] While this particular point was not a matter of public speculation, Kent nevertheless spent the last part of his life trying to clear his name. In April 1963 he filed a libel suit against Kennedy, his former ambassador, for his comments on the case. The ambassador's son Robert, then Attorney-General in his brother's administration, managed to suppress the action, but not until there had been a succession of memoranda within the Justice Department on the question of whether the department itself would have to defend the action.

Until his death in 1988, Kent continued to proclaim his innocence. His name began to appear in scholarly articles, and shortly before his death he appeared in a BBC television *Newsnight* programme. While the case was never again likely to make the headlines, a new generation, reinterpreting the outbreak of the Second World War and America's entry two years later, had discovered a man who could so easily have changed the course of history.[84]

In retrospect what was Kent's importance? In at least one way his actions proved beneficial. The case resulted in an improvement in the pay and position of code clerks. Breckinridge Long musing on the episode came

> to the conclusion that it is necessary for us to establish a career service for clerks and pay them higher salaries and to protect particularly the code clerks. This one incident involves our whole system of communications, and it just shows how dependent the Government is upon a comparatively few confidential key positions.[85]

Whatever was the truth behind Kent's lifestyle in Moscow, Long was evidently determined to pursue the economic interpretation of agent recruitment.

Yet a number of the accusations levelled at Kent at the time do not stand up to scrutiny. Kennedy claimed in his September 1944 interview that Kent's actions meant that

> right at the time of the fall of France, the United States Government closed its confidential communicating system and was blacked out from private contact with American embassies and legations everywhere. At this critical time, with decisions of the highest importance needing to be made and communicated hourly, no private message could be sent or received from the President, Mr Hull or anyone else. This lasted from two weeks to a month and a half – until a new unbreakable code could be devised in Washington and carried by special couriers to our diplomatic representatives throut [*sic*] the world.[86]

An FBI memorandum repeated the claim: 'His actions when discovered caused a four to six weeks delay in the handling of confidential information from and to United States Embassies around the world until new codes could be furnished these Embassies.[87] It is very hard to find evidence to support such allegations. The messages that Kent stole were generally neither in top-grade code nor even in the Grey Code, which was a non-confidential code with no security implication.

It is by no means clear that Kent would have betrayed code secrets even when messages were encoded, so lax – or perhaps calculatingly relaxed – were American encryption procedures. The Grey Code had been broken in 1924, and by 1939 was being intercepted and read by the codebreakers of most countries. In fact when Mussolini invaded Ethiopia, Roosevelt used the Grey Code to send a message to the American embassy in Rome, knowing that Mussolini would read it but would be unable to protest. On 6 December 1941, when Roosevelt released his 'Peace Plea' to Hirohito, he said, 'Send it in the Grey Code. I don't care if they do read it'.[88]

The confidential codes were brown, A, B, C and D of which the most confidential was D. Kent later explained:

> In the case of the 4 latter codes, the tables were changed every 3 or 4 months, that is to say, the arrangement of the

letters in the five letter groups were changed. In the case of these codes the text was encoded twice; once in a basic five letter group which did not change, and then a second time in another set of five-letter groups which changed as I have indicated above. An interesting sidelight on the 'Brown' code is that Kennedy wired the State Department that 'the British have got the Brown code', because as he stated, they knew what he was going to say at a certain conference at the Foreign Office. Nonetheless Kennedy continued to use the Brown regularly thereafter.[89]

Perhaps one of the most intriguing aspects of the Kent case is the light it throws on the use of diplomatic double-talk via the sham secrecy of long-broken codes.

As the case against Kent on the ground of being a Nazi is as unconvincing as that against him for being an isolationist, and as his imprisonment seems to have been a mere matter of political convenience, there remains the problem of explaining his motive in stealing items from the Churchill–Roosevelt correspondence. Can one take a leaf from the book of the economic historian, and argue counter-factually? If he was neither an isolationist nor a Nazi spy, how can one explain his actions? Could he have been a Soviet spy?

At first, Kent was of course treated as a German spy, an opinion encouraged by reports from the American embassy in Moscow.[90] But it will be recalled that Kennedy's initial telegram to Hull of 20 May had spoken of 'a gang of spies working in the interests of Germany and Russia'.[91] And even during the war, despite Russia being now an ostensible ally of the United States, the Tyler Kent case was reclassified. A fragment in an FBI memorandum dated 4 March 1944 records: 'At the present time it would appear that Kent was actively engaged in espionage for the Russian Government' (someone deleted the rest of the text).[92]

The suspicions persisted after the war. An FBI memorandum marked 'Tyler Kent/Internal Security' and dated 21 November 1950 notes that Kent 'may have been connected with Soviet Espionage instead of with German Espionage as was then believed'.[93] Further files relating to the internal investigation of Kent over the next three months are noteworthy for the number of deletions and for their indefinite nature. A former colleague at the Moscow embassy, when interviewed, expressed the belief Kent was 'working for both sides based on his expressions of enthusiasm for Moscow and Russia and his apparent efforts to infiltrate "White Russian" circles in London', though he later admitted that this 'was based merely on a hunch rather than any concrete information'.[94]

The case for saying that Kent was a Soviet spy is no more flimsy than the too-readily-believed alternative theories. We know that the investigation into his case concentrated on a number of unexplained Russian links. Whereas his motive for helping the isolationists or Nazis would have been ideological, his spur for working for the Russians, in London as in Moscow, could have been pecuniary. When he was arrested in May 1940, he was found to be in possession of a £50 note. Much was made of this in the subsequent case against him in the 1950s. During his interview on 18 September 1951, Kent told the FBI that he 'was paid by the American embassy in British currency'. But an FBI search of the payroll records for the spring of 1940 showed 'there was no indication that the subject or any employee was paid in British pounds'. Neal Borum, the administrative officer in the London embassy while Kent was there, 'stated that American citizens employed in the embassy were paid in United States Treasury checks or in American dollars and never to his knowledge were they paid in British currency including Bank of England notes or bank drafts'.[95]

Kent during his interviews in the 1950s at first denied having dealt with any NKVD agents.[96] This was doubtful in some cases, untrue in others. A memorandum of 17 February 1954 notes Kent 'was associated with Tataniya Alexandrovna Ilovaiskaya, a reported NKVD Agent'. While he disputed whether or not Tatiana was an agent, Kent did admit 'that some time during the year 1936 Tatiana gave him the impression that she was "sounding him out" as to whether or not he would cooperate with the NKVD'. [97]

The FBI also questioned him carefully about his acquaintanceship with Mrs Mandakulatura Vishvanata Gangadharan, otherwise known as Truda. She worked in the office of the US military attaché Phillip Faymonville and had given Kent German lessons. When pressed, he agreed that she could well have been an NKVD agent.[98] The code clerk had met her at the home of John Marsalka, an employee in the American embassy. 'Kent stated that Marsalka definitely had pro-Soviet leanings but that, to Kent's knowledge, he was not an NKVD agent nor was he engaged in espionage activities'.[99] Kent did however accept that he knew an NKVD agent, one Calligos, a 'Roumanian Greek whom he met in 1934 while both were living at the Metropole Hotel in Moscow', and that Calligos had tried to obtain political information from him.[100]

In themselves these friendships did not constitute proof that Kent was a Soviet agent. It is unremarkable that the Russians should target him as a potential source of information and try to win his confidence – they would have done this as a matter of routine to anyone in his position. Kent's social life did, however, show him to be unwise in his choice of companions, and suspicions were raised by the fact that he had not previously reported these contacts himself.

Not surprisingly, the FBI were suspicious about both the contacts and the standard of living that Kent as a junior code clerk was able to enjoy in Moscow. Here were involved matters of risk, as well as of expense: Charles Bohlen has written of the period 'that any attempt by a foreigner to get in touch with a Soviet citizen was the equivalent of signing an order for his arrest, if not his execution'.[101] And yet when Kent departed from Moscow

> he left a briefcase with some colleagues, to be forwarded to him later by [diplomatic] pouch. The contents of the briefcase included: inter alia, a Smith and Wesson 38-calibre hand gun with ammunition; three photographs of his Moscow mistress (Tatania Alexandrovna Ilovaiskaya) one clothed, two nude; a photo of a nude Russian actress; and a photo of a nude man and woman (unidentified).'[102]

This seemed to indicate a lifestyle that was in some way protected, as well as subsidised.

Kent was further unable to explain the mysterious Mrs Straker who had introduced him to Anna Wolkoff in London. She was supposedly a childhood friend of his mother from Virginia, but there is no evidence that she did anything more than effect an introduction. It seems strange that she never visited Kent in prison or corresponded with him. Straker supposedly worked for the Russian Red Cross, which often doubled as a Soviet front organisation, and it is not impossible that she was used in order to bring Kent and Wolkoff together.[103]

The later FBI investigations were conducted at the height of the McCarthy era and one therefore needs to treat the suggestion that Kent was involved in Soviet espionage with some caution. The head of the FBI, J. Edgar Hoover, was determined to find 'Reds' where they did not exist. On examination, however, the FBI's handling of the Kent inquiry seems to have been conducted fairly and efficiently.

Perhaps weight should therefore be attached to the FBI's negative findings. They were unable to find the necessary evidence to convict Kent of spying for the Russians. An early FBI memorandum concluded that 'the current investigation of Kent has revealed no indication of espionage or subversive activities in the United States since his return from Europe in 1945'.[104] Another memorandum concludes; 'There is nothing in the investigation which is good and clear cut on the question of whether Kent might have been working for the Russians'.[105] Yet another noted retrospectively that the 'subject could furnish no pertinent information concerning Soviet Intelligence or CP activities. The plan to have him appear before a Grand Jury was abandoned and the investigation was apparently closed'.[106]

On the other hand, of course, the case may be unproven rather than disproved. Tyler Kent may well have taken the truth of his involvement with the Russians to the grave. Certainly there is enough circumstantial evidence to suggest that he had been compromised by them, perhaps unwittingly. Was he recruited as a future potential agent of influence whom they then abandoned, possibly as part of a wider deception plan or to protect another source?

While Kent was in Moscow he had a car accident. This is one of the best-known recruitment ploys used by the Russians. An accident, often fatal, is staged and the offender taken into custody. In return for not pressing charges the authorities then ask the culprit for a 'favour'. The entrapment process has then begun. Kent may also have opened himself up to another form of blackmail while in Moscow. An FBI memorandum refers to: 'a report allegedly submitted in 1939 from the embassy at Moscow concerning personnel at the embassy and homosexual activities thereof . . . It appears that his might be tied in with the Kent case.[107]

It is more likely, however, that Kent's womanising and currency smuggling may have made him vulnerable to blackmail. Given his access to the code room, he was an obvious target for a Russian approach, and it would be surprising if such an approach had not been made. Kent himself during his trial admitted to having stolen documents while in Moscow, and this may have been part of his apprenticeship as a spy.[108]

A number of commentators on the case have noted Kent's strong anti-communist views. Malcolm Muggeridge, for example, described Kent as having 'a maniacally hostile attitude towards the Soviet regime'. This by no means clears him of the charge of being a Russian agent.[109] It is not unusual for Soviet agents to feign anti-communist views: witness Guy Burgess and Kim Philby.

Yet it is just as possible that Kent worked for the Soviet Union while in London without being fully conscious of the fact. He may not have realised that he served their interests, as well as his own isolationist views: by passing material to Anna Wolkoff. Hayden Peake, a former senior CIA officer, has concluded: 'Kent may really have been as pro-Hitler and anti-communist as he is portrayed, with the NKVD having found a pressure point based on the facts reported above, which allowed them to use him for their purposes.'[110] He could in short have been both an isolationist and a spy.[111]

The Kent case is a cautionary tale. Its complexities are too great to allow simple assumptions about isolationist partisanship or Nazi sympathy to pass unexamined. It does seem likely that Kent was subject to an approach by the NKVD while in Moscow. Yet, if he was recruited as a Soviet agent, did it matter?

If Kent was indeed a Soviet secret agent, it is difficult to see what damage he inflicted. Certainly he was, as a code clerk, privy to the most secret information passing through the American embassy in London. Yes, he would have known of the various peace initiatives made during the phoney war, information of great interest to the Russians, who feared that Germany might turn eastwards as soon as peace had been made in the west. Given, however, that most of the Churchill and Roosevelt correspondence was in an easily breakable code, he could have revealed little there that was not known already, perhaps making him expendable. In any case, if the Russians knew about the correspondence, they appear to have made no use of the knowledge. To appreciate the historical significance of the Kent case, one needs to consider the light it sheds on sham secrecy.

One of the most important ramifications of the Kent case was the public revelation in 1941 that Churchill and Roosevelt had begun a secret correspondence soon after the outbreak of the war. By delaying Kent's trial and holding it *in camera* in Britain, the British authorities kept quiet the full extent of Kent's embarrassing disclosures. The British colluded with the Americans, in effect, to secure the re-election of Roosevelt.

As Halifax had anticipated, post-war revisionist historians made much of this collusion. Charles Beard, for example, dwelled at length on the matter, and on the significance of the Kent case.[112]

Kent himself had strong views about the orthodoxy of such communication.

> To give a foreigner [i.e. Churchill] carte blanche to transmit
> a message without examination by the Ambassador through a
> diplomatic channel is, to say the least, a highly unusual and
> extraordinary procedure. There is no question about the fact
> that the sending of these messages constituted an erosion of
> the British censorship on the part of Churchill.[113]

However, Joseph Kennedy's biographer Richard Whalen has
argued that the telegrams were in the Grey Code and therefore
secret only to the public at large:

> Apparently Roosevelt was unconcerned about the strong
> possibility that his exchange with Churchill would be over-
> heard; or else there may have seemed no way of preventing
> it. For in wartime England, the government cable office rou-
> tinely turned over to British cryptographers copies of all
> coded messages sent and received by foreign embassies. By
> using the Grey Code for messages of which the British pos-
> sessed the original clear text, the embassy gave the British
> only what they presumably had, and did not risk compromis-
> ing a more valuable code.[114]

The public never did become fully aware even of the full *extent* of
the secret Churchill–Roosevelt correspondence. Though most of
the telegrams have now been released, some are still closed and
therefore no one quite knows the extent of the exchange. Leutze
claims that there were thirteen messages between 11 September
1939 and 10 May 1940, of which four were from Roosevelt and nine
from Churchill. He writes: 'It is sage to conclude therefore, that
although dramatic and unorthodox, the early Churchill–Roosevelt
correspondence was not vast.[115] The historian Warren Kimball has
only eight Churchill telegrams for the period, with three more on
15, 18 and 20 May. He notes that five of them were in Kent's
possession.[116] The file marked 'Churchill' found in Kent's flat and
since recovered from the FBI files had eleven telegrams, including
four of the telegrams Kimball identifies as having been in Kent's
possession.[117] Kent did not have copies of the telegrams of 5 and
16 October, 7 January, and 7, 15 and 18May 7th, May but he did
have six new ones. Intriguingly Kent, admittedly not the most

reliable source, told Richard Whalen that 'of Roosevelt–Churchill communications there might have been from 30 to 50'.[118] Whalen accepted this figure when he later wrote up the Kent case.[119] Careful cross-checking might well reveal hitherto unknown telegrams between the two leaders which would shed new light on their relationship.

The mystery about the extent of the Roosevelt and Churchill correspondence continues. So too does that about the real motive behind the actions of the young code clerk in 1940. In the absence of proof of Kent's isolationist or Nazi undercover connections, speculation must remain alive about the possibility of a Soviet connection. Yet, in the absence of proof of *that*, his precise role in intelligence history must remain obscure. But the case, as illuminated by declassified FBI files, is now well enough documented to throw a disconcerting light on code practices and on the motives behind them. It serves to highlight the continuing uncertainties of the intelligence background, and therefore of the diplomatic background, to the shifting German–Soviet–British–American relationship in the years 1939–40.

Notes

1. Richard Whalen, 'The strange case of Tyler Kent', *Diplomat (Nov. 1965)*, 1. cf. Richard Thurlow, *Fascism in Britain* (Oxford: Blackwell, 1987), p. 195 and Anthony Masters, *The Man Who Was M* (Oxford: Blackwell, 1984), p. 84.
2. *Washington Times-Herald*, 6 Sept. 1944.
3. Richard Whalen, *The Founding Father* (London: Hutchinson, 1965), p. 311.
4. Nigel West, 'Moscow's moles and the Nazi spy', *Times*, 10 Dec. 1983, p. 12; cf. Christopher Andrew and Oleg Gordievsky, *KGB: The inside story of its foreign operations from Lenin to Gorbachev* (London: Hodder & Stoughton, 1990) p. 181.
5. United States Federal Bureau of Investigation (FBI) file 65–27850–10. FBI memos of 19 April 1944 and 25 May 1944 state that while at Princeton Kent 'was reportedly liberal in his views and enthusiastic about the Russian form of Government'. This chapter draws substantially on the fruits of freedom-of-information enquiries to the FBI. The documents obtained through these enquiries are identified in the notes by date. Where available, identifying serial numbers from the FBI's own indexing system are also supplied.
6. Memo, 18 Sept. 1951, FBI file 65–27850–134.
7. Memo, 19 April 1944, FBI file 65–27850–11.
8. Memo, 18th Sept. 1951, FBI file 65–27850–134.
9. 14 June 1934, State Department file 'Tyler Kent'. Loy Henderson, another colleague of Kent in the Moscow embassy, thought him 'an honest and intellectually capable person and one of the best linguists he ever employed'. Quoted letter Barnes to Whalen, 6 Feb. 1964,

in Whalen collection lent by kind permission of John Costello. The author assisted Mr Costello in researching *Mask of Treachery: Spies--buggery and betrayal the first documented dossier on Anthony Blunt's Cambridge spy ring* (New York: Morrow, 1988).

10. Memo, 18 Sept. 1951, FBI file 65–27850–134.
11. Memo 25 May 1944, FBI file 65–27850–40. To further complicate matters Kent claimed in the 'Dear Pucia' letter, found among his possessions, that 'Bullitt had done everything possible to have me fired from Moscow, because Lange and I were REDS.' Letter to A.J. Barratt, 1 July 1937, Department of State Decimal Files, National Archives, Washington, DC (hereinafter NADS) 123 Kent, Tyler/6–440.
12. For an account of the Sumner Welles mission see Stanley E. Hilton, 'The Welles mission to Europe February-March 1940: illusion or realism?' *Journal of American History*, 58 (June 1971) 93–120.
13. Memo, Herschel Johnson, 28 May 1940 NADS 123 Kent, Tyler/5–3040.
14. *Ibid.* Cf. Masters, *M*, p. 84; Anthony Read and Ray Bearse, *Conspirator* (New York: Doubleday, 1991), p. 64 for the view that Matthias was a Soviet agent.
15. For Ramsay's background, see Thurlow, *Fascism*, pp. 79–80.
16. For Anna Wolkoff's background, see W.A. Jowitt, *Some Were Spies* (London: Hodder & Stoughton, 1954), pp. 65–68.
17. Memo, 18 Sept. 1951, FBI file 65–27850–134.
18. For background, see Richard Griffiths, *Fellow Travellers of the Right* (London: Constable, 1980).
19. For background, see Charles Higham, *Trading With the Enemy* (New York: Delacorte, 1983).
20. See Joan Miller, *One Girl's War* (Dublin: Brandon, 1987). The book is, however, not entirely accurate.
21. For further accounts of Miller's penetration of the Right Club, cf. Nigel West, *MI5: 1909–1945* (London: Bodley Head, 1981) and Bernard Newman, *Spy and Counter-Spy* (London: Hale, 1970).
22. Whitehall seemed to know about the spy in the American embassy. A letter marked 'this should have been put in the green file, i.e. closed for 100 years', dated 26 March 1940, from the Ministry of Economic Warfare to Sir Alexander Cadogan, Permanent Under-Secretary at the Foreign Office, reads: 'Many thanks for your secret letter A1945/G of the 18th March about conversations with members of the United States Embassy. I am seeing that all those concerned here are warned that the Embassy's report of these conversations may become available to the enemy'. FO 371/24460.
23. For examples from the 'Kennedy' file see FO 371/24251. Cf. Michael R. Beschloss, *Kennedy and Roosevelt: The uneasy alliance* (New York: W.W. Norton, 1980), p.195.
24. Liddell to Johnson, 7 Feb. 1940, NADS London Embassy Files 820–02.
25. *Ibid.*
26. Letter, Johnson to Dunn 14 Feb. 1940, NADS London Embassy Files 820–02. Cf. John Costello, *Ten Days that Saved the West* (London: Bantam, 1991), p. 139, for background information on Janke and Pfeffer.
27. *Ibid.*

28. 4 April 1940, Breckinridge Long Diary, Manuscript Collection, Library of Congress.
29. Robert T. Crowley, former senior CIA officer, letter to John Costello, n.d. Lent to the author by kind courtesy of Mr Costello.
30. Cf. Read and Bearse, *Conspirator*, p. 131 for the view that 'the Doctor' may have been the German chargé d'affaires in Washington, DC.
31. Beschloss, *Kennedy*, p. 194.
32. Taped interview of Tyler Kent by John Costello, 1982. Lent to the author by kind courtesy of Mr Costello.
33. Johnson memo cited above, n. 13, p .6.
34. Thurlow, *Fascism*, p. 182.
35. US Dept of State Press Release No. 405, 2 Sept. 1944.
36. Thurlow argues that Kent was 'the trigger mechanism for the immediate internment of British fascists': Thurlow, *Fascism*, p. 194. Cf. Masters, *M*, p.90.
37. Memo, Franklin Gowen, 28 May 1940, NADS 123 Kent, Tyler/5–3040. Kent does not comment on her in his article 'The Roosevelt legacy and the Kent case', *Journal of Historical Review*, 4 (summer 1983), 175.
38. Gowen memo, pp.4, 13. Hayden Peake, a CIA officer who later took an interest in the case has speculated that she was working for the British: Hayden Peake, 'The putative spy', *FILS*, 5 (March–April 1986), 1, 7–8 (May–June 1986), 3–5. Even if she had been a British agent, one assumes MI5 would have gone through the motions of taking her in for questioning. Cf. taped telephone call of Irene Danischewsky by John Costello, 1982, in Costello Collection.
39. For full inventory, see NADS 123 Kent, Tyler/6–440.
40. For full interrogation, see NADS 123 Kent, Tyler/5–3040.
41. NADS 123 Kent, Tyler/68. Italics added.
42. NADS 123 Kent, Tyler/69–72.
43. NADS 123 Kent, Tyler/74.
44. NADS 123 Kent, Tyler/75.
45. Telegram, Kennedy to Hull, NADS, 123 Kent, Tyler/88.
46. *New York Times*, 2 June 1940.
47. Report of talk by Mrs Kent on 20 July 1944, quoted in Whalen, *Founding Father*, p. 313. Long noted in his diary at the time: 'The arrest of Kent in London and the disclosure of his activities in our Embassy, coupled with known leaks of his information which we have been unable to account for but which concerned our correspondence with London and which had appeared at Copenhagen, Berlin and Bucharest – all have made it apparent that he may have accomplices and confederates or that there may be other cells of an aggressive diplomacy of another Government representing their interests in our own offices abroad': 4 June 1940, Breckinridge Long Diary.
48. NADS 123 Kent, Tyler 91–11.
49. Kent Trial Transcript, Tyler Kent Papers, Sterling Library, Yale University, p. 58.
50. *Ibid.*, p. 153.
51. *Ibid.*, p. 157.
52. Quoted in Jowitt, *Some Were Spies*, p. 47.
53. *Ibid.*,p. 48

54. Trial Transcript, p. 18.
55. Jowitt admits 'there was no evidence that she had passed any secret
    information to such attaché: Jowitt, *Some Were Spies*, p. 53. How-
    ever, British cryptographers had broken the German diplomatic
    codes and they knew that the German ambassador to Rome, Hans
    Mackensen, had copies of the Churchill and Roosevelt telegrams.
    They also knew from a tip from Luigi Barzini, Jr, an Italian-American
    journalist, that the leak came from the American embassy in London
    and the last cable was on the 16 May 1940:Warren Kimball and
    Bruce Bartlett, 'Roosevelt and prewar commitments to Churchill:
    the Tyler Kent affair', *Diplomatic History*, (fall 1981), 303. Ladislas
    Farrago says there is proof that Kent was the leak but does not
    provide it. Ladislas Farrago, *Game of the Foxes* (New York: David
    McKay, 1971), pp. 338–45.
56. For a graphic account see Muggeridge's autobiography, *The Infernal
    Grove* (New York: Morrow, 1975), pp. 112–15.
57. Trial Transcript, pp. 198–9.
58. Director of Public Prosecutions to Herschel Johnson, 17 Feb. 1941,
    Herschell Johnson Papers, Southern Historical Collection, Chapel
    Hill, North Carolina.
59. *Washington Post*, 23 July 1961.
60. Quoted in a letter to the Secretary of State from Herschel Johnson,
    12 Aug. 1941, Johnson Papers. For a further account, see *The Times*,
    1 Aug. 1941.
61. Quoted in Gerald L.K. Smith, *The Cross and the Flag: The story of
    Tyler Kent* (New York, privately published, 1944), p. 3.
62. James Leutze, 'The Secret of the Churchill–Roosevelt Correspon-
    dence, September 1939–May 1940', *Journal of Contemporary His-
    tory* (1975), 467.
63. Quoted in Smith, *Cross*, p. 3.
64. John Howland Snow, *The Case of Tyler Kent* (New York: Long
    House, 1946), p. 38.
65. *Washington Times-Herald*, 18 June 1944. Cf. 4000 House of Com-
    mons Debates.
66. *Washington Times-Herald*, 29 June 1944.
67. FO 371/38704.
68. FO 371/44628 for Driberg's request for the release of the trial tran-
    script.
69. *Washington Times-Herald*, 18 July 1944.
70. Copy of the press release, 'Tyler Kent' file, Westbrook Pegler Papers,
    Herbert Hoover Presidential Library, West Branch, Iowa.
71. Quoted in Snow, *Case of Kent*, p. 26. Cf. *Washington Daily News*,
    5 Sept. 1944.
72. Smith, *Cross*, p. 4. Another pamphlet about Kent, by John Howland
    Snow and already cited above, was published two years later. Entitled
    The Case of Tyler Kent, it tended to concentrate on the Pearl Harbor
    aspect of the story. 'Kent takes a dim view of Snow's brochure and
    stated that we might consider it about 75% reliable. It was written
    and published during an election year and while the facts appear to
    be well authenticated, they were somewhat embellished to fire public
    opinion, and some generous latitude was taken with interpretations.'
    Charles Hiles interview with Tyler Kent 19-29 Oct. 1963, Whalen
    Collection.

73. Snow, *Case of Kent*, p. 23.
74. *Ibid.*, p. 24.
75. 'O.A.' Harker was presumably A.W.A. ('Jasper') Harker.
76. FO 371–44628. The file contains the full correspondence with the Home Office about the possible release of the trial transcript.
77. *New York Post* and *New York Daily News*, 4 Dec. 1945.
78. An FBI report dated 26 Nov. 1963, FBI report 65–27850–180, has the tantalising but inaccurate passage: 'Bureau files disclose information indicating that Mrs William P. Kent allegedly was at one time married to A. Dana Hodgdon'. It is hard to believe that Tyler's mother should have married her daughter-in-law's former husband!
79. Memo, 10 March 1953, FBI file 65–27850–16.
80. Memo, 6 June 1950, FBI file 65–27850–37.
81. Memo, 18 Sept. 1951, FBI file 65–27850–134.
82. Letter to Kent from William Foley, Dept of Justice, 30 Oct. 1951, Kent Papers.
83. FBI memo, 24 Feb 1966.
84. Obituary, *Daily Telegraph*, 17 Feb. 1989.
85. Long Diary, 22 May 1940.
86. Quoted in *Washington Daily News*, 5 Sept. 1944.
87. Memo, 23 Nov. 1962, FBI file 65–27850–173.
88. Quoted in a letter to a Dr Barnes from 'Lawrence',[19] Feb.19th 1964, from the research files of the historian Warren Kimball (hereinafter 'Kimball Collection', by John Costello's kind permission.
89. Letter, Kent to Whalen, 16 Feb. 1964, Whalen Collection. The problem of State Department codes is discussed in David Kahn's *The Codebreakers: The story of secret writing* (New York: Macmillan, 1967), pp. 488–501.
90. NADS 124.613/1192.
91. NADS 123 Kent, Tyler/68.
92. Memo, 4 March 1944, FBI file 65–27850–9.
93. Memo, 21 Nov. 1950, FBI file 65–27850–40.
94. Memo, 2 May 1951. This colleague was presumably the A. J. Barratt mentioned below.
95. Memo, 20 Sept. 1951, NADS 105–1396.
96. Memo, 18 Sept. 1951, FBI file 65–27850–134.
97. *Ibid.*
98. *Ibid.*
99. *Ibid.*
100. *Ibid.* Calligos, a close associate of the head of the NKVD, Genrikh GrigoryevichYagoda, was revealed in the 1936 purge trials to be an NKVD agent and later executed.
101. Charles Bohlen, *Witness to History 1929–1969* (London: Weidenfeld & Nicolson, 1973) p.45.
102. Quoted Peake, 'Putative spy' (May–June), 4. For a full list, see NADS 123 Kent, Tyler/66.
103. It has been suggested that Kent shared a flat with Mrs Straker's son, who is still alive, but all attempts to trace him have failed. tape-recorded interview with Kenneth de Courcy by the author, 1 April 1989. Secretary to the independently-financed Imperial Policy Group, De Courcy was a Russian emigré who spied unofficially for MI6 chief Stewart Menzies.
104. Memo, 17 March 1951.

105. Memo, 1 Sept. 1953.
106. Memo, 21 April 1962.
107. FBI memo 4 March 1954.
108. Masters, *M*, p. 83.
109. Quoted in Peake, 'Putative spy' (May–June), 4.
110. *Ibid.*, 4.
111. For another view see Whalen, 'Strange case', p.2.
112. Charles A. Beard, *President Roosevelt and the Coming of the War: A study in appearances and realities* (New Haven, Conn. Yale Univ. Press, 1948), pp. 265–73. Beard observed that Anna Wolkoff's 'designs in the case were obscure' (p.266).
113. Letter, Kent to Whalen, 3 Feb. 1964, Whalen Collection.
114. Whalen,'Strange Case', p. 3.
115. Leutze, 'Secret', 469.
116. Kimball Collection. Professor Kimball compiled and edited *Churchill and Roosevelt: The Complete Correspondence*, 3 vols. (Princeton, NJ Princeton Univ. Press, 1984). An earlier publication lists 548 pieces of 'secret' correspondence exchanged over the whole wartime period; the post-Pearl Harbor items are, of course, less controversial: Manfred Jonas, Harold D. Langley and Francis L. Loewenheim, eds., *Roosevelt and Churchill: Their secret wartime correspondence* (New York: Saturday Review Press, 1975).
117. The other, dated 20 May, clearly had not been put in the 'Churchill' file.
118. Letter Kent to Whalen, 1 March 1964, Whalen Collection.
119. Whalen, 'Strange Case', p. 2.

4

Democracy goes to war: politics, intelligence, and decision-making in the United States in 1942

DAVID WALKER

The United States' first offensive action of the Second World War in the west, the invasion of Vichy French North Africa – codenamed Operation Torch by Winston Churchill, began on 8 November, 1942. Both at the time and subsequently, Torch has come under criticism from journalists, historians and professional soldiers. These critics have argued that the operation was ill-conceived, strategically pointless, and actually detrimental to the Allied war effort because of its necessary compromises with fascistic Vichy personnel.[1] My aim here is to re-examine Operation Torch, especially from the policy-making and intelligence perspectives, and to ask why the operation was launched, what it achieved and how much merit there is in the criticism levelled against it.

Though this essay is influenced by recent writing in intelligence history, it differs in one respect from most existing works.[2] This difference stems from my methodology, for I attempt to put the intelligence and policy-making relationship into a broader context. In the first part of this essay, I argue that President Roosevelt's temperament and style of governing, as well as United States domestic politics, were crucial determining elements in the final decision to launch Torch. These elements were independent of intelligence and raise the question of whether Roosevelt would have listened to competent intelligence (possibly warning of the dangers involved in invading North-West Africa) even had it existed, which, I go on to argue, it did not. In the second part of the essay, I examine the principal intelligence source for Operation Torch – the agents and analysts of the newly formed Office of Strategic Services (OSS). This organisation, which is usually regarded as the forerunner of the CIA, boasted of several new

intelligence capabilities, including an ability to assess enemy motivation. I argue here that the OSS was bureaucratically weak in
1942, and that its personnel, especially its ambitious chief General
William 'Wild Bill' Donovan, were eager to please FDR and other
United States leaders and to prove the value of their organisation
to the war effort, and that this coloured their assessment of the
situation in Vichy French North Africa. Franklin Roosevelt wanted
Torch to succeed, and William Donovan wanted the OSS to succeed; together this made for a happy congruence, but at the expense
of objective reporting and analysis in North Africa. Finally, I discuss
some of the repercussions of Operation Torch, for intelligence and
policy-making in the United States, and also for the future course
of the war. My discussion draws on some original sources. But I
should stress that the bulk of my work here is interpretative, relying
on biographies of Franklin Roosevelt, organisational histories of the
OSS and accounts by military historians of the planning and
execution of Operation Torch.[3] Additional research needs to be
done by future scholars to promote a more thorough understanding
of the workings of intelligence and its influence on policy-making
in the United States during the Second World War. I hope this
essay will be a modest contribution to the framework for such future
enquiries.

During the Second World War, President Franklin D. Roosevelt,
unlike the leaders of the other leading combatant nations, usually
refrained from becoming involved with major military or strategic
decision making. He preferred the 'experts', in this case the professional military men, to decide among themselves on such issues
as when and where to launch a particular offensive, or how many
resources to commit to strategic bombing.[4] This approach, moreover, was characteristic of his presidential style as a whole. For most
of his presidency he wished, both in appearance and in actuality, to
be 'above' politics as much as possible and to leave the details, the
necessary persuasion, and, more importantly, the responsibilities
of day-to-day decision making to others. If things should go wrong
the appropriate people could be reprimanded or fired, and hopefully as little fall-out as possible would land on the President. Only
in the last resort would he intervene directly, either because the
members of his administration could not agree over a particular
policy, or in times of crisis when he felt that there was no alternative
to his personal involvement, although he often used indirect
methods, such as secrecy and especially patronage, to assert his
leadership at other times.[5]

Roosevelt's presidential style has been likened to that of a constitutional monarch or broker of factions.[6] His style reflected his own temperament and choice of governing methods, but it is also important to point out that the structure of the United States Constitution, with its separation of powers, allowed him and to an extent encouraged him to act in this way. Roosevelt was also strongly influenced by the example of President Wilson's personal and political hubris over the Treaty of Versailles and the League of Nations. As Assistant Secretary of the Navy between 1913 and 1921 and Democratic vice-presidential candidate in the election of 1920, Roosevelt had experienced directly the catastrophic consequences of Wilsonian self-assertion. Experience cautioned him against becoming too closely involved with a controversial policy.[7]

In 1942, however, Roosevelt modified his style of leadership with regard to military strategy, and played a more direct role in its creation than he had done previously or would do later. This was in part because he was forced to – there was at the time disagreement between his own military chiefs and the British over the timing and location of the projected second front in the west. But more than this, Roosevelt was acutely sensitive to, almost obsessed with, the domestic political situation in the United States, and he determined that, whatever the military objectives of the second front should be, United States forces had important political tasks to accomplish in 1942.[8]

In the months following Pearl Harbor, Roosevelt was uncertain of the extent of the American people's commitment to the war. He feared latent isolationism and Japan-firstism, the notion, now embraced by some influential former isolationists, that America should concentrate its resources on an effort to defeat Japan, the immediate aggressor, and not Germany, the greater threat to American national security. He was shocked at evidence in Gallup polls and elsewhere that revealed how little understanding many Americans had of the reasons for their involvement in the war.[9] What was also clear in early 1942 was that the public was impatient for both action and success after being subject to a long series of Axis (especially Japanese) victories. The April 1942 Doolittle Raid, the dropping of a few bombs on Tokyo by carrier-launched bombers, was militarily worthless, but it caused such wild excitement that it underscored the American people's need for victorious action.[10]

Roosevelt came to believe that a successful early offensive involving United States forces in the west would serve several political functions. First, it would fulfil the public's need to strike back, and to be seen to be winning. Second, it would make the war tangible for Americans by involving many GIs – with families back home – in combat, with all the hardship and pain that that implied. Third, by being an offensive launched (however indirectly) against Germany, it would make it clear that Germany was an enemy of the United States and would hopefully lead to public appreciation that the 'Germany First' strategy, agreed by the British and Americans at the Arcadia Conference in December 1941 on the basis of Germany being the greater threat, was correct. Finally, it was also important to FDR that 1942 was a congressional election year: success on the battlefield would, he hoped, pay large political dividends, though he imagined that these would be in the broader sense of returning supporters of the war to Congress rather than the narrower sense that President Wilson had required in 1918–20, of returning Democrats as such.[11]

Some historians have argued that a major reason for Roosevelt's ordering of Torch was a promise he had made to Soviet Foreign Minister Vyacheslav Molotov, on the latter's visit to Washington, DC between 29 May and 1 June 1942, to open a second front in Europe in 1942. This promise was made, it is said, only in part for military reasons, the main aim being to prevent the Soviet leadership from insisting upon British and United States recognition of the Soviet Union's 1941 frontiers. These frontiers included the annexations of the Baltic states, eastern Poland and parts of Finland, and had been made possible by secret protocols in the Nazi–Soviet Pact of August 1939. Their recognition would almost certainly have caused widespread public resentment in the United States and Great Britain, but Stalin and Molotov declared that doing so was essential to maintain the morale of the Soviet people, threatened at a critical juncture by the Nazi 1942 summer offensive (Operation Blue), and to cement the alliance between the Soviet Union and the western Allies. The argument runs that FDR insisted on mounting Operation Torch at least in part to pre-empt these Soviet demands in eastern Europe, by proving that the United States was pulling its weight in the war and was indeed a faithful ally of the Soviet Union, without having to recognise any new frontiers.[12]

This is unconvincing. First, Roosevelt did not actually promise a second front in Europe to Molotov in 1942; he merely stated that 'we expect the formation of a second front this year'.[13] Second, although Roosevelt was always aware of the diplomatic picture, and also United States public opinion, the question of the Soviet 1941 frontiers was a moot one in early 1942, when the very survival of both the Soviet Union and the anti-Axis alliance was in doubt. Roosevelt knew that the Soviets had no alternative but to fight on, and decided to deal with the frontier question by ignoring it as much as possible until it became a significant issue, which it did by the end of the war. Finally, Operation Torch was by no stretch of the imagination a 'second front in Europe'. It was too peripheral strategically to help the Soviet Union in 1942, and by its diversion of Allied strength to Africa, away from Europe, it strongly suggested that a second front would not be possible to help the Soviets in 1943 either. The Soviet leaders would have perceived that Torch was no substitute for an invasion of France, the only way the western Allies could have helped the Soviet Union militarily in an efficacious manner, and it seems unlikely that members of the British and United States governments could have believed that they could fool the Soviets with a sideshow.[14]

Other historians have pointed to the strong British promotion of Operation Torch, and have argued that the British leadership's high degree of influence over FDR in 1942 was probably decisive in winning his approval for the operation.[15] This influence has been exaggerated, however. Despite Roosevelt's admiration and affection for the British in general and Churchill in particular, it is unlikely that he allowed them to influence policy-making in any important way. Roosevelt did not trust British motivations entirely: specifically, he did not wish to see United States forces used to preserve the British Empire. He did not like colonial empires, and there is evidence to suggest that even in 1942 he was taking steps to weaken that of the British – for example, in his attitude towards Indian independence.[16] Moreover, in early 1942 British military fortunes and prestige, following the fall of Singapore, were at their lowest ebb. It is hard to believe that Roosevelt would have ignored this when he was listening to British advice on what military undertakings he should and should not proceed with.

It is also inaccurate to portray the British as united promoters of Torch. Churchill certainly supported the operation, but there were dissenting voices within the British leadership, especially in the British Army, with certain generals agreeing with their American counterparts that Torch was a pointless diversion of resources.[17] Where the British were united was in their opposition to Sledgehammer, the planned invasion of France in 1942 (and the major strategic alternative to Torch) advocated principally by the United States Chief of Staff, General Marshall, which they regarded as militarily suicidal. Since British participation in Sledgehammer was essential to that operation's chances of success, their effective veto of it certainly cleared the way for Torch, but by no means determined that it would go ahead.

In this essay, then, I argue that political reasons lie at the heart of President Roosevelt's decision to order Operation Torch to proceed in 1942. But it is important to emphasise that this decision was not mandated by the current state of domestic politics in the United States. Rather, Roosevelt chose to act in this way.

Roosevelt's military advisers were unanimous, if at different levels of intensity, in their opposition to Torch. They explained that it was very risky and also essentially peripheral in nature.[18] But in the end, because of British opposition to Sledgehammer, the only real alternative to Torch became Roundup. This was a cross-Channel invasion of France, but on a more ambitious scale than Sledgehammer. While Roundup had great military potential, as it was intended to bring Allied armies directly into the heart of Europe, it was politically unappealing to FDR because it could not go ahead before the spring of 1943 at the earliest.

Roosevelt might have swallowed this and gone over to the political offensive, educating the public on the need to deal with the Nazis before the Japanese, and also stressing the need for patience while full mobilisation of the war economy was taking place. In the meantime he could have pointed to less spectacular but very real signs of success, such as increases in production of war *matériel* or greater frequency in U-boat sinkings. After all, earlier presidents had accepted the challenge of guiding or initiating public opinion, and had advanced controversial policies in order to overcome a crisis. This is how Lincoln had acted in the Civil War over the emancipation of the slaves.[19] Roosevelt himself had shown comparable initiative in the summer of 1935 when he pushed the New Deal leftward during the 'second Hundred Days'.[20]

In 1942, however, he decided not to seize the initiative in this way. For Roosevelt did not perceive that there was a crisis which required his personal intervention. He was, of course, aware of the potential seriousness of the problem of public opinion – that ignorance and apathy on the one hand and the need for quick victory and revenge on the other could, if not dealt with, lead to a clamour to deal with the Japanese first or to rapid war weariness and demoralisation. But he thought that a second front in the west in 1942 would solve all these problems for him. He listened to his military advisers' misgivings on Torch and would have happily endorsed an alternative if one had been available. But since none was, he opted for Torch.

Roosevelt also did not share his military's pessimism over Torch's prospects. Although he was aware to some extent of the weaknesses of his intelligence sources in North Africa, their confidence in Torch's good prospects for success none the less did much to reassure him, as we shall see. More importantly, however, his intuition or instinct, influenced no doubt by the need to have United States forces involved in an offensive in the west in 1942, told him that somehow everything would be all right once the operation was actually under way. He felt sure that the officers and men of the Vichy French Army of North Africa, on whom the success or failure of Operation Torch depended, would not put up more than a token resistance once it was made clear that United States forces came not as conquerors, but as friends and liberators. Roosevelt thought that this would be so because of the 164-year history of friendly relations between the United States and France, a history which had often seen the two nations fighting on the same side against 'enemies of liberty', as for example in the First World War. In keeping with the historical nature of this scenario, Roosevelt deemed it necessary that British participation in Torch be minimised. Also, the President believed that the Free French movement and its leader, General de Gaulle (to whom he had developed an aversion), should not be involved at all, because this would antagonise elements in Vichy which regarded the movement as an attempt to usurp the authority of both the French Army and the French state.[21]

While there is nothing intrinsically wrong in using intuition to help shape policy – political leaders have often done so and have had to rely on it when intelligence sources have proven deficient or ambiguous – for it to come close to being effective, it has to be grounded in at least something. Adolf Hitler, for example, whose mind was usually antithetical to rational and systematic thinking, and whose intelligence services had widespread problems of bias, nevertheless in many instances had a good grasp of his enemies' strengths and weaknesses.[22] This was based on personal experience (his service in the German Army in the First World War being important here), a wide if disorganised reading knowledge, and a good brain. In Führer Directive No. 51, for example, issued on 3 November 1943, he revealed his keen sense for British and American strategymaking and its consequences for Germany, expressing the realisation that their threat, although not serious up to now, would soon become so:

> The hard and costly struggle against Bolshevism has demanded extreme exertions ... The danger in the east remains, but a greater danger now appears in the west: an Anglo-Saxon landing. The vast extent of territory in the east makes it possible for us to lose ground, even on a large scale, without a fatal blow being struck to the nervous system of Germany. It is very different in the west. Should the enemy succeed in breaching our defences on a wide front here the immediate consequences would be unpredictable. Everything indicates that the enemy will launch an offensive against the Western Front of Europe, at the latest in the spring, perhaps even earlier. I can therefore no longer take responsibility for further weakening the west, in favour of other theatres of war. I have therefore decided to reinforce its defences, particularly those places from which long-range bombardment of England [with pilotless missiles] will begin.[23]

It seems unlikely that Roosevelt would have been capable of making a strategic appreciation like this. Although he had gained some understanding of modern warfare when he was Assistant Secretary of the Navy, this knowledge was necessarily limited because the United States Navy did not play a major role in the First World War. Also, apart from a brief tour of the western front in the summer of 1918, Roosevelt's administrative duties kept him in Washington, away from the centre of the war's activity in Europe.[24]

As far as travel and knowledge of countries outside the United States went, again Roosevelt did have some experience and also curiosity, probably more than many United States presidents, but it was none the less not enormous. His travels abroad were mostly made when he was a boy, and consisted of vacations to Europe with his parents, part of the general education that those of his patrician background thought it important to acquire at that time.[25]

Some historians have argued that he was always strongly interested in foreign affairs, and in fact was a lifetime Wilsonian internationalist, although he had to disguise this during the 1920s and 1930s because of the power of isolationism in United States politics.[26] This view strains both logic and the evidence. Roosevelt's passive stances on the rise of Nazi Germany, Imperial Japan and

Fascist Italy in the 1930s reveal an internationalism that is so latent that it might as well not be there.[27] And after Pearl Harbor, when isolationism was discredited and he had an opportunity to display his supposed internationalist colours, he did not do so. In fact his ideas on international relations were often at variance with those of Wilson. Roosevelt's 'four policemen' plan, his scheme to maintain the peace in the post-war world by entrusting its upkeep to four powers only – China, Great Britain, the Soviet Union and the United States – with all the other nations effectively disarmed, reveals an authoritarian approach that is far removed from Wilson's championing of the rights of small nations, and more closely resembles the thinking of Prince Metternich and Tsar Alexander at the Congress of Vienna. Roosevelt's cavalier attitude towards smaller nations is also evident in his treatment of French sensibilities at the time of the planning for Torch. Nor did he mellow with the passage of time. Towards the end of the war he found himself having to conceal many of his foreign policy aims from a public that was becoming increasingly Wilsonian in outlook, in a manner that was reminiscent of his confrontations with isolationists in 1940 and 1941. This is evident in the discussions over the proposed United Nations Organisation, when FDR made public speeches which emphasised the importance of small nations, while at the same time planning to make the UN only a talking shop, with real power lying in the hands of the 'four policemen'.[28]

What often struck visitors to the wartime White House, especially foreigners, was not the President's competence in international affairs but his amateurishness, and his lack of self-awareness in this respect. British Foreign Secretary Anthony Eden, who had several days of meetings with Roosevelt in March 1943, later wrote in his memoirs:

> Though I enjoyed these conversations, the exercise of the President's charm and the play of his lively mind, they were also perplexing. Roosevelt was familiar with the history and geography of Europe. Perhaps his hobby of stamp-collecting had helped him to this knowledge, but the academic yet sweeping opinions which he built upon it were alarming in their cheerful fecklessness. He seemed to see himself disposing of the fate of many lands, allied no less than enemy. He did all this with so much grace that it was not easy to dissent. Yet it was too like a conjuror, skillfully juggling with balls of dynamite, whose nature he failed to understand.[29]

Roosevelt's confidence in Torch therefore, based on his intuition, rested on very shallow foundations.

Let us now examine the intelligence picture in North-West Africa – what existed, what its quality was, and the degree of influence it exerted over the President. The historian David Kahn has argued that there were six main foreign intelligence sources available to American leaders in 1941. They were: diplomatic reports; information from friendly nations; military attachè reports; radio intelligence; the press; and information from private individuals.[30] Several of these sources existed in French North Africa in 1942, in particular diplomatic reports from career diplomat Robert D. Murphy, Roosevelt's special representative in the area, as well as press reports and information from British sources in the region. In addition to these, United States leaders had an even more significant source, one which did not appear in Kahn's purportedly all-embracing list. This was the United States' only effective espionage ring then in existence, the vice-consuls organisation run by the OSS.[31]

The OSS's role in Vichy French North-West Africa was extensive and went back some time. Indeed, the establishment of an American spy network in the area in the form of the vice-consuls organisation preceded both the formation of the OSS in June 1942 and the founding of the OSS's predecessor organisation, the Office of the Co-ordinator of Information (COI), in July 1941. The vice-consuls organisation was set up in May 1941, following the Murphy–Weygand economic agreement of 10 March 1941, whereby certain American goods could be imported into French North-West Africa, circumventing the British blockade of the area, if the Vichy authorities in return allowed American observers in to watch over the destinations of the goods and ensure that they did not fall into the hands of the Germans or Italians. This was the ostensible role of the vice-consuls.

In reality, the vice-consuls' task was to collect information for the United States government on all aspects of North-West African affairs, especially Axis penetration of the region. They were to do so by any means available to them, including espionage. United States officials were aware of the dire strategic consequences should the Axis come to control the area – the coast of Brazil could be easily threatened by German and Italian naval forces stationed in West Africa.[32] Interest in the region intensified after American entry into the Second World War in December 1941, when Winston Churchill suggested at the Arcadia conference that North-West Africa would be a good site for the launching of America's first military offensive.[33] General Donovan's COI, which was now directing the activities of the vice-consuls, broadened the range of their duties to include organising guerrilla groups, looking into the possibility of arranging a pro-Allied coup within the Vichy French Army of North Africa, and assessing motivation within that army.[34]

The OSS, when established in June 1942, was not an independent agency responsible only to the President, as COI had been, but was part of the Joint Chiefs of Staff (JCS) system, and thus had military overseers. Its standing was uncertain. As a new and 'upstart' organisation, it had many enemies in the government bureaucracy, and incorporation into the JCS meant that OSS personnel had to work hard to justify to their military superiors their organisation's continued existence.[35] They proceeded to do so by giving the JCS every assistance they could in the planning and execution of Operation Torch. The main responsibilities of OSS agents in the field were the collection of military intelligence (for example, details of possible landing sites for Allied troops, and of the strengths and dispositions of French forces) and the operation of guerrilla units. The latter, to be recruited in the main from pro-Allied Frenchmen but also including some Arabs, were to be used to assist Allied troops when the invasion actually took place. Furthermore, the OSS maintained links with disaffected officers of the Vichy Army of North Africa, and it was on the basis of evidence supplied from this source that OSS agents claimed that the resistance of the Vichy French to a primarily American invasion of North Africa would be minimal. It was the OSS's job, here, to build on political disaffection in the French Army. Later, this would include the recruitment of a distinguished French soldier, General Henri Giraud, to the Allied side, in an attempt to persuade the French forces in Africa not to resist the Allied landings. This was by far the most important of the OSS's tasks; indeed, the OSS's optimistic claims in this area undoubtedly helped to reinforce Roosevelt in his belief that Torch would meet with success.[36] Were the OSS's claims justified?

Taking the collection of purely military intelligence first, it is clear that the OSS's work here was of excellent quality. Information on conditions that Allied forces could expect to meet in North Africa, from the level of surf at the Casablanca beaches to details about North Africa's roads and railways, was all furnished on a lavish scale, as was information on the strengths and dispositions of French forces in North Africa – harder to obtain, but delivered nevertheless by the pro-Allied Frenchmen in the French forces.

This is clear not only from primary material on the vice-consuls, but also from the accounts of various American generals commanding at the time of the actual invasion, who praised the accuracy of the intelligence they had received prior to the landing, stressing its value to Torch.[37]

This reflected well on the OSS, but was not enough to justify its existence as a separate organisation. After all, the United States Army's Military Intelligence Division (MID) could have done the same job, as it had done similar jobs in the past. The OSS had to demonstrate that it was capable of achieving success in new areas in order to convince the Joint Chiefs that it deserved to survive.

OSS personnel believed that they did have more to offer the Joint Chiefs than just military intelligence. Specifically, they claimed to have carried out extensive investigation into the motives which might govern the response of the Vichy Army of North Africa to an Allied invasion, for it was these forces that Allied armies would have to deal with if Torch went ahead. Although investigations into enemy motivations had been carried out before by American military intelligence services, these had mostly looked at the likely will to fight of individual enemy units, rather than at the whole army of a neutral nation, which was what the OSS was attempting to do in North Africa.[38] In addition, the OSS believed it had reached a new level of sophistication in this area with its Research and Analysis (R and A) branch, a body composed of scholars who investigated problems in the world in order to assist the policy-making process within the United States government. R and A (whose personnel included many scholars of French history and politics) was asked to report on the readiness of the French Army of North Africa to welcome a possible United States invasion there. R and A concurred with the vice-consuls' optimistic view of the likely reaction of the Vichy French to an American invasion, although it must be stressed that much of the information on which they based this judgement came from the vice-consuls themselves.[39]

Finally, the OSS offered the American military the support of disaffected Frenchmen in North Africa, many of them military personnel. In the event of an invasion by US forces, it was hoped that the Vichy French would not resist. But if they did, and even the optimists in the OSS expected at least some initial resistance from the French armed forces, then these disaffected Frenchmen could be called upon to go into action to support the American invasion, carrying out various sabotage tasks. It was hoped that the existence of this guerrilla group would encourage other Frenchmen in North Africa to join the Allies.[40]

The basis of the OSS agents' belief that the Vichy French would offer little or no resistance to an American invasion was that, confronted with a large number of American troops, the French would be forced to decide which side they wished to fight on, Axis or Allies. It was as inconceivable to Roosevelt as it was to the OSS that the French would wish to join the Axis by resisting the invasion. So it was to be expected that the French would allow American forces to occupy North Africa, and would then join the Allies.[41] Thus the prediction was that there would be a swift occupation of French North Africa. This would allow Allied forces to move swiftly on to Libya. The Axis forces there – Rommel's Afrika Korps – would then have to face assaults from two sides, a primarily American force (from Torch) from the west, and a strengthened British force from the east. The whole of the southern shore of the Mediterranean would be in Allied hands in a matter of weeks. According to John S.D. Eisenhower, General Eisenhower's son:

> The real purpose of the whole effort [Torch] was to reach Tunisia in time to cut off Rommel from the rear. And after the Eighth Army's victory at El Alamein [October 1942], Allied possession of all North Africa now shone as a glittering, attainable prize. Rommel and his forces were important, but the greater objective of this particular campaign was to gain vital real estate.[42]

The confidence of OSS personnel in this scenario was so immense that soon the American military came to accept it too. But a number of American commanders, including General Eisenhower, who was to lead Allied forces in the Torch invasion, had grave doubts about the whole operation. Allied troops allocated to Torch were few in number, and would find it hard going indeed if the French did choose to resist wholeheartedly.[43] In the event of the French accepting German aid in such a situation, the Allies might face a catastrophic defeat. The military thus needed reassurance on the question of the likely attitude of the Vichy forces to an American invasion, and this the OSS supplied.[44] The military did not just accept the OSS's word on the situation, for other Allied intelligence organisations, most notably British Military Intelligence, or MI6, were also active in North Africa. But, in practice, the voice of the OSS's personnel was the loudest and most confident, as the other

Allied intelligence organisations did not have intelligence resources of a comparable size in French North Africa.[45] President Roosevelt's demands for an offensive in 1942 also put pressure on American military planners who might otherwise have raised objections to Torch. If they had believed that the French would probably put up fierce resistance to an invasion, however, it is likely that they would have gone to Roosevelt with the request that, because the invasion was too risky, an offensive elsewhere should be undertaken, or, failing that, all major operations should be postponed until 1943.[46]

We can, of course, only speculate on what Roosevelt would have done in such circumstances. But given his strong desire for a United States offensive in the west in 1942, it seems likely that he would have ignored all but the blackest of intelligence pictures from French North Africa and, trusting in his intuition, would have given Torch the go-ahead anyway, in spite of warnings from intelligence sources. But, as we have seen, the OSS's reporting from North Africa did not contradict Roosevelt's optimistic picture of the situation there; on the contrary, it strongly reinforced it.

In fact, the OSS's assessment of Vichy French motivations was poor, as was forcefully demonstrated on 8 November 1942, the day Operation Torch was launched. Encouraged by Marshal Philippe Pétain, the Vichy head of state, the French put up a fierce resistance to the American forces everywhere.[47] In three days of fighting, 1,400 Americans and 700 Frenchmen died.[48] The OSS's guerrilla teams were a manifestly unsuccessful failure, almost all of them failing to achieve their objectives.[49] One reason for this may have been that the OSS's guerrilla plans were too ambitious, especially when the French chose to resist wholeheartedly. They may have been drafted merely to impress the military.[50]

Two events which the OSS could not have predicted came to the aid of the Allies in their hour of need. The first had its origin in the presence in Algiers of the Vichy head of armed forces, Admiral Jean Darlan. Darlan had arrived in Algiers to be at the side of his son, who was stricken with polio. When the Americans appeared at Algiers he was made a virtual prisoner, and necessity soon drove him to co-operate with the Americans to arrange a ceasefire. What was needed to make the French stop fighting, and this had been foreseen by the OSS, was an order to do so by a high-up French military leader. OSS agents and Robert D. Murphy had tried to use General Giraud to accomplish this, but he had proved uncooperative. Darlan had the authority to order a ceasefire and was prepared to do so, but when Marshal Pétain learnt of his manoeuvres he dismissed him. Yet this, as we shall see, was not to be the end of the Darlan affair.

The second event to benefit the Allies was Hitler's decision to invade the unoccupied zone of France, thus breaking the 1940 armistice. Why Hitler chose to invade the unoccupied zone at this moment is unclear, but he had never trusted the French and probably believed that they were about to come to an accommodation with the Allies anyway, an accommodation that might include the handing over to the Allies of the powerful French fleet based at Toulon, a fleet Hitler himself wished to acquire.[51] In the event, Hitler's hasty action precipitated the event he feared – namely, French agreement to a ceasefire with the Allies.

With Pétain soon becoming a prisoner of the Axis, French personnel in North Africa accepted Darlan as head of Vichy, and the reinstated leader promptly arranged a ceasefire with the Americans. Apparently, the OSS's face had been saved by accident, and all was now well.

However, the 'deal with Darlan', the ceasefire arrangement by which the French agreed not to fight the Americans any more in return for the Americans allowing Darlan to remain in control of French North Africa, created many problems for the Allies. Darlan had collaborated with Hitler: among other acts of collaboration he had agreed to ship food and trucks from Tunisia to Rommel's Afrika Korps. For the Allies to make arrangements with him seemed to imply that arrangements might be made with Hitler and Mussolini also.[52] A storm of protest arose in Allied countries, and Allied propaganda suffered a serious setback because of this seemingly cynical deal.[53]

There is another, controversial, twist to this sorry tale. The American military leaders who, with Robert Murphy's help, had negotiated the 'deal with Darlan' have been represented as having had no choice, for the apparent alternative was to continue to fight the French and suffer heavy casualties.[54] But J. Rives Childs, a State Department official stationed in Tangier at the time of Operation Torch, argued that the 'deal with Darlan' was unnecessary, as the bulk of the French forces would have ceased resisting the Americans upon hearing of the German invasion of the unoccupied zone on 10 November 1942. Childs holds Robert Murphy responsible for the deal, as it was Murphy's job to advise the American military leaders on political matters. Murphy, who is known to have had considerable sympathy for Vichy leaders and perhaps shared their right-wing leanings, may not have wished to avoid a 'deal with Darlan'.[55] Murphy went on to enjoy a distinguished career in the United States government, often maintaining his links with intelligence organisations such as the CIA. He was to be one of Operation Torch's more debatable bequests to posterity.[56]

In a more important and immediate sense, however, the OSS's failure to predict the initial French reaction to Torch had dire consequences for the future of the Allied war effort. This was because the Allies were unable to foresee that they would fail to take Tunisia in the first few days of the campaign. Tunisia is closer to Italy than Libya is, and in the context of the Second World War African campaigns this was important, for after Operation Torch the Axis were able to occupy Tunisia, thus establishing much shorter and hence less vulnerable supply lines than they had previously had to Libya. The British had wanted landings in Tunisia as part of Operation Torch, but Eisenhower had ruled them out as being too dangerous. Allied forces were supposed to move east quickly from landing sites in Algeria to occupy Tunisia, but, because the unanticipated French resistance held them up, the Axis were able to deploy powerful forces there first. French forces in Tunisia, belying their supposed pro-Allied orientation as presented by OSS agents, made no attempt to prevent this.[57]

Indeed, benefiting from their short supply lines, Axis forces were able to hold out in Tunisia until May 1943, almost seven months from the initial launching date of Torch. This delay meant that forces allocated to Roundup, the planned cross-Channel invasion of France in 1943, had to be committed to Tunisia instead, and the cross-Channel invasion had to be postponed until 1944, when it was renamed Operation Overlord. As a result of the long-drawn-out Tunisian campaign the Allies drifted into a peripheral strategy, making relatively small-scale attacks against Hitler's Europe, as in the Sicilian and Italian campaigns, but never coming to grips with the bulk of Hitler's forces until Overlord in 1944. Thus it can be argued that the OSS's failure to predict the extent of the initial French resistance to Torch helped to prolong the war because it reduced the strategic options available to the western Allies in 1943, especially the cross-Channel option.

It is, of course, easy to say with hindsight that the OSS made mistakes with its assessments of the morale and temperament of the Vichy Army of North Africa. The question is, did the OSS make errors of judgement with the information it had on hand at the time? The answer is yes. The example of the Syrian campaign of

May 1941, in which Vichy French forces strongly resisted an invasion force of British and Free French troops, ought to have given the OSS an idea of what course of action the French would take when their territory was invaded by outsiders.[58] Marshal Pétain, indeed, was asked by Admiral Leahy, American ambassador to Vichy, what his reaction would be to an American invasion of North Africa. Pétain replied that he would order French forces to resist any invasion strongly, and that he expected his orders to be carried out.[59] OSS personnel chose to ignore this and other evidence, and to believe instead the advice of their vice-consuls that American forces would be welcomed. While the vice-consuls were in general probably not as incompetent as has been alleged in certain quarters, asking them to predict what the likely attitude of the French Army of North Africa to an American invasion was expecting too much.[60]

OSS personnel were correct in assessing that the French were fundamentally pro-Allied. What they did not understand was that the French were also prepared to defend their own national interests, and would obey the orders of their leaders. The OSS partially realised the importance of honour and obedience in the French Army – this is why they wanted General Giraud to act on their behalf, although their expectation that he would be able to order the French to lay down their arms was much too optimistic. Giraud had few supporters in North Africa, and was also politically naïve. This over-optimistic assessment of him, however, was mainly the fault of Murphy, whose considerable political sympathies for the Vichyites led him to overrate their abilities.[61]

The main problem facing French pro-Allied sentiment at the time of Torch was that there was no clear indication that the Allies would win the war. In early November 1942, the Axis powers still appeared to be beating the Russians (this was just before the Russian counterattack at Stalingrad which began on 19 November) and might well emerge the victors in the war. The plan of Vichy's leaders, as determined in 1940, was to reach an accommodation with the Axis in the belief that the Axis would ultimately win the war, and that the interests of France would best be served by collaboration with Germany.[62] Torch aimed to reverse that policy overnight, and it was just not possible. Only political naïvety, false optimism and the selective use of intelligence material could have produced the prediction of such a sudden switch in French attitudes, and these charges can be laid straight at the door of Donovan's OSS as it existed in 1942.

Donovan's enthusiasm for Torch arose partly from his perception that if OSS performed well in this instance, its bureaucratic position at home would be that much stronger. Although the OSS had made repeated blunders regarding the abilities of its North African subordinates and its assessment of the motivation of the Vichy French Army of North Africa, these were forgotten in the light of the apparent success of Torch and of the OSS's good military intelligence work. American military leaders, too busy fighting the war to examine the OSS's work for Torch too closely, believed that the OSS had done a good job. This judgement helped the OSS, with the backing of the military, to establish itself on a permanent wartime basis in 1943, thus partially justifying Donovan's presumed assessment of the importance of Operation Torch to his organisation's future: '[Torch] put OSS into the big time as far as American military leaders in Europe were concerned and insured Donovan the support of both Roosevelt and Eisenhower.'[63]

One can conclude by reiterating that the OSS misjudged the attitude of the majority of the officers and men of the Vichy French Army of North Africa to an American invasion. Although the vice-consuls had made contact with pro-Allied groups in the French Army, these groups were in a minority. The bulk of the French Army wished to follow the policy of the Vichy government and withdraw as much as possible from the war-torn world. Loyalty and honour were strong forces linking the French Army of North Africa to the Pétain government, and in retrospect Operation Torch's attempts to break those links or force the Vichy government on to the Allied side seem misguided and naïve.

Part of the explanation for the OSS's poor assessment of the French Army of North Africa lies in the inexperience of its personnel, especially the vice-consuls, in political matters. They were not initially meant to pass much comment on the state of French North African politics, their main job being to watch out for Axis penetration of the area. But they themselves quickly became confident in their abilities in the field of political intelligence, and OSS headquarters encouraged this tendency uncritically.

The main cause of the OSS's false optimism over French North Africa, however, was Donovan's desire to see things this way. The OSS was under pressure, and needed an opportunity to prove itself. When Donovan heard of the opportunities open to his organisation in North Africa from the vice-consuls, he wholeheartedly embraced the case for an American landing there. His need for the project and his enthusiasm blinded his judgement, however, and this almost brought about, if not the destruction, then at least the severe mauling of the forces involved in Operation Torch at the hands of the French.

Operation Torch was saved by two things, neither of which could have been predicted by the OSS. The first was the availability and willingness of Admiral Darlan to help the Allies; the second, Hitler's decision to make an enemy of France by terminating the 1940 armistice. Despite the OSS's failures in the fields of both political assessment and guerrilla warfare, the organisation came out of Torch with credit, for the results if not the causes of its action were roughly what had been expected by the Allied command and President Roosevelt. In addition, Operation Torch was regarded as one of the great early turning-points of the war – the others being the battles of El Alamein (October 1942) and Stalingrad (November 1942–February 1943) – thus further increasing the OSS's reputation. American military leaders were impressed by this and by the OSS's high-quality military intelligence work for Torch, and gave their considerable backing to the OSS in the bureaucratic battles in late 1942 and early 1943, battles which the OSS was ultimately to win, establishing itself on a permanent wartime basis in March 1943. Damage to the Allied cause, through the 'deal with Darlan' and the commitment to the peripheral Mediterranean strategy, went largely unnoticed in the Allied camp, and the OSS did not suffer as much as it perhaps deserved.

Thus, intelligence did not serve United States leaders well in 1942. As I argued earlier, better intelligence might not have made a great difference as the national leadership, President Roosevelt in particular, was indisposed to listen. In fact, Roosevelt does not seem to have changed his habits even after the 'deal with Darlan' resulted in a significant drop in Allied morale, the antithesis of his main objective for Torch.[64] The implications of these circumstances were ominous for the future war effort, and for the ensuing peace.

Notes

1. See, for example: B.H. Liddell Hart, *History of the Second World War* (1971; rpt. New York: Perigree, 1982), chapter 21. John Keegan, *The Second World War* (New York: Viking Penguin, 1990), p. 542. Maurice Matloff, 'Allied strategy in Europe, 1939–1945', in Peter Paret, ed., *Makers of Modern Strategy: From Machiavelli to the nuclear age*, (Princeton: Princeton, NJ: Univ. Press, 1986), pp. 683–687.
2. I have been influenced in my thinking by Lawrence Freedman, *US Intelligence and the Soviet Strategic Threat*, 2nd edn. (Princeton, NJ: Princeton Univ. Press, 1986), Ernest R. May, ed., *Knowing One's*

Enemies: Intelligence assessment before the two world wars (Princeton, NJ: Princeton Univ. Press, 1986) and Rhodri Jeffreys-Jones, *The CIA and American Democracy* (New Haven, Conn.: Yale Univ. Press, 1989), as well as by Roy Godson, ed., *Intelligence Requirements for the 1980s: Analysis and estimates* (New Brunswick, NJ: Transaction Books, 1980) and Roy Godson, ed., *Intelligence Requirements for the 1980s: Intelligence and policy* (Lexington, Mass.: Lexington Books, 1986).

3. My main sources are: (1) Roosevelt biographies: James MacGregor Burns, *Roosevelt: The lion and the fox* (New York: Harcourt Brace Jovanovich, 1984, 1956); James MacGregor Burns, *Roosevelt: The soldier of freedom* (New York: Harcourt Brace Jovanovich, 1970); Robert Dallek, *Franklin D. Roosevelt and American Foreign Policy, 1932–1945* (New York: Oxford Univ. Press, 1981). Robert A. Divine, *Roosevelt and World War II* (Baltimore MD: Johns Hopkins Press, 1969); Frank Freidel, *Franklin D. Roosevelt: A rendezvous with destiny* (Boston, Mass.: Little, Brown, 1990). (2) Organisational histories of the OSS: Bradley F. Smith, *The Shadow Warriors: OSS and the origins of the CIA* (New York: Basic Books, 1983). Richard Harris Smith, *OSS: The secret history of America's first central intelligence agency* (Berkeley, Calif.: Univ. of California Press, 1981); Thomas F. Troy, *Donovan and the CIA: A history of the establishment of the Central Intelligence Agency* (Frederick, Md: Univ. Publications of America, 1981). (3) Military history: John S.D. Eisenhower, *Allies: Pearl Harbor to D-Day* (Garden City, NY: Doubleday, 1982); George F. Howe, *The Mediterranean Theater of Operations: Northwest Africa–seizing the initiative in the west* (Washington, DC: Office of the Chief of Military History, Department of the Army, 1957); Liddell Hart, *History of the Second World War*; Keegan, *Second World War*; Maurice Matloff and Edwin M. Snell, *Strategic Planning for Coalition Warfare, 1941–1942* (Washington, DC: Office of the Chief of Military History, Department of the Army, 1953). Richard W. Steele, *The First Offensive, 1942: Roosevelt, Marshall, and the making of American strategy* (Bloomington, Ind.: Indiana Univ. Press, 1973). Russell F. Weigley, *The American Way of War: A History of United States military strategy and policy* (Bloomington, Ind.: Indiana Univ. Press, 1977). In addition, I have worked at the Hoover Institution Archives, Stanford, California, the location of a sizeable batch of primary material on the activities of OSS-directed agents in French North-West Africa.

4. Keegan, *Second World War*, pp. 540–1; Freidel, *Rendezvous*, p. 459.

5. See, for example: Burns, *Roosevelt: The lion and the fox*, Burns, *Roosevelt: The soldier of freedom*.

6. See, for example, John Keegan's characterisation of him as a Renaissance prince: Keegan, *Second World War*, p. 540.

7. It may be conjectured that this affected Roosevelt to the end of his life. In 1944, after he had watched a movie about Wilson's losing battle over the League, his doctor noted a significant rise in the President's blood pressure: Freidel, *Rendezvous, p. 556.*

8. On Roosevelt's changing role with regard to military strategy in 1942, see Matloff, 'Allied Strategy in Europe, 1939–1945', p. 686, and Keegan, *Second World War*, p. 542. On Roosevelt and public opinion, see Dallek, *FDR*, chapter 12.

9. It can be argued that, to a large extent, he himself was responsible

for this by failing to educate the American people at an earlier stage on the urgency and nature of the Axis threat to the United States, and by failing to take much action to deal with it. See Burns, *Roosevelt: The lion and the fox*, pp. 399–400. See also, Dallek, *FDR*, p.358.

10. Dallek, *FDR*, p. 334. Keegan, *Second World War*, pp. 270–2.
11. Dallek, *FDR*, pp. 360–1.
12. See, for example: John Lewis Gaddis, *The United States and the Origins of the Cold War, 1941–1947* (New York: Columbia Univ. Press, 1972), pp. 16–17; Mark A. Stoler, 'The "second front" and American fear of Soviet expansion, 1941–43', *Military Affairs*, 39 (Oct. 1975), 136–41; Freidel, *Rendezvous*, pp. 449–50.
13. Divine, *Roosevelt and War*, p.90.
14. On Hitler's acknowledgement of the importance of an Allied invasion of France, see Führer Directive No. 51, cited below.
15. See, for example, Freidel, *Rendezvous*, p. 410 and following.
16. Dallek, *FDR*, p. 319.
17. Winston S. Churchill, *The Second World War IV, The Hinge of Fate* (Boston, Mass.: Houghton-Mifflin, 1985 1950), pp. 396 ff.
18. Matloff, "Allied strategy in Europe, 1939–1945', pp. 683–687.
19. See Eric Foner, *Reconstruction: America's unfinished revolution, 1863–1877* (New York: Harper & Row, 1988), chapter 1.
20. Burns, *Roosevelt: The lion and the Fox*, pp. 220–226.
21. See, for example, Freidel, *Rendezvous*, p. 453.
22. David Irving, *Hitler's War* (New York: Avon, 1990). On Hitler's intelligence services, see David Kahn, *Hitler's Spies: German military intelligence in World War II* (New York: Collier, 1985, 1978) and Michael Geyer, 'National Socialist Germany: The politics of information', in Ernest R. May, ed., *Knowing One's enemies: Intelligence assessment before the two world wars* (Princeton, NJ: Princeton Univ. Press, 1986).
23. Quoted in Keegan, *Second World War* p. 30.
24. Freidel, *Rendezvous*, pp. 22–32; Burns, *Roosevelt: The lion and the fox*, chapter 3.
25. Freidel, *Rendezvous*, chapter 1; Burns, *Roosevelt: The lion and the fox*, chapter 1.
26. See, for example, Dallek, *FDR*, part 2, 'The internationalist as isolationist, 1935–1938'.
27. Burns, *Roosevelt: The lion and the fox*, chapter 19.
28. Divine, *Roosevelt and War*, part 3, 'Roosevelt the realist'.
29. Quoted in Freidel, *Rendezvous*, p. 466. Note Freidel's agreeement with Eden's judgement, *ibid.*, p. 467. See also Charles De Gaulle, *War Memoirs*, 5 vols. (New York: Simon & Schuster, 1955–60).
30. David Kahn, 'The United States views Germany and Japan in 1941', in May, ed., *Knowing One's Enemies*, p. 479.
31. See David A. Walker, 'OSS and Operation Torch', *Journal of Contemporary History*, 22 (1987), 667–79.
32. Dallek, *FDR*, p. 251.
33. *ibid.*, p. 321.
34. Bradley F. Smith, *Shadow Warriors*, chapter 2. Richard Harris Smith, *OSS*, chapter 2.
35. Troy, *Donovan and CIA*, chapters 7–8. Bradley F. Smith, *Shadow Warriors*, chapters 3–4.

36. Bradley F. Smith, *Shadow Warriors*, pp. 149–50. Richard Harris Smith, *OSS*, pp. 57–8.
37. Notes, apparently by Leland Rounds, vice-consul at Oran, Oct. 1941, Leland Rounds Papers, box 1, section j, Hoover Institution Archives. Intelligence Report, North Africa, 10 March 1942, M.P. Goodfellow, OSS Deputy Director for Operations, M.P. Goodfellow Papers, box 3, section a, Hoover Institution Archives. On the praise of American generals for the intelligence furnished at Torch see Martin Blumenson, ed., *The Patton Papers* II: *1940–1945* (Boston, Mass.: Houghton-Mifflin, 1974), pp. 103–11. Mark Clark, *Calculated Risk* (New York: Harper, 1950), pp. 81–7. This may not have been the view of General Eisenhower, however: see John S.D. Eisenhower (General Eisenhower's son), *Allies*, pp. 143–4.
38. See, for example, Emanuel V. Voska and Will Irwin, *Spy and Counterspy* (New York: 1940). Voska was a Czech-born American citizen who worked for American military intelligence in the First World War. In 1918 he was assigned the task of evaluating the morale of Austro-Hungarian units, many of which were supposed to be on the brink of collapse, on the Italian front.
39. Bernard David Rifkind, 'OSS and Franco-American relations: 1942–1945' (George Washington University Ph.D., 1983), pp. 176–7; William L. Langer, *Our Vichy Gamble* (New York: Knopf, 1947); author's telephone conversation with Ken Kent, nephew of Sherman Kent, head of R and A North Africa, 30 Aug 1984 (Sherman Kent was, due to illness, unable to answer the author's questions in person, but instead answered some of them through his nephew, Ken Kent); Ray S. Cline, *Secrets, Spies and Scholars: Blueprint of the essential CIA* (Washington, DC: Acropolis, 1976), pp. 70–71.
40. Allied Force Headquarters, SO Operation Instructions to Lieutenant-Colonel W.A. Eddy, USMC, Naval Attaché, Tangier 14 Oct. 1942, Leland Rounds Papers, box 1, section h, Hoover Institution Archives; copy of letter, David Wooster King, vice-consul at Casablanca, to Stafford Reid, 12 Dec. 1947, David Wooster King Papers, box 1, section b, Hoover Institution Archives; Richard Harris Smith, *OSS*, p. 56. Bradley F. Smith, *Shadow Warriors*, p. 149.
41. Alfred Cobban, *A History of Modern France*: III *France of the Republics, 1871–1962* (Harmondsworth: Penguin, 1982, 1965), pp. 191–2. Bradley F. Smith, *Shadow Warriors*, p. 148.
42. Eisenhower, *Allies*, p. 199.
43. *ibid.*, p. 144. One estimate put Allied casualties at around 60,000, approximately two-thirds of the initial invasion force, if the French resisted vigorously: 'Eisenhower, Allies's African gamble', by Brigadier-General Julius C. Holmes, Leland Rounds Papers, box 1, section k, Hoover Institution Archives.
44. Bradley F. Smith, *Shadow Warriors*, pp. 149–50.
45. *ibid.*, p. 152; George January Slowikowski to F.H. Hinsley, 23 March 1981, M.Z. Rygor-Slowikowski Papers, box 2, section c, Hoover Institution Archives. George January Slowikowski was the son of M.Z. Rygor-Slowikowski, who had operated a small-scale Polish espionage network in French North Africa for MI6. F.H. Hinsley was the major contributor to *British Intelligence in the Second World War*, 4 vols. (London: HMSO), *Its Influence on Strategy and Operations*, I (1979),

II (1981), III Part 1 (1984), III Part 2 (1988); *Security and Counter-intelligence*, IV (1990).

46. Steele, *First Offensive*, p. 69.
47. Eisenhower, *Allies*, p. 198. Bradley F. Smith, *Shadow Warriors*, pp. 153–4.
48. Richard Harris Smith, *OSS*, p. 61.
49. Bradley F. Smith, *Shadow Warriors*, p. 154. Richard Harris Smith, *OSS*, p. 60.
50. The actual plans convey the impression that this was the objective of some OSS personnel. See Allied Force Headquarters, SO Operation Instructions to Lieutenant-Colonel W.A. Eddy, 14 Oct. 1942, Leland Rounds Papers, box 1, section h, Hoover Institution Archives. Center Task Force, OSS Tasks to be carried out, Leland Rounds Papers, box 1, section h, Hoover Institution Archives.
51. Cobban, *France of the Republics*, p. 192. In fact, there is little indication that the French intended to hand over their fleet to the Allies.
52. See Arthur Huge Pitz, 'United States diplomatic relations with Vichy France from 1940 to 1942' (Northern Illinois University Ph.D., 1975), chapter 8.
53. See Eisenhower, *Allies*, pp. 198–9. Clark, *Calculated Risk*, p. 123. The Darlan deal may have poisoned Franco-American relations for decades, see Rifkind, 'OSS and Franco-American relations: 1942–1945', pp. 160, 277.
54. Eisenhower, *Allies*, p. 198. Clark, *Calculated Risk*, p. 125.
55. J. Rives Childs, 'Thirty Years in the Near East', chapter 6, J. Rives Childs Papers, Hoover Institution Archives.
56. In the mid-1970s Murphy was the head of a commission investigating the organisation of the government in respect to the conduct of foreign policy, whose report featured a chapter on the importance of the CIA in this process: Cline, *Secrets*, pp. 237–41.
57. Eisenhower, *Allies*, pp. 198–9.
58. Pitz, 'Relations with Vichy', pp. 222–4.
59. Steele, *First Offensive*, p. 73.
60. For a damning criticism of the vice-consuls, see Leon Borden Blair, 'Amateurs in diplomacy: the American vice consuls in North Africa, 1941–1943', *The Historian*, 35 (1973), 607–20. Notes on Nazi memo (secret) on Vice-Consuls, 3/16/42, Richard Harris Smith papers, box 1, North Africa section, Hoover Institution Archives.
61. See Arthur L. Funk, 'Eisenhower, Giraud, and the command of Torch', *Military Affairs*, 35 (1971), 103–8; Richard Harris Smith, *OSS*, p. 70. Murphy should have been aware of Giraud's political nävety. This nävety is evident in Giraud, 'The causes of the defeat' (translation), 26 July 1940, Henri Honoř Giraud papers, box 1, Hoover Institution Archives. In this exposition, Giraud is strong on the military reasons for French defeat, but out of his depth in attempting to connect them to failings in pre-war French politics and society. He blames the 1940 military defeat on the decline of the French work ethic and on politicians, thus refusing, in a flight of self-deception, to attach any responsibility to the French Army.
62. Cobban, *France of the Republics*, p. 186.
63. Cline, *Secrets*, p. 70. Also see Bradley F. Smith, *Shadow Warriors*, pp. 156–7.
64. Freidel, *Rendezvous*, chapter 33.

5

The OSS and the Burma Road 1942–45

RICHARD B. LAIDLAW

Special Operations Unit, Detachment 101, has a unique standing in the folklore of the Office of Strategic Services (OSS). The detachment was the OSS's first-born clandestine, irregular warfare unit, staffed with the cream of volunteers, credited in admiring accounts with strenuous feats of arms, inflicting imposing casualties on the Japanese and playing an essential if not indispensable role in operations to reopen the supply road from Burma to China. But, in the British 'official' history of the Far East War, that unit warrants but a few part-line, shared entries amid five volumes packed with detail.[1] Initially, my objective in undertaking research on this subject was to correct the partisanship displayed on both sides, and that remains one of my goals. But, as so often happens in the course of an investigation, a new question arose: namely, what on earth were the OSS doing in Burma in the first place?

I must declare an interest. A lifetime ago, while preparing for the Army Staff College at Camberley in Surrey, I was required to study the campaigns of Field Marshal Sir William Slim. Then, briefly, towards the end of his life, I met my hero. We shared convalescence at Queen Victoria's Palace on the Isle of Wight. In pain, the Field Marshal was not in reflective mood, but his eyes sparked and the famous but now tired chin came up when we touched on the subject of his American contemporary, General Joseph Stilwell. Slim humoured over their relationship, restated his qualified but lasting respect for 'Vinegar Joe' and firmly recorded his regret, indeed anger, at the way that fighting man had been treated and finally abandoned by his political masters.

As a sequel to this encounter, I became determined to find out why a unit of the secret American intelligence service spent three years in one of the world's worst tropical rain forests, committing officers and men to minor local forays and pitting aboriginal tribesmen against a highly professional Japanese Army.

Neither the Americans nor the British will emerge from my account with a great deal of credit. In explaining the OSS's presence in Burma, one must concede that the Americans had a poor strategic overview of events in South-East Asia. Others have remarked, and I can only confirm, that the OSS was an agency in search of a mission, with a national leadership prepared to invent roles for itself. On the ground, OSS officers appear to have deceived both themselves and, more tragically, Third World tribesmen – the credulous Kachins delivered military co-operation in response to speculative American talk of independence.

The explanation of 101's presence in Burma augurs well neither for one's assessment of its strategic significance nor for one's assessment of the degree to which it succeeded in its enterprise. It is hardly surprising that 101's Burma mission suffered from muddle and poor tasking. With a faltering British Empire clinging anachronistically to the vestiges of world power, Anglo-American distrust and friction compounded the difficulties over mission definition.

To understand why the OSS became so unproductively enmired in the Burma campaign, one must examine its activities in the context of the waters muddied by turmoil all over southern Asia. One must attempt to understand what its officers were up to in China and India, as well as in Burma. What was Eifler doing in China? Why did Johnson and Phillips fail in India?

The answers to these questions help to explain why the OSS was marginalised in Burma, and why the Burma Road itself was a sanguinary irrelevance to the outcome of the war. To make our narrative of these complex events intelligible, we shall be tackling each in chronological order.

The story starts early in 1942 when, although the fight-back against Japan could only be America's war, there seemed no part in it for the ambitiously led OSS. The island-hopping assault westwards from Hawaii was planned as a purely naval offensive utilising carrier groups and amphibious forces. Their intelligence arm was to concentrate on enemy fleet manoeuvres and signals intercepts. The Office of Naval Intelligence would ward off friendly intruders just as keenly as it would the agents of its Japanese antagonists. General Douglas MacArthur's return north through Indonesia and the Philippines was the army's contribution, with the South-West Pacific commander maintaining his military intelligence wing inviolate, especially against the OSS.[2] Britain narrowly retained control of an India in turmoil, apprehensively awaiting Japanese incursion. Having no place with the navy, unwanted by the army and unwelcome in India, the OSS seemed excluded from the Pacific theatre. China alone offered faint hope as an immediate and further potential theatre of operations; and that avenue, by fate and misfortune, stranded the OSS on the Burma Road.

It was the application of lend-lease to China in January 1941 which, in raising the possibility of a revitalised Nationalist Army engaging the Japanese in serious hostilities, stimulated American interest in the Burma Road. From 1937 the Japanese had sequentially sealed off all ports of entry, rivers, roads and rail communications to the interior of China. The long overland route from the USSR dried up as war loomed in Europe.[3] The French colonial railway line from Haiphong through Hanoi was forcibly shut down.[4] A rude, ancient, 700-mile pack trail from the Irrawady River in Burma to the communication centre at Kunming in China was the one remaining back-door link. By 1939 the Nationalists had upgraded this track to a motor road using slave labour.[5] They then launched a propaganda campaign, portraying a poor, united, isolated country manfully defending itself against Japanese incursion, and hence warranting the fullest backing and support from the democracies. Newsreel films of the road contained spectacular footage of daunting obstacles and the apparent success and density of traffic.[6] But the overall impression was false, and Western intelligence agencies were well aware of the deceit.[7] The quantity of arms exported over the Burma route, even if the exaggerated estimates were accepted, was trivial.[8]

Following Allied defeats at Pearl Harbor and in the Philippines, Singapore and the Dutch Indies, China was seen as the only viable theatre for operations against the enemy, a place where the Japanese effort could be contained to allow time for America to arm and train its new army.[9] The Magruder military mission, named after its author, Brigadier General John Magruder (then in army intelligence, later in charge of the OSS's intelligence services), had forecast, unrealistically, that thirty Chinese divisions could be re-equipped and launched on an aggressive land campaign.[10] In consequence, General Joseph W. Stilwell (the aforementioned 'Vinegar Joe') was selected by Roosevelt to co-ordinate American aid and, in effect, to direct such a campaign.

There can be little doubt that the Office of the Co-ordinator of

Information (COI), the OSS's direct ancestor, was active in the preoperational planning for the new campaign. As Stilwell's staff were being appointed, Miles Goodfellow (then deputy director of special activities at the COI) proposed that a secret intelligence and special operations detachment should accompany the general to China.[11] In January 1942 General William J. Donovan, chief, successively, of both the COI and the OSS, sought to arrange this matter, and to square it with the military. Goodfellow's proposal was at first rejected, with Stilwell a leading sceptic. It was later confirmed, but made conditional on its leader being personally selected by, and remaining totally subordinate to, Stilwell. Furthermore, the general was to exercise control over the activities of the whole party. Captain Carl Eifler was chosen to command, and was afforded cover as assistant military attaché to the US embassy in Chungking, Nationalist leader Chiang Kai-shek's headquarters in central China.[12]

Though Detachment 101 was assembled quickly, indeed hastily, a great deal happened in the few months between its inception and the arrival of its advance party in India. While recruitment and training were still under way for the irregular warfare group, the Japanese struck. They launched a military offensive from Siam on 20 January 1942, and by May the British and the Chinese had been driven out of Burma. This knocked out the sole supply route from America to China. There was now a real possibility that the Chinese Nationalists, isolated by the latest Japanese thrust, might conclude a separate armistice. Without the lifeline of the Burma Road, China's potential status slumped overnight from that of formidable partner to that of a weak and wavering protégé.[13]

Detachment 101 was already in danger of being overtaken by events. Japan's crack 18th Division (conquerors of Singapore) held the key road, rail and airfield complex of Myitkyina in upper Burma. They exerted a stranglehold over both air and land communications to China, and maintained it for three years. The American Chiefs of Staff, recognising resupply as the key to retaining Chiang's armies in the war, overrode British opposition to a land campaign, and ignored their proffered military alternative of a seaborne assault on Sumatra opening the way to Singapore. For the time being, the Allies would supply Chiang's forces by air, flying perilously over that Himalayan protrusion which separates North Burma from the western Chinese province of Yunnan. The fliers christened it 'The Hump', and 'over the hump' entered the English language as a metaphor for hard tasks accomplished.

It was with an eye to heavier, overland shipments and the construction of a fuel pipeline that the Chiefs of Staff directed Stilwell to clear the Japanese out of North Burma. They required him to build an all-weather bypass road from India over the mountains and jungles of Assam, past the small town of Ledo to Myitkyina, whence it could be spliced into the established Burma Road.[14]

Proper field and strategic intelligence resources would have diminished Stilwell's difficulties. Field Marshal Slim in his memoir, however, complained of the inadequacy of such resources: 'The extreme inefficiency of our whole intelligence system in Burma was probably our greatest single handicap.'[15] Thanks to the subsequent declassification of intercepts, we now know that Slim was, up to a point, being economical with the truth: America's codebreakers were doing useful work.[16] At the same time, it is true that the OSS worked no miracles. Eifler wasted a month in China, having flown to Chungking following his June 1942 arrival with 101's advance party in Karachi. Avoiding embassy contacts but utilising his diplomatic cover, he tried unsuccessfully to build the nucleus of an intelligence-gathering network. He similarly failed to organise even the most elementary semblance of partisan resistance.[17] The Chinese did not want the OSS.

Moreover, the Office of Naval Intelligence had pre-empted the OSS and established prior rights over local intelligence. The Chinese had moderated their inherent distrust and dislike of foreigners in order to accommodate the ONI's head of station, Captain Milton (Mary) Miles. An old China hand, Miles had for years co-operated with the Nationalists' secret police in their counter-revolutionary activities.[18] The Chinese could safely regard him as having been taken on board. Like its close Chinese associates, the ONI was prepared to accept neither dilution nor displacement, so the OSS was doubly excluded.

Yet another factor adversely affected Eifler's fortunes. Stilwell was losing out to General Claire Chennault in the competitive contention over allocations of supplies arriving by air over the Hump. As the army commander's influence in Chunking dwindled, so, by association, did the standing of his associates – the OSS. Eifler returned to Assam, defeated.

Excluded from China by Captain Miles and the Chinese secret service, barred from operations in India by the British, prohibited from participation in the South-West Pacific by General MacArthur and unwanted in the 'island chain' assault led by Admirals Chester William Nimitz and Ernest Joseph King, the OSS were at a loss to find an entry to the Pacific war. With no active theatre of operations, they had no justification for their presence. No presence meant no contacts, no contacts no intelligence, no intelligence no influence! From this apparent impasse comes a strong impression that Stilwell employed 101 merely as a soft option that carried less aggravation than an attempt to disband them locally or to send them home as failures. Immersed in his multiple problems, the fate of a few officers of little influence, no matter what their pedigree, could really be of small consequence to the general. As a fighting soldier, he could not see their potential rise above that of a minor sabotage and tactical intelligence unit. The façade of an independent strategic intelligence source was discarded. Department 101 was committed to disrupt the Japanese supply lines south of Myitkyina.[19]

Elsewhere in South-East Asia, however, the OSS had an additional, more covert role. This role stemmed, in large part, from the impediments imposed by Japanese military success, for the Japanese dominated the Bay of Bengal and bombarded Ceylon with impunity. The port of Calcutta was of necessity closed, so imports destined for points east had to be landed from the Arabian Sea and transported across the belt of India, over an inadequate railway system. This meant that the Burma Road effectively started at the port of Karachi.

But the subcontinent was seething with discontent against British colonial rule, and this posed a special political problem. William Phillips, the former OSS London station chief who now served as President Franklin D. Roosevelt's special representative in India, later expressed it this way:

> Not only was it necessary to transport a large part of the supplies across India to Assam, but vast assembly and repair centres had been constructed in Karachi and other points further East and South. Peaceful conditions in India were therefore necessary to the success of our operations.[20]

Roosevelt and his advisers believed that 'peaceful conditions' should be brought about through an Allied commitment to Indian independence. So did the OSS. This factor further complicated and bedevilled any attempt to launch co-ordinated Anglo-American intelligence and guerrilla operations, and compounded the effects of Japanese domination of the Bay of Bengal.

It should be stressed that the OSS's sense of mission in India was deep-seated, and independent of external political pressures.

Historians have already alluded to and speculated upon the OSS's
antipathy to British imperialism. This antipathy is all the more
intriguing because Donovan was ostensibly an Anglophile in close
co-operation with the British. Most recently, Kenton Clymer has
directed our attention to that early aversion, estimating that it
began in the days of the COI, long before that organisation's transformation (on 13 June 1942) into the OSS. He thinks it commenced
just 'a few days after the attack on Pearl Harbor [7 December
1941]'.[21]

However, the Donovan papers, lately made available at the US
Military History Institute at Carlisle Barracks, Pennsylvania, reveal
an OSS interest in imperial problems which antecedes even Pearl
Harbor and American entry into the war. They contain a report on
India dated 12 November 1941 by the COI's Research and Analysis
division, which highlights the COI/OSS interventionist spirit and
their unmistakably role-seeking intent:

> No other nation could hope to bring India and Britain to
> agreement for wholehearted prosecution of the war. Our good
> offices might even help to reconcile the Hindu–Muslim con-
> flict.
>
> Mr Norman Brown, our expert in India, and Conyers Read,
> Head of the British Empire Section, have discussed the
> matter with competent people, all agree that the United
> States is in a position to exercise an effective and salutary
> influence upon India's war effort.
>
> Public revelation of an American interest in India might
> take the form, as in the analogous case of the Harriman mis-
> sion to Russia,[22] of an American mission to study India's war
> needs from America and her own war effort. Such a mission
> would quite properly have to consider public opinion in India
> as it affects war effort. On these grounds it could then make a
> thorough investigation, hear all parties, and perhaps discover
> some basis for the accommodation of differences. If the Ameri-
> can representative were wisely chosen, he might win the
> confidence of all parties and even be invited to act as
> mediator.
>
> . . . the one or ones charged with assessing public opinion
> in India, should be chosen with the greatest care. No one
> should be employed who has reached final decision on the
> issues involved or has passed public judgement on them, in
> speech or in writing.

> The COI would not itself act in the whole matter, except in an advisory capacity.[23]

This ambitious thinking lay at the root of initiatives which were to supercede the initial, fruitless activities of Carl Eifler. Donovan's old friend E. Edward Buxton, working for the COI out of New York, laid the groundwork for an American delegation to advise and assist the government of India on the upgrading of the subcontinent's war economy. Colonel Louis A. Johnson, a former Assistant Secretary of War (and future Secretary of Defense) was to be in charge. Significantly, Buxton co-ordinated personal introductions through Sir Vivian Gabriel of British Information Services, bypassing the Department of State. Nevertheless, Johnson, unlike other members of the American delegation, received diplomatic credentials – as minister plenipotentiary by presidential appointment.[24]

The timing of the Johnson delegation coincided with that of the British mission headed by Sir Stafford Cripps, a parliamentary group seeking resolution of the vexatious problem of Indian instability, and carrying an offer of partial self-government. Johnson's claims to have been instrumental, indeed to have acted as broker, in the final agreements between Cripps and the Congress leaders have now been substantiated. An apparently successful compromise solution having been realised, Cripps signalled Prime Minister Winston S. Churchill on 9 April 1942: 'Largely owing to the very efficient and wholehearted help of Col. Johnson . . . I have hopes scheme may now succeed. I should like you to thank the President for Col. Johnson's help on behalf of HMG.'

But London overruled the 'Cripps Compromise'. The offer to the Congress leaders was withdrawn, and Churchill despatched a rebuff, that same day, an insult that was to send Johnson home: 'Col. Johnson is not President Roosevelt's personal representative in any matters outside of the specific mission dealing with Indian munitions and kindred topics on which he was sent.'[25] This first American intervention in pursuit of peaceful conditions had failed.

The Quit India movement gained momentum, but through a rapid, highly organised internal security programme the British interned thousands of the Congress leaders, and halted the revolt with what, it is clear in retrospect, was a minimal loss of life. The whole process was made easier by Gandhi's insistence on nonviolence. There was only limited resistance. The lid was tied down tightly, and held there by a large paramilitary operation and the devastating social consequences of the Bengal famine.

With Johnson gone, America was without primary representation in India. Roosevelt chose as his second emissary William Phillips. His new choice was a career diplomat, a former ambassador to Canada and Italy, twice an under-secretary of state, a very senior man who, on his repatriation from Rome, had been snapped up by William Donovan to enhance the prestige of the OSS and, as we have noted, had become station chief in London – where *The Times* had openly hailed the arrival of this supposedly undercover official.[26]

Phillips did not return to America for briefing, nor did he receive communication directly from his President. We have his formal record of appointment, processed by the State Department through his ambassador in London. It is filled with restraints, limitations and admonitions, spelling out what he must not do, how he must not be seen to become involved and how he must stay clear of any political manoeuvring, any intrigue of the type which brought down his predecessor. But it says little of what positive actions he should take and nothing of the declared policy of his government.[27] Perhaps, as Riley Sutherland later found with China, there was no Washington policy.[28]

Phillips suffered from State Department constraints on what he could and could not do, and the British, their suspicions of OSS men mounting by the minute, placed further restrictions on whom he could and could not see: for example, he was denied access to Gandhi during the Mahatma's highly publicised fast in gaol. His telegraphic reports through OSS channels testified to what he clearly perceived to be a lack of progress. On 25 January 1943, not long after his arrival in India, he said in a despatch:

> I am greatly impressed by the lack of faith in the British official promises. It seems to me the nub of the problem, and I cannot but feel that a new approach from the British is essential. Without it, Indians themselves would defer all serious efforts to compose their own differences. Such an approach must be more advanced than either the Cripps offer, or the 1935 India Act.[29]

Discouraged, Phillips returned home to his President. He prepared a confidential report. The gist of it is conveyed in a key-feature summary prepared either by Phillips or by his assistant, Richard Heppner:

If Gandhi dies [during his fast], there will be no hold over civil disobedience.

Churchill is psychopathic over the India situation.

The Viceroy, Lord Linlithgow, is a shallow, stubborn Scot and should be replaced.

The large army recruited in India is inferior and is hardly likely to be used against the Japanese. Its purpose is not clear. Its morale is poor.

There are two single track railways running from Bombay to Karachi which would be extremely vulnerable to any sabotage or civil disturbance.[30]

These findings, exposing the intransigence of the British, infuriated Under-Secretary of State Sumner Welles, who leaked the substance of the Phillips report to the newspaper columnist Drew Pearson. The latter's revelations created a furore ending with Phillips being declared *persona non grata* by the government of India.[31]

America's attempts to influence directly the Indian independence problem had failed twice, and were now ended. OSS officers, however, continued to worry about the situation – about the capabilities of the Indian transportation systems, the effects of the Bengal famine on the war effort, and the need to distance US military personnel from British repressive measures. An army intelligence team supplemented this effort, reporting on the Indian Army's recruitment problems and preparedness for chemical warfare, as well as 'the internal security situation in India'.[32] The fact remains that, by the end of 1943, there was political stability in India not in consequence of any political agreement, but because of British suppression of Indian civil rights through the use of force. The Americans were obliged to accept this state of affairs, a bitter and demoralising pill for them to swallow.

In spite of the improving conditions in India, 101 had not made much progress. Politically isolated, they were left to themselves. They did establish a small administrative cell in Delhi, a base training camp in Assam and a very restricted field role in Burma. But their efforts amounted to little in the face of Japanese advances.[33] Over a year had passed from inception, and they were hardly off the ground.

One problem was that Detachment 101 could not obtain intelligence of sufficient quality and quantity to facilitate effective guerrilla action. The acquisition of intelligence is the work of agents. Caucasians could not pass as Burmese. Tribesmen, too, were easily recognised, so native Burmese agents were sought amid the refugee camps in India. But a critical gap in intelligence remained in lower Burma, in the villages and amid the traffic along the valleys from Mandalay to Rangoon. Both the Mongoloid Shan and the Burmese, who peopled these areas, were hostile to the British and their friends. During the great British retreat, the bulk of the population had remained at home, happy to co-operate with the advancing Japanese, while those who fled were mainly Indian in origin – the despised traders, money lenders and businessmen who dared not go back. There was an indigenous underground resistance movement, the communists. But the Americans had no contact with this group and the British shunned them – the communists were as opposed to British imperialism as they were to Japanese occupation.

In the north, there did seem to be a glimmer of hope. There, local hill tribesmen, the Karens and the Kachins, were in a position to gather local intelligence. Both groups were antagonistic to the valley people, and had recently suffered a backlash consequent to their residual loyalty to the British Raj – the British had recruited to the Burma Rifles almost exclusively from the hill people. Now, the Strategic Operations Executive, the guerrilla specialists affiliated to the Secret Intelligence Service (MI6) and originally established in 1940 – in Churchill's words, to 'set Europe ablaze' – set out to ignite Asian passions. SOE Detachment 136 began to infiltrate the hills, seeking support from the Karens. The Americans sought to do likewise with the Kachins. So began the folklore of the OSS guerrilla capability.[34]

By maintaining a small vociferous presence in Burma, by relying on their own primitive administrative channels and semi-independent supply system, by co-operating with the SOE as little, or as much, as was necessary, the OSS kept their foot in the door of the Far East theatre. To back up their very limited operations they bartered man to man with the US 10th Airforce over the most precious of local commodities, air supply and light aircraft. They promised and maintained a Himalayan rescue service for crews 'downed' on the Hump. Indeed, at one stage, more effort was expended there than against the Japanese. This was hardly a strategic role, but it gave them a visible presence and made them pseudo-indispensable. Yet, as late as August 1943, their field strength remained as low as twenty-one officers and enlisted men.[35]

In late 1943 the British, desperately hoping to switch their offensive lines away from Burma to an amphibious assault through Indonesia to Singapore, were permitted a theatre reorganisation.

Hitherto, the headquarters of South-East Asia Command (SEAC: dubbed 'Save England's Asiatic Colonies' by wise-cracking Americans) had been in India. Now Admiral Lord Louis Mountbatten, a grandson of Queen Victoria and SEAC supreme commander, moved with his staff to Ceylon. This brought in its train changes for the OSS and, whatever the British intended, new hopes for its role in South-East Asia. Under the reorganisation, a new 'P Division' was created within SEAC, with the duty of co-ordinating undercover activities throughout Asia. To be the American deputy staff to the British leader of P Division, Donovan selected Lieutenant Commander Edmund Taylor. The newly appointed officer had served in OSS headquarters, had promoted the OSS cause in the Torch Operation and, up to this point in his career, had been a rampant Anglophile – Donovan might have been forgiven for assuming that Taylor would be an emollient influence within SEAC. In a further move, Donovan sought to consolidate the OSS's position within SEAC. He created a new unit, Detachment 404, tasked to organise all South-East Asian operations. He placed Richard Heppner in command. The British remembered only too well this officer and his association with that advocate of Indian independence, William Phillips.

In a conference with Mountbatten, Donovan had secured agreement on the sequestration of the small-scale operations in Burma from overall clandestine operations in Asia. Those suspicious of the OSS director's ambitions no doubt hoped that the granting of some autonomy in one limited region might have the effect of a sanitary cordon against the others. Edmund Taylor recalled in his 1971 memoir: 'Stilwell, dreading [OSS] contamination by the British, was no less reluctant than British traditionalists to see the OSS operate anywhere in the [China–Burma–India] Theatre outside North Burma . . . Donovan as usual was empire building.'[36]

Operations apart, Mountbatten had to concede to the OSS the right to gather intelligence independently, through their own agents, as United States interests dictated.[37] There now began a competition between Allied intelligence agencies, a race to structure an underground, to establish presence, to influence, perhaps even dominate, the emerging nationalist groups. This point is illustrated in the 1943 OSS report on the CBI (China–Burma–India) theatre. The report forecast twenty-seven projects. The commentary on one of the projects explains why the British regarded OSS expansion as ominous. It referred to an impending trip by Colonel

Robert Hall, the China–India specialist for the OSS's Research and Analysis branch:

> New Delhi. Col. Hall and eight officers will arrive in mid December. Their task will be to prepare:
>
> a. Political and psychological intelligence, maintaining overall personality files.
> b. Topographical and terrain intelligence.
> c. Economic, staff strategic and tactical economic intelligence, as required by OSS ops and R & A Washington.

The British were reluctant to allow such operations to be carried out under sole OSS control. Indeed, the more conservative elements in the colonial establishment and the SOE were opposed to any American clandestine presence whatsoever. Their objections were to no avail in the face of a man as determined as Donovan, who stated that if the British shut the door on his OSS personnel, he was 'prepared to slip them in through the transom'.[38] This combative approach towards those who sought to shackle the OSS is indicated in a confidential 'history' of its role in the China–Burma–India theatre completed in 1944: 'It is safe to predict that it [the OSS] will broaden the scope of its activities and increase its usefulness to the armed forces of the US, provided it is unhampered by restrictive agencies within other powers.'[39]

Sir Andrew Gilchrist, the senior SOE operative in Bangkok, confirmed that the mistrust within Allied intelligence communities was mutual: 'Relations between British and US organisations are characterised by intrigue, suspicion and absurd duplication of activities in all fields.'[40] Records in the Donovan Papers amply confirm what Gilchrist and official SOE historian M.R.D. Foot have already told us, that British–American intelligence relations in the CBI area were poor. They indicate further that, on the American side, both anti-imperialist sentiment and bureaucratic ambition were responsible for what the British regarded as difficult behaviour.[41]

Poor intelligence relations undermined Allied co-ordination, and helped to convert the Burma Road into a strategic albatross. To be sure, the tide turned against Japan in Burma. Field Marshal Slim had managed to preserve British morale and discipline after the difficult retreat of 1942. Appointed commander of the 14th Army in December 1943, he was to enjoy the satisfaction of ejecting the Japanese from Mandalay and Rangoon. The battle of Imphal (March to June 1944) was the worst defeat sustained by the Japanese on land, and, as the British fought through the 1945 monsoon, they brought irregular forces into play successfully. OSS units helped to protect the flank of the Allied advance. Nor were these events without parallel further north. In February 1945 an inaugural jeep train finally advanced up the Burma Road in company with a formation of Chinese-manned tanks. OSS officers were present.[42]

But such episodes were mere flickers in an intermittent fire. Other major events were by now taking place in the Far Eastern war, while the Burma Road remained forever peripheral. In theory, it is true, the Road still had a potential strategic role. In the Pacific, the Japanese had shown their determination to fight to the death. It was feared that the very strong Japanese military contingent based in mainland China would emulate their Kamikaze comrades on the Pacific islands, requiring a major, and politically unpopular, new offensive to eject them. As usual, Donovan was in these circumstances determined to play his part. In February 1945 he told Heppner, now head of OSS China, to revive plans for the training of Chinese guerrillas.[43] In April he demanded the procurement of agents qualified to penetrate the Japanese zones in Korea and Manchuria, and even the home islands.[44] And, what concerns us here, there was a plan, at last, to deploy armed forces in significant strength by means of the Burma Road.

The American Chiefs of Staff had decided to assault Japan through Luzon and Okinawa in preference to Formosa and the port of Amoy on the Chinese mainland. But, on account of the danger that residual Japanese resistance would continue in China, they were required to prepare for such an eventuality. They formulated a plan for a simultaneous assault up the Burma Road with seaborne landings on the South China coast.[45] The OSS launched complementary projects. To the coast was despatched a photographic and topographic reconnaissance team. Inland, they sent an expert on 'terrain intelligence assessment' to prepare information in readiness for tank offensives.[46]

The Burma Road, however, fell far short of being a strategic lifeline. It was beset with an array of problems both natural and man-made. Monsoons wreaked their havoc, bridges proved unreliable, smuggling and corruption were rife, and Chiang Kai-shek banned the use of American black soldiers, the very men whose expertise as road builders and truck drivers was vital to the success of that arterial link.[47] It is unlikely that the projects were in a serious military sense anything other than a contingency plan. In the words of President Harry S. Truman (paraphrasing his Secretary of War, Henry Stimson): 'The campaign against Japan was based on the assumption that we would not attempt to engage the masses of the Japanese Army in China with our own ground forces.'[48] The OSS's own Research and Analysis branch had reached a conclusion which cast doubt on the strategic utility of the Burma Road. Its head, William Langer, accompanied Donovan on a tour of the CBI theatre at the turn of 1944–5. He concluded that, if the American assault on the home islands succeeded, Japanese resistance in China would collapse.[49]

In terms of grand strategic design, the OSS's involvement in the Burma Road campaign makes a story which is picturesque, revealing and yet unimpressive. Can one, nevertheless, make the claim that the OSS and their local allies scored at least a tactical success, in tying down significant numbers of the enemy and imposing on them heavy casualties? According to figures cited in both American and British official sources, Detachment 101 strength at the start of 1945 stood at 131 officers, 418 enlisted men and 9,000 locals. In the course of hostilities, 101's guerrillas claimed to have killed 5,428 Japanese, with a further 10,000 either killed or seriously wounded. They admitted to losses of fifteen Americans and 184 guerrillas.[50]

These figures invite critical scrutiny. The first point that needs to be made is that most of the Japanese casualties were sustained when they were already in retreat and in a disorganised state. Secondly, figures collected in the course of confused, irregular warfare are notoriously suspect.[51] Another consideration is that, according to a reliable scholarly estimate, the total death toll among the Japanese forces facing the Allies along the 'Irrawady line' was not more than 6,000 men. Yet, the OSS guerrillas were only a small part of the combined opposition.[52] It is unlikely that they killed such a disproportionate number of the enemy. We know that only three of the fifteen American deaths occurred in the course of behind-the-lines combat. Air and road accidents claimed most of the others.[53] Finally, it should be remembered that only one-sixth of the total Japanese forces in Burma were deployed in that sector where the OSS were active.

The achievements of Detachment 101 nevertheless continue to be glorified. Until recently, most of the books written about the OSS have had little to say about its Research and Analysis division, and devote themselves to narratives of adventure and heroism.[54] Even those who are critical of the OSS's emphasis on action instead of analysis have lavished praise on its exploits. Ray S. Cline, a former deputy director of the CIA, thinks the OSS was 'remarkably successful'; Bradley F. Smith, a leading authority on OSS history, believes 'Detachment 101 and the Kachins provided extraordinarily valuable intelligence and guerrilla support'; on the more popular level, the authors of a 1989 'book-of-the-television-series' publication describe the OSS–Kachin operations as 'brilliantly successful'.[55]

It is, of course, important not to overreact against OSS self-advertisement. Detachment 101 did make the most of limited opportunities in difficult circumstances. If their inflated victories do not merit the 'in-house' adulation of pro-OSS historians, then neither do their achievements warrant the denigration by omission accorded by the British. The unit's valid claim to fame rests on its experience with the Kachin Rangers. This experience may confirm Stilwell's worst expectations about OSS officers being contaminated by contact with the British, but it does, within a limited time-scale, represent a successful application of an imperial pattern of partisan warfare – white officers directing locally recruited troops.

However, it is possible not only to question the more glowing accounts of 101's achievements, but also to point out some deleterious consequences. Donovan's men were unwitting and therefore uncritical practitioners of partisan warfare. They supplied, trained and directed their native irregulars. They did not need to differentiate then, and have failed to differentiate since, between such externally directed partisan action and the self-contained insurgency practised by Mao Tse-tung's followers in China.[56] This failure to discriminate left an unfortunate legacy. In the context of the 1960s phase of the Vietnam War, it helps to explain the misplaced interdiction of the Ho Chi Minh trail, the mistaken contentions over North-to-South reinforcements and the confusion in American minds over the spontaneous, indigenous and self-generating nature of the Viet Cong insurgency in the South.

A further mistake is again reminiscent of older imperialist practices. As we have seen, by pure circumstance 101 were forced to operate in the tribal areas of the Kachins. Once recruited, Kachin fighters proved to be superb in combat. But their aim was independence, not just from Japan, but also from British control – and from the national government of Burma. That national Burmese government had treasured the limited autonomy granted by the Japanese 'liberators', and regarded the Kachins, even if American directed, as puppets of British imperialism. With Japanese collapse imminent in 1945, Mountbatten instructed the British SOE Force

136 to arm the Burmese government on condition that it performed a volte-face and turned on the Japanese. (In fairness, it must be stated that both Slim and the OSS opposed this decision.) After the war, the tribes faced a period of armed repression and quite rightly felt abandoned.

From the Kachin point of view – and this viewpoint heralded the future disillusionment of the tragic Meo tribe in Laos – they had been betrayed. The Americans might be more relaxed and more friendly than the traditional imperialists, but in the long run they looked and tasted exactly the same, mouthing their few words of pidgin, conversing second-hand through the unknown qualities of local interpreters. The problem in this case lay not so much in the OSS, but in the manner in which its officers had been deployed.

Lieutenant-Colonel William R. Peers, who in early 1944 took over from Eifler to become 101's second and last commander, became in due course the accredited military expert on guerrilla warfare. While an instructor at the Army War College in 1948, he prepared a handbook on the subject. It ends, prophetically: 'The outstanding difference, the one not always understood, is that our cause is not always the guerrilla's cause.'[57]

As for the Burma Road itself, some parts, mainly the line from Assam to the Irrawaddy, are now barely perceptible even in the most detailed of satellite photographs – a devastating epitaph to the politics of war. For, with Mao's triumph, Chiang's defeated Nationalist troops were driven back into the wild country of the lower Salween River, that inhospitable region part-claimed by China, Burma and Thailand. They attempted a foray into China in 1951, but suffered heavy losses and were obliged to withdraw. The Burmese government understandably prefers to let the Road in that area fall into decay, regarding it as an avenue of dangerous ingress. This is the area of the world which became the opium-producing 'golden triangle', with such fateful implications for the CIA and for millions of addicts.

The supplementary question raised at the beginning of this essay was: what on earth were the OSS doing in Burma in the first place? My answer is that Donovan and his men forced their way in for reasons of ambition. They either shared the faulty perception of the Chinese capacity to resist and the value of the Burma Road as a supply axis, or they simply opted to grab and assimilate any role open, however questionable.

My view of their effectiveness, once there, is critical. While 101 had its local minor successes, it was involved in counterproductive bickering with the British. Such bickering might have yielded fruitful results elsewhere. But in India OSS personnel failed to develop such differences and formulate a compensatory philosophy on decolonisation. Their critique was purely destructive.

Detachment 101 was effective in just one area – the creation of a retrospective aura of guerrilla expertise and invincibility. But on closer inspection its legacy and teachings must be deemed of dubious inspiration. The overall verdict must coincide with the view which R. and A. chief William Langer confided to his memoirs: 'I believe the OSS as a whole had no important part in the war in the Pacific.'[58]

Notes

1. Contrast the expansive description in *Donovan and the OSS* (London: Hale, 1970) by OSS veteran Corey Ford (who had early, privileged access to the papers of OSS chief William J. Donovan) with the almost non-recognition in the HMSO publication, *The War Against Japan*, 5 vols., ed. Woodburn Kirby (London, 1969).
2. For one of many references to MacArthur's jealous attitude, see *Ronald Lewin, the American Magic: Codes, ciphers and the defeat of Japan* (Harmondsworth: Penguin, 1983), p. 178.
3. See statement by André Vischinski, *Foreign Relations of the United States* (Washington, DC: Government Printing Office, henceforth *FRUS*), 1940, vol. IV, p. 671; Edgar Snow, 'Will Stalin sell out China?', *Foreign Affairs*, XVIII, (April 1940), 450–63; Arthur N. Young, *China and the Helping Hand, 1937–1945* (Cambridge, Mass.: Harvard Univ. Press, 1963).
4. The French dilemma is clearly explained in two reports: *FRUS, 1939*, vol. III, *Report by Ambassador Bullit in Paris dated 4 April 1939, Serial 4092, and FRUS*, 1940, vol. IV, French Ban on Armament Shipments, p. 481.
5. For the best of many first-hand descriptions of the Road's construction and natural hazards, see Squadron Leader Gerald Samson, *The Burma Road* (London: London China Society, 1946).
6. The films were probably shot by Nicol Smith, correspondent, camera man, adventurer and later OSS captain: Nicol Smith, *The Burma Road* (New York: Garden City Publications, 1940).
7. For a pastiche of the confusion, mal-administration, corruption and blatant mismanagement on the Road, see various papers and correspondence in *Pacific Affairs*, vols. XIII–XV (1940–1).
8. See the report by America's ambassador to Japan, Joseph C. Grew, to the Secretary of State, *FRUS*, 1940, vol. IV, p. 40.
9. See the statement by Secretary of War Henry Stimson quoted in Ronald Spector, *Eagle against the Sun* (London: Viking, 1985), p. 329.
10. Charles F. Romanus and Riley Sutherland, *Stillwell's Mission to China* (Washington, DC: Government Printing Office, 1953), pp. 25ff, 42.
11. Romanus, *Mission*, p. 31 and fn. 91.
12. Elements of this story are told in Richard Harris Smith, *OSS: The secret history of America's first central intelligence agency (New York: Dell, 1973), chapter 8, 'The Chinese Puzzle'. See, also William Peers*

and Dean Brelis, Behind the Burma Road (Boston, Mass.: Little, Brown, 1963).

13. Leland M. Goodrich, ed., *Documents on American Foreign Policy*, vol. V, 1942–3 (Boston, Mass.: World Peace Foundation, 1944), p. 478; Spector, *Eagle*, p. 330.

14. See Barbara Tuchman's comments on Operation Saucy in her *Stilwell and the American Experience in China 1911–1945* (London: Macdonald, 1981 (1970), pp. 372 ff.

15. William Slim, *Defeat into Victory* (London: Cassell, 1956), p. 120.

16. See John Costello, *The Pacific War* (London: Pan, 1985), p. 415.

17. Richard Dunlop, *Behind Japanese Lines* (Chicago, Ill.: Rand McNally, 1979), p. 108. The British were similarly frustrated. See C. Cruickshanks, *SOE in the Far East* (Oxford: Oxford Univ. Press, 1983), pp. 77–9.

18. Contrast the two different approaches to this story in Milton E. Miles, *A Different Kind of War: The unknown story of the US Navy's guerrilla forces in World War II, China* (Garden City, NY: Doubleday, 1967) and Michael Schaller, 'SACO and the US Navy's secret war in China', *Pacific Historical Review*, 34 (1975), 527.

19. Dunlop, *Behind Japanese Lines*, p. 109.

20. William Phillips, *Ventures in Diplomacy* (Boston, Mass.: Beacon, 1952), p. 344.

21. Kenton J. Clymer, 'FDR and Louis Johnson: India and anti-colonialism; another look', *Pacific Historical Review*, 57 (1988), 261–84.

22. The millionaire and diplomat William Averell Harriman led a special mission to Moscow in 1941, following the application of lend-lease to Russia.

23. R & A report No. 11, 12 Nov. 1941, in Vol. 'India', part 3, Box 41A, Papers of William J. Donovan (henceforth WJD), US Military History Institute, Carlisle Barracks, Pennsylvania. OSS officials continued their critical monitoring of the situation in India: Norman Brown, 'The exclusion of India from the Atlantic Charter', 19 Nov. 1941, Box 41, WJD, and 'Tentative notes on the British War Cabinet's proposals for India', 31 March 1942, Sit. Rep. Report No.6, Folio 6, WJD.

24. 'New York, SI, OP 58, Folder 5', n.d., Entry 106, Box 43, Record Group 226, Records of the OSS, Modern Military Archives Division, National Archives, Washington, DC (henceforth, OSS/NA); memorandum, Berle to Roosevelt, 29 Jan. 1942, *FRUS*, 1942, vol. I, p. 599; *FRUS* 1942, vol I, pp. 617 and 618 n. 32.

25. The quotations are from Nicholas Mansergh, ed., *India: The transfer of power, 1942–47*, 12 vols. (London: HMSO, 1970–81), I, serial 556 and 564.

26. *The Times*, 22 July 1942.

27. Secretary of State Cordell Hull to the US ambassador in London, John Winant, 20 Nov. 1942, in *FRUS*, 1942, vol. 1, p. 746.

28. Riley Sutherland, 'Commentary' to George M. Elsey, in Elsey, *Roosevelt and China* (Wilmington, Del.: Glazier, 1979) and subsequent correspondence with Walter LaFeber in *American Historical Review*, 81 (1976), 703 ff. It must be allowed that Phillips may have received his instructions by other means. The Donovan papers show that he frequently used the transatlantic telephone, and (to avoid British as much as enemy intercepts) he may have used couriers: for example,

Richard Heppner, who had been a junior member of Donovan's law firm, and who was to be active in the China–Burma–India theatre.

29. Special Intelligence 5, 25 Jan. 1943, Box 102A, WJD. The 1935 India Act's proposal for the transformation of the Indian Empire into a partly self-governing federation was never fully implemented, though it did remove Aden and Burma from the jurisdiction of the government of India.

30. R & A 923, 10 June 1943, India Part III, Box 41A, WJD. Phillips had every right to suspect the morale and loyalty of the Indian Army. Of the 45,000 Indian troops surrendered by the British at Singapore, more than half, within a month, had volunteered for service with the Indian National Army: see Joyce C. Lebra, *Japanese Trained Armies in SE Asia* (Hong Kong: Heinemann Education (Asia), 1977).

31. Mansergh, *Transfer of Power*, IV, serial 661.

32. See compilations in Records of US Military Attachés, Serials DF 322.095, 341, 350.05, 360.33, May 1942–April 1943, Washington National Records Centre, Suitland, Maryland.

33. Dunlop, *Behind Japanese Lines*, p. 59.

34. See Cruikshanks, *SOE*. In chapter 7, Cruikshanks explains that there was a schism and demarcation dispute between the SOE and the OSS.

35. Citation request, Donovan to Roosevelt, 18 Aug. 1943, Box 124B, WJD.

36. Edmund Taylor, *Awakening from History* (Boston, Mass.: Gambit, 1971).

37. Ford, *Donovan*, pp. 255ff.

38. Christopher Thorne, *Allies of a Kind: The United States, Britain and the war against Japan, 1941–1945* (New York: Oxford Univ. Press, 1978), p. 402.

39. 'History of OSS/CBI', Oct. 1944, RG 226, E99, Box 58, OSS/NA.

40. Andrew Gilchrist, *Bangkok Top Secret* (London: Hutchinson, 1970), p. 199.

41. M.R.D. Foot, *SOE* (London, 1984). Edmund Taylor, in his memoir *Awakening from History* (1971) assumed that Donovan was already building the foundations for a post-war intellence agency on a scale fitting for a superpower.

42. See the full description in Oliver J. Caldwell, *A Secret War: Americans in China, 1944–45* (Cabondale, Ill.: Southern Illinois University Press, 1972).

43. Directive of 2 Feb. 1945 in folio 259, Box 67A, WJD.

44. Directive of 4 April 1945 in folio 3, Box 100, WJD.

45. Robert Ross Smith, 'Luzon v. Formosa', in *Command Decisions*, ed. Kent R. Greenfield (Washington, DC: Government Printing Office, 1960).

46. Undated authorisations for Project Aqua and the Amoraider mission in Serial 255, Box 67A, WJD.

47. Romanus, *Time Runs Out*, pp. 247, 348. George A. Shepperson, Professor Emeritus of Commonwealth and American History at the University of Edinburgh, who served with the King's African Rifles in Burma in 1944, recalls seeing black American soldiers in Calcutta and other Indian cities, but none in Burma: personal communication dated 11 October 1990.

48. Harry S. Truman, *Memoirs*, 2 vols.: I, *Year of Decisions* (Garden City, NY: Doubleday, 1955), p. 236.

49. William Langer, *In and Out of the Ivory Tower* (New York: Watson, 1977).
50. Cruickshanks, *SOE*, appendix 3; US Department of War, *Presidential Distinguished Units Citation* (Washington, DC, 17 June 1946).
51. Nevertheless, eminent authorities on intelligence sometimes accept them at face value: see Roger Hilsman, 'Burma Ambush', *Marine Corps Gazette*, 16 (1962).
52. On the Allied side of the line were arrayed, in addition to the OSS forces, three Chinese divisions, one American brigade, three Chindit columns and, in the final phase, a fresh British division. On the casualties, see Louis Allen, *Burma: The longest war* (London: Dent, 1984), appendices 1 and 3.
53. Dunlop, *Behind Japanese Lines*, pp. 182–87.
54. Bradley F. Smith began to rectify the position in his book *The Shadow Warriors: OSS and the origins of the CIA* (New York: Basic Books, 1983), which contains a chapter on R and A (pp. 360–89), and in 1989 scholarship took a stride forward with the publication of B.M. Katz's *Foreign Intelligence: Research and analysis in the Office of Strategic Services, 1942–1945* (Cambridge, Mass.: Harvard Univ. Press).
55. Ray S. Cline, *The CIA under Reagan, Bush & Casey* (Washington, DC: Acropolis, 1981), p. 94; Bradley F. Smith, *Shadow Warriors*, p. 321; Ernest Volkman and Blaine Baggett, *Secret Intelligence* (London: W.H. Allen, 1989), p. 40. The title of the last book was also the title of a television series devised by its authors for Community Television of Southern California.
56. For an expansion of this theme based on different examples, see Larry E. Cable, *Conflict of Myths: The development of American counterinsurgency doctrine and the Vietnam War* (New York: New York Univ. Press, 1986), pp. 4–7.
57. William R. Peers, *Guerrilla Operations in North Burma* (US Army Command and Staff College, 1948), loose within the special collection of 101 papers and photographs in WJD. For a sympathetic account of the fortunes of the Meo in northern Laos, their recruitment by the CIA, their eventual abandonment by the Americans and the subsequent near-extinction of the tribe, see Peter Scholl-Latour, *Eyewitness Vietnam* (London: Orbis, 1979), pp. 126ff and 319.
58. Langer, *Ivory Tower*, p. 187.

6

The Missouri Gang and the CIA

DANNY D. JANSEN AND RHODRI JEFFREYS-JONES[1]

Here is how the Central Intelligence Agency (CIA) was founded, according to the apologists and the official historians.[2] In the Second World War, William J. ('Wild Bill') Donovan forged the Office of Strategic Services (OSS) into an effective intelligence agency. Donovan presented his wise superior, President Franklin D. Roosevelt, with a plan for the continuation on the OSS in peacetime. But Roosevelt died, the war ended and the new President, Harry S. Truman, committed an appalling blunder. He disbanded the OSS. He made no proper provision for its replacement, and forced Donovan to return to private business. Like Andrew Johnson in the wake of Lincoln's death, Truman showed himself to be inexperienced, bereft of political finesse and lacking in foresight. Psychologically debilitated by the sudden weight of office, he fell back on the comforting but ill-informed counsels of his 'Missouri Gang' of cronies.[3] Only after a potentially damaging delay did the new President address the strategic problems and set up a peacetime central intelligence organisation. By 1947, when the National Security Act established the CIA, it was obvious to every patriotic citizen that the Soviet Union was posing an increasingly serious threat to United States national security. Even now, it took an inspired campaign by intelligence partisans to direct a stumbling President on to the right path. By the early 1950s, however, wisdom had prevailed and, the apologists conclude, the CIA was at last becoming an effective organisation.

Common sense suggests, and the scholarship of some sympathetic historians confirms, that the harsher judgements on Truman need to be mellowed. Like Lincoln, FDR died at a time which was opportune for his political reputation. He left to his successor the task of facing grave post-war problems without the benefit of a public united by martial spirit. Truman's performance must be judged against the difficulties of the tasks facing him. Moreover, his words and actions suggest that he was by no means laggardly in his reaction to international communism: for better or worse, Truman has a claim to have been a pioneer in the modern cold war.[4]

This chapter carries the process of revision still further, for Donovan was a political liability and, in this sense, an inappropriate intelligence leader in a democracy that was now at peace. 'Wild Bill' had alienated a good number of the people he would have had to work with, including Truman himself. Mr Truman was by no means irresponsible in releasing Donovan and dismantling the OSS. He acted with due deliberation. In particular, he was wise in establishing the interim agency, the Central Intelligence Group (CIG). The CIG held a place open, within the Washington bureaucracy, while plans were carefully made for a more permanent institution. Historians writing about immediate post-war intelligence have allowed their loyalties to the OSS and 1950s CIA to blind them to the role and virtues of the CIG. They have also neglected Admiral Sidney W. Souers – the first Director of Central Intelligence, the first executive secretary of the National Security Council, and a man who served in the latter capacity to the end of the Truman administration.[5] Souers, it is true, was one of Truman's Missouri cronies. Truman did have an aversion for élitist Washington insiders. But, one must ask, which phenomenon is more deserving of critical attention – Truman's reluctance to appoint East Coast establishment personnel, or that establishment's resentment at his selection of non-establishment appointees? The neglect of Souers' achievements certainly cries out for redress, for Souers has a claim to have been one of the principal architects of the CIA.

While not uncritical of Truman and Souers, this chapter represents an effort to redress the balance, and to show that these individuals did something constructive in the years 1945–7. Hitherto, lack of information, as well as anti-Truman bias among some historians, has made such an effort unfeasible. We have lacked a first-hand account, by Souers and Truman themselves, of what they were trying to achieve in the intelligence field, for, unlike some of their successors, they observed the dictates of absolute discretion – not just while in office, but for some years thereafter. Yet, both Truman and Souers did leave a record of their opinions. Truman's dismay at the Bay of Pigs fiasco was an important spur to some trenchant public remarks by the former president. In the absence of verifying evidence, most historians missed their significance. Privately, however, both Truman and, what is crucial from the verification standpoint, Souers did elaborate on the former President's viewpoint. The occasion was Ludwell Lee Montague's embarkation on a classified history of the CIA in the Truman years.[6] The Truman and Souers reminiscences were delivered amidst elaborate security precautions, but are now declassified.[7] Helped by the new evidence, we shall now examine Donovan's failings, Souers' tenure as Director of Central Intelligence, and the arrangements Souers made for the future of secret intelligence and the creation of the CIA.

Personalities had an important effect on the early post-war history of American secret intelligence. The contrasting relationships between Roosevelt and Donovan, on the one hand, and Truman and Donovan, on the other, had an effect on that history.

The man who took the oath of office for the presidency of the United States on 12 April, 1945 was very different from his predecessor, Franklin Roosevelt. Whereas President Roosevelt was a member of the so-called East Coast establishment, and born into the world of the privileged upper and middle class, Harry Truman was the son of Missouri 'hard scrabble' farmers, and an outsider to the game of Washington power politics.

Roosevelt had his own, private sources of information and at the same time allowed William Donovan what appeared to be a free hand in the running of the Office of Strategic Services. Donovan played to the President by making sure that the reports which were sent to Roosevelt were of a style that the President enjoyed reading. Generally this meant that they were short summaries of successful OSS operations, which read more like stories than intelligence reports.[8] President Roosevelt was by nature secretive, and he aimed to keep the lid on feuds between various groups in his administration more through appearing to agree with the person with whom he was speaking than by making any decision regarding the matter in hand.

In contrast, Truman wanted his best people to give him their best estimates of a given situation, and he would make the decision. This proved to be an irritant to many in Washington who had expected the man from Missouri to be easily controlled and dominated. They were caught off-guard, for Truman was made presidential by the office. Truman had never expected to become President of the United States, or even a United States Senator. He had been genuinely surprised at his nomination as the vice-presidential candidate of the Democratic Party in 1944 (had the President's ill health been common knowledge in the party at that time, it is doubtful that he would have been an acceptable nominee). Now that fate had propelled him into the highest office of his nation, he was determined to be the President in more than just title.[9] He was to prove successful in his quest to live up to his responsibilities.

Among the organisations and people Truman inherited from Roosevelt were the OSS and its director, Donovan. The OSS was technically under the command of the Joint Chiefs of Staff (JCS). But, due to the secret nature of its work, it was not required to account for its operational funds. With these unaccountable 'black' funds, the OSS exercised much more freedom in its decision making than the JCS would have liked. In a confidential memorandum, Truman's Chief of Staff, Admiral William Leahy, referred to Donovan as a 'loose gun on the deck'. He recommended that the free-wheeling head of the OSS be brought to heel, and that the agency itself be placed under tighter presidential control.[10]

Truman did indeed bring Donovan and his agency to heel, by ridding himself of both man and organisation at the same time. His action may be explained, in part, by the lingering prejudices of his small-time political outlook. But the interpretation in this chapter is that his decision was more in keeping with his determination to supply firm and appropriate leadership in the intelligence field. And, in understanding the President's decision, it is important to appreciate the degree to which General Donovan had become a liability.

For one thing, the operational effectiveness of Donovan's OSS in the war was open to question. The organisation failed in its attempts to penetrate Nazi Germany, and failed to gather information about Japan in an active manner through the use of agents. Donovan appreciated and publicly endorsed the painstaking efforts of Dr William Langer and his team at the OSS's Research and Analysis branch, and the analysts did record some successes, such as the use of inferential evidence to supply accurate estimates of German battle casualty figures. But the OSS leader succumbed to the dictates of popular taste: it was obvious that the news-hungry public of a nation at war preferred to read about the gallant exploits of the dashing Jedburgh teams[11] and cloak and dagger adventures in occupied Paris, rather than about the development of a cross-filing system which allowed easier access to information to

researchers – even if it was that system which allowed the agency
to produce helpful reports in that pre-computer age. Donovan
appeared to have given Americans what they wanted, not what
they needed.

Donovan was a flamboyant activist. He undertook constant trips
abroad. Some of these trips seemed unnecessary and a few were
dangerous. Notably, Donovan went ashore on the second day of
the Normandy invasion just to have a look around. For the head
of an intelligence service to expose himself to the risk of capture
by the enemy during a fluid ground combat situation was at the
very least a foolish act. The story would later go around Washington
that, after getting ashore, Donovan's assistant told him that he had
forgotten to bring along his suicide pill. Donovan replied that it
was all right, he had two and would give one to the assistant – but,
after going through his pockets, it seemed he had forgotten his
too.[12] While Donovan found the story amusing and told it often, it
was not seen as humorous by those who were aware of what kind
of information Donovan carried around in his head.

Donovan's maverick style, his globe-trotting liberty, his lobbying
of the high and mighty inside and outside Congress, and his privileged access to President Roosevelt alienated him from 'turf-defens-
ive' colleagues in the wartime intelligence network. Souers later
recalled that senior army and navy intelligence leaders resented
his usurpation of their authority. Generals George Strong and
Marion Miles of Army G2, as well as Admirals Ernest King and
Robert Inglis, the Navy Chief of Staff and head of the Office of
Naval Intelligence respectively, had been long-time and intractable
foes of Donovan's organisation, especially in light of its failure to
provide the tactical intelligence necessary for operations in the
field.[13] Truman would have been aware, of course, of the doubts
about the OSS chief's operational effectiveness. As a politician, he
was also obliged to take note of the fact that Donovan's style had
made him powerful enemies.

The fact that the President himself was one of those enemies
sealed Donovan's fate. Their lack of temperamental affinity
stretched back many years. For example, in the First World War,
Donovan had been decorated for his bravery in command of the
New York 69th Infantry, the 'Fighting Irish', and had attracted
major press publicity. This helped him on his way to being a
successful Wall Street lawyer. Truman had also acquitted himself
well in combat as a captain of artillery, but suffered obscurity and
business difficulties when the war was over. In Truman's eyes,

Donovan was an arrogant opportunist. Donovan's 1943 performance before the Senate War Investigating Committee confirmed this impression. The committee was an expenditure watchdog. Truman had been the prime mover for its creation, and was its chairman. When Donovan appeared before the committee, he used his legal skills and courtroom experience to work his way around issues that the committee wanted to discuss, and on more than one occasion excused silence for 'reasons of National Security'. Whether he really felt that he should keep certain secrets out of the hands of the committee or viewed himself as protecting 'his' agency is debatable. What is not debatable is the fact that to refuse information to a Senate hearing is politically dangerous, and that, by doing so, Donovan probably alienated several members of the powerful committee, as well as its chairman.[14] While one interpretation of Donovan's post-war misfortune may be that he was the victim of the provincial, 'pay back' politician in the White House, another must be that he failed to think politically, and in consequence lost both his job and his agency.

OSS staff had worked on plans for a peacetime central intelligence agency under civilian control, and in April 1945 Donovan sent Truman a memorandum outlining a plan.[15] Had the OSS's wartime record been more impressive, or had Donovan been politically persuasive, the plan might have received serious consideration. But, in the absence of such pressures, other considerations thrust themselves to the fore: a press campaign against anything that smacked of the Gestapo, fears about manipulation by British intelligence (Truman was especially reluctant to be manoeuvred into supporting the old European empires), and the need to preserve presidential prerogatives. At the root of Truman's decision, however, lay, his deep-rooted reservations about the wartime organisation. He wrote to his press secretary and 'Missouri Gang' confidant Charlie Ross that he had come to the conclusion that the OSS was tainted, both by 'reds' and corruption, and was therefore not an organisation which should be trusted by the rest of government.[16] Though these charges would be difficult to sustain, the animosity behind them is unmistakable.

Souers' recollection of the conduct of the Joint Chiefs of Staff at this point suggests that they were more diplomatic than Donovan. Aware of the likely disbandment of the OSS, they had established a group to study the issue of what might be salvaged from the agency, and to whom it should be assigned. They sent a message to the President that, in their opinion, the OSS should be kept intact, but inactive until the study was complete. Souers recalled that the message arrived several hours after Truman issued the executive order for the dismantlement of the OSS on 18 September 1945.[17] It is unclear whether the message from the Chiefs was intentionally late. But they had diplomatically demonstrated their support for the President's action, while avoiding the appearance of – and responsibility for – plunging in the dagger. Their skill contrasts with the blunders of the OSS chief.

The next day, Truman sent a curt note to Donovan thanking him for his contribution to the war effort and dismissing him from his post.[18] Donovan had paid the penalty for being a headline-grabber, a self-promoter and a man who could not get along with the President. The unfortunate interaction of personalities between him and Truman forms a background that is in telling contrast to the more constructive dialogue that ensued.

Rather than make a snap decision on the post-OSS shape of American secret intelligence, Truman opted for a process of gradual reappraisal. He and his officials did not act on their findings until 1947. In the meantime, the President realised that he needed an intelligence arrangement to tide him over, and to keep open the space vacated by the OSS, into which a new organisation could be placed. The structure of the new organization, and of its durable successor, was a matter of fierce debate. Survivors of the OSS, now redeployed in the State and War Departments, favoured an independent agency.[19] Those who accepted the need for secret intelligence agreed with them. But there were differences of opinion about the functions of such an agency, the subjects of accountability and control, and the issue of civilian as distinct from military leadership. In his effort to steer a sensible course, Truman fell back on the counsel of a man whom he trusted.

Sidney W. Souers was born in Dayton, Ohio, in 1892. After graduating from Miami University in the same state, he engaged in several business ventures in New Orleans, becoming president of that city's Mortgage and Security Company, and of the First Joint Stock Land Bank. In 1930 he moved to St Louis, Missouri. There, he demonstrated the trouble-shooting skill and disregard for the niceties of legal precedent that were to be his hallmarks in government, as well as in business: when he saved the General American Life Insurance Company from financial ruin, the legality of his methods was questioned by newspapers across the state.[20]

In Missouri, Souers consolidated his already resounding business success. Some of his enterprises began to point him in the direction of his future government service. He was an active member of the board of directors of the Aviation Company, an investment banking concern which loaned money to McDonnell Douglass, Lockheed, Boeing and other groups working in the field of both military and civilian aircraft. He became an influential director of the *St Louis Post Dispatch*, a newspaper which had opposed Truman in the 1920s, but which now boosted Missouri's native son and in due course supplied him with his presidential press secretary, Charlie Ross.

Souers was no stranger to public duty. He had been turned down for service in the First World War for medical reasons, but joined the Naval Reserve and became a lieutenant-commander in 1929. From 1932 to 1940 he was on inactive status as an intelligence officer. Recalled to active duty in 1940, he served as intelligence chief for the Caribbean Sea zone, then, in 1944, he became assistant director of the Office of Naval Intelligence in Washington, DC.

Though a man of abundant talent, Souers owed his promotion, at least to some degree, to Secretary of the Navy James V. Forrestal. Forrestal had a perspective on life which made him acceptable to Truman: he had never forgotten his treatment at Princeton, where more privileged classmates made him feel unwelcome. Forrestal, indeed, survived in the Truman cabinet longer than any other Roosevelt appointee, and became the first Secretary of Defense. With insight into the outsider's viewpoint, Forrestal realised that the new President might well find Souers congenial. Thus, Souers could prove to be a vehicle for the advancement of his own plans and ambitions.

In the latter stages of the war, Forrestal commissioned Ferdinand Eberstadt, former chairman of the Army–Navy Munitions Board, to prepare a report on army-navy unification, and on post-war civilian-military relations. Eberstadt delegated portions of the job, and asked Souers to prepare the chapter on intelligence. As Souers later noted, he had had pre-war business dealings with both Forrestal and Eberstadt, who were, like himself, investment bankers.[21] He told one researcher that he had known them 'well'.[22] The men who were to help Truman in his delicate task were compatible individuals who could work together.

On 23 January 1946 Souers took charge of the Central Intelligence Group. Truman had issued a directive establishing the new agency on the previous day. The CIG would be formed with staff seconded from the Departments of State, War and Navy. Those departments would jointly administer its funds, paying seconded staff and splitting administrative costs. The CIG would work under a Director of Central Intelligence (DCI), a presidential nominee. The director would receive intelligence from the heads of the various civilian and military intelligence groups. These intelligence providers were also to band together and provide the director with advice as the Intelligence Advisory Board. Both the director and the board would be responsible to the National Intelligence Authority, consisting of the Secretaries of State, War and Navy or their representatives, along with a presidential representative who would preside as chairman. The authority would, in turn, be responsible to the President.

The indications are that Truman meant to stay in firm control, and that Souers had provided him with the means to do so. One such indication is that the representative of the major Washington bureaucracies, the Intelligence Advisory Board, had no command or control functions within the CIG. The CIG director's official job designation is another indication of presidential intent. The director was to correlate and evaluate intelligence from all sources and to perform 'such other duties affecting the national security as the President and the National Intelligence Authority may from time to time direct'.[23] That Truman intended to keep the new agency on a short lead is demonstrated by the choice of the word 'and' instead of 'or'. Truman, or so he would claim in 1964, did not envisage any need for the CIG to mount any clandestine or covert operations: 'Both the CIG and the CIA were set up by me for the sole purpose of getting all the available information to the President. They were not intended to operate as international agencies engaged in strange activities.'[24] Truman wanted a 'tame' intelligence agency headed by someone willing to remain in the shadows, and not another OSS.

Truman's need to have an intelligence director who would do his bidding dictated the fact that such a person would be beholden to nobody else in government. Souers met this requirement in several ways. He had no taint of OSS connections with their old-boy loyalty connotations. He was a naval reservist, not a career officer with promotion and loyalties to worry about. He was of independent means, and, in 1946, keen to return to private business:

> While I agreed to accept the appointment of DCI, it was understood I would serve only until I could recommend a successor who would be acceptable to the members of the

NIA and the President.[25] [The NIA was the acronym for the National Intelligence Authority, a committee of senior military and civilian officials that supervised the CIG.]

In fact, Souers did return to government after leaving the CIG, and did become a lifelong consultant and confidant of Truman, but this was from choice. He could tread on powerful officials if he wanted to. He was free to do the President's bidding.

Nevertheless, certain circumstances gave the CIG the appearance of being an ineffective organisation squeezed into the chronological gap separating two more robust agencies, the OSS and the CIA. One of these circumstances was that, however independent Souers may have been, his staff was dependent on the various contributing departments. The CIG did not have the power to hire, fire or promote its own staff. Members of that staff were loyal less to the CIG than to the agencies which paid them, and where their future careers lay. Though the OSS's table of organisation was fixed at sixty-six people, there was a feeling of dependency on the funding departments. In-fighting broke out between CIG employees serving the sectional interests of their parent bodies.

A second circumstance that seems to diminish the significance of the CIG is that Truman neither assigned its director a clear policy function, nor gave the group a specific task to perform. It is true that the CIG was providing the President was a daily intelligence summary within weeks of its formation, in an attempt to meet Truman's insistence that he be directly and reliably informed, and not led astray by bureaucrats with vested interests. But, according to Souers' recollection, Truman felt that the cold war would not last long. Prior to the Soviets' explosion of an atomic device in 1949, moreover, it was felt that the United States was in an unassailable position owing to its sole possession of atomic weapons. The tasking of the CIG was not an urgent problem.[26]

All this is unimportant, however, for Truman appears to have had in mind a special role for the CIG. Souers, at least, was in no doubt on the matter:

> I did not consider the Executive Order of January, 1946 setting up the CIG as anything but a preliminary step. The next most important step was to give permanence to a Central Intelligence organization by Congressional Act, along the lines set out in the Executive Order. We were to act as a holding

agency, until such time as a fully functional agency took over our intelligence tasks.[27]

Within days of the new agency's inception, the lack of legal knowledge on the part of Truman and his helpers made itself known. The agency's own employees discovered that the President could not, except during time of war, form a group like the CIG to last more than a year without statutory authorisation from Congress.[28] The investigation of just what statutes were needed, and the drawing up of these for Congress, were to become the primary focuses of the Souers group.

Souers appointed Larry Houston general counsel, or senior legal officer, of the CIG. Houston was on loan from the Strategic Services Unit of the War Department. He supported the concept of a separately funded agency, and went on to become the general counsel for the CIA. By February 1946 Houston and his team were at work developing possible legislation for the permanent establishment of an intelligence agency under civilian control. They examined precedents in American intelligence history, searching for ways of circumventing legal impediments which had existed in the past. They considered the code-breaking unit, the Black Chamber, whose activities Secretary of State Henry Stimson had curtailed in 1929 on the ground that they were dubious. They also reviewed, of course, the legal difficulties encountered by the OSS. Finally, they produced a concept paper regarding future roles for a central intelligence agency, and a long administrative draft on its possible makeup. At the same time, they drafted enabling legislation.

In describing the work performed by those assigned to the CIG, one should note that they did perform some useful intelligence assignments. They were able to exploit their experience in the intelligence world, and their connections in the military and in state. A handful of OSS Research and Analysis veterans who had survived the cuts and migrated to the CIG reported usefully on ethnic frictions in the Eastern bloc, collating limited materials supplied by other agencies with their own more ample research in an open source, the amply stocked Library of Congress.[29] But the main emphasis within the small agency was on preparations for a more substantial successor. The largest numbers of staffers worked under Larry Houston, preparing the report on and the legislation for the new agency.[30] Souers' main brief had been to lay the groundwork for a more substantial agency which would follow the CIG and which would not be reliant upon other agencies or departments for funding and personnel. He succeeded in this mission. The work was completed in late May and presented to Souers' replacement, Major-General Hoyt Vandenberg, on his first day in command of the CIG.

The selection of a successor had presented Truman and Souers with a political challenge. The navy having supplied Souers, the next DCI would have to be an army man. He would need to be of sufficient rank and public standing to pull weight and advance the desired cause, yet he would have to be respectful of civilian authority, and supportive of the idea of an independent civilian agency. Souers made sure of the last point, in the case of the ambitious Army Air Corps general, Hoyt Vandenberg. The new appointee had a respected public persona as a 'flying glamor boy' of the recent war. Vandenberg's ambition was to see an independent air force established, and to become its senior officer. In 1946 a 'dogfight' was in progress over the issues of armed-forces unification, of an independent air force, and of who should get the top jobs in any new structure. Assuming command of the CIG was an honourable way for Vandenberg to remove himself from the line of fire, while others took chances with their careers. In due course, the National Security Act of 1947 did establish an independent air force (as well as promoting military unification, and authorising the CIA). The astute Hoyt Vandenberg was to serve as Chief of Staff, US Air Force, 1948–53.

The President and Souers had interested a figure of some substance to take a post not yet, by any means, imbued with the prestige it was to acquire in later years. In so doing, they expected a political bonus. Hoyt's uncle was the redoubtable Arthur Vandenberg. A senior Republican figure, Arthur Vandenberg was about to become the chairman of the Senate Foreign Relations Committee. He was in an excellent position to support his nephew's new group, and to back Hoyt's ideas on the intelligence community and what role the new CIG should play in it. As Souers later put it: 'it was nice that [Hoyt] was a nephew to the Senator, because we had to keep in mind that we needed to finally set up the agency as an independent agency under the President'.[31]

Hoyt Vandenberg soon seized the opportunity presented by the report which Houston and his colleagues had written, and which was waiting for him when he took over the Central Intelligence Group in June 1946. Within ten days of assuming command, Vandenberg presented a draft directive to the National Intelligence Authority which was aimed at strengthening the Director of Central

Intelligence's position with regard to that body, and at upgrading the status of the CIG. It proposed that the DCI should have direct control of all intelligence activities, including the clandestine collection of information. It further proposed that the director should be appointed 'executive agent' of the NIA to ensure those policies were properly enforced.[32] After much discussion and not a little horse trading and infighting within the NIA, a less aggressive version of the Vandenberg directive was issued as NIA Directive Number Five in July 1946.

The way was now open for the establishment of the CIA. The 1947 National Security Act and the 1949 Central Intelligence Act established the permanent peacetime clandestine organisation. It was a tribute to the political skills of the founding fathers – with Souers still 'serving as a consultant to Vandenberg' even during his fleeting return to civilian life before resuming public service with the NSC – that the legislation went through with a minimum of fuss.[33] Souers, far from being a myopic provincial intent on feathering his own nest (the image conjured by the phrase 'Missouri Gang'), was proving to be a responsible public official. He helped to ensure that the Director of Central Intelligence had real powers and that the NSC, which replaced the NIA and became the CIA's supervisory body, was not under military domination. The following passage illuminates both the intentions and the determination of Souers and Truman:

> Messrs Eberstadt and Forrestal felt strongly that the NSC office should be in the Defense Department but the President insisted that it be in the White House. At Forrestal's urgent request, it was agreed that the Executive Secretary (who was I) would have another office next to the office of the Secretary of Defense, but this turned out to be temporary because I knew that the Executive Secretary could serve the President and members of the NSC better being directly under the President and Chairman of the Council.[34]

Truman later testified in the clearest terms to his own motives and intentions:

> the Army, Navy, and the new Air Force had intelligence agencies in nearly every country in the world. The Department of Agriculture, the Department of Commerce, and the Department of Labor also had such organizations, but the

President had no way of finding out what those agencies were doing behind his back. So I set up the CIA . . . The President must have all the information he can get . . . the cabinet Departments have an idea he will be there 'only four years' and they don't have to pay any attention to him.[35]

Truman wanted an intelligence agency he could control. But did he want an agency that would engage in covert operations? In search of legitimacy for some of the agency's activities in later years, some of those who have depicted him as hesitant in reaching the right intelligence formula have nevertheless insisted that he was contrastingly firm in his authorisation of undercover work. However, both Truman and Souers stressed, in looking back on their White House years from the perspective of the 1960s and 1970s, that they had not intended the CIA to engage in risky adventures.

Two developments in the intervening period help to explain their responses. The first was the emergence, in the 1950s, of a powerful CIA which engaged in covert operations – under the leadership, some have stressed, of Ivy League-educated members of the East Coast establishment. The second was the notorious Bay of Pigs disaster, the CIA's attempt, with President John F. Kennedy's authorisation, to overthrow the Fidel Castro regime in Cuba. The attempted Cuban counter-revolution was based on a paramilitary operation involving CIA-trained Cuban exiles. The CIA came under fire for a number of reasons, prominent amongst which was its refusal to inform the military about its plan, which meant that it did not avail itself of professional advice on paramilitary tactics.

In December 1963, following Kennedy's assassination, an article appeared under Truman's name in the *Washington Post* and in several other newspapers. It contained the following observations:

For some time I have been disturbed by the way the CIA has been diverted from its original assignment. It has become an operational and at times a policy-making arm of the government . . .

I never had any thought when I set up the CIA that it would be injected into peacetime cloak and dagger operations. Some of the complications and embarrassment that I think we have experienced are in part attributable to the fact that this quiet intelligence arm of the President has been so removed from its intended role that it is being interpreted as a symbol of sinister and mysterious foreign intrigue – and a subject for cold war enemy propaganda.[36]

There have been various attempts to discount the significance of the former President's outburst. According to one CIA publication, a Truman aide confessed that, at a time when his boss was going senile, he had forged the document in the name of the former President. Allen Dulles, the CIA director who fumed at his dismissal following the Bay of Pigs and threatened to publish a memoir, privately claimed that he confronted Truman in 1964, and that the former President admitted that he had made 'a very unfortunate impression' in his article. A recent historian of the CIA has suggested without further elaboration that 'Truman never found it difficult to rewrite history', a charge that appears to reflect the view that political memoirists usually tell the gospel truth.[37]

Another explanation of the 1963 article is perhaps too prosaic to be considered by popular historians, but is surely more convincing. This is that it was indeed Truman's work, and that it reflected both his opinions and his true recollections of events in the 1940s. Here, the reactions of Souers supply conclusive corroboration. Commenting on the article in a letter to Truman, he wrote:

> This was a splendid statement and I am delighted you made it, because it needed to be said . . .
> Allen Dulles caused the CIA to wander far from the original goal established by you, and it is certainly a different animal than I tried to set up for you.
> It would seem that its principal effort was to cause revolutions in smaller countries around the globe . . .
> With so much emphasis on operations, it would not surprise me to find that the matter of collecting and processing intelligence has suffered some.[38]

This was not just a spontaneous burst of sentimental loyalty. Several months later, Souers wrote to the CIA's official historian:

> I always felt, as did the President, that the CIG and later the CIA had no business to get involved in covert operations of a para-military type. After the very unfortunate experience in the Bay of Pigs campaign in Cuba, I was told, and I hope accurately, that the CIA would not conduct such campaigns in the future.[39]

This language does not mean that the intention was to prevent all types of covert operation. Neither 'psychological' operations, such as bribery, blackmail and disinformation, nor the clandestine collection of information were precluded. But one can see why Truman was opposed to using the CIA in paramilitary operations, fearing as he did another OSS type of agency.

Souers felt that the rot had set in the moment Truman left the White House in 1953, and that responsibility for the wrong turn in the CIA's history lay, to a considerable extent, with the Dulles brothers, John Foster, who became Secretary of State, and Allen W., the new director of the CIA. He thought General Walter Bedell Smith 'should have been permitted to continue in his job as DCI because the head of CIA should not be changed automatically when an Administration changes'. Even President Eisenhower, Souers claimed, was uneasy about John Foster Dulles.[40] Perhaps he imagined that Eisenhower, as a fellow-Midwesterner, would feel the same as he and Truman did about Princeton graduates and other Ivy Leaguers who seemed to have taken over the CIA. His own and Truman's ire about such people welled up in the wake of the Bay of Pigs. In his 1963 letter to Truman, Souers ripped into Richard Bissell, one of the brightest stars of the 1950s CIA:

> As bad as [fomenting revolutions] was, it was worse to try to conduct a 'war' invading Cuba with a handful of men and without air cover. The campaign had been designed and carried out by Mr. Bissell who was on my staff at the NSC. He had been a professor at Harvard and wrote good staff papers, but he had little or no experience in practical warfare. As a matter of fact, it is my understanding that he has never worn a uniform.[41]

Souers and Truman still shared a similar outlook. Truman reciprocated the high regard Souers had for him: 'You can depend on this guy', he had noted in 1954, 'he was one of my greatest assets.'[42] The dictates of loyalty made each present the other in a good light. But their stories are too consistent for the Truman article to have been a forgery, the product of a senile mind or a travesty of history. They did believe that the 1950s CIA was different from the 1940s CIA. And the Missouri Gang is entitled to a fair hearing.

The CIG period of American intelligence history has suffered from neglect and distortion. One reason for this, and for the resulting confusion, has been a strange inversion of the historiographical process. Normally, the executive officials responsible for public policy in a particular period are the first to publish their version of events – anxious, as they are, to defend their record, and privileged in their prior access to the facts via secret documents and their own recollections. But when Truman published his memoirs in the 1950s, he did not detail his efforts to pioneer a modern intelligence community. With the exception of his 1963 article, he remained silent. The first accounts of intelligence history in the 1940s were therefore coloured by the loyalties of writers who had been active in the CIA in the 1950s. It is only now, with the onward march of progressive declassification, that we can begin to piece together the story as Truman and Souers perceived it.

It would be a mistake to imply that there was a drastic contrast between the 1940s CIG and CIA, and the CIA as it operated under President Eisenhower. Yet, distinctions may be and have been made. Some intelligence veterans have taken pride in the fact that the 1950s CIA could claim inspiration by and descent from Wild Bill Donovan's OSS. Moreover, there are those who deplore the perceived departure from OSS values in the 1960s. On the other hand, Truman and Souers scorned Donovan, priding themselves on their responsible, pragmatic approach, and on their firm control of both the CIG and the CIA. They emphasised intelligence work, as distinct from the wilder varieties of covert activity, and deplored the CIA's adventurism in the 1950s.

Truman and Souers were undoubtedly partisan, in the party-political sense as well as personally, in attacking the Republican Eisenhower legacy. But their critique must be taken seriously. They were, after all, senior figures. Their accounts were obviously based on first-hand knowledge of the 1940s and of presidential intent in that decade. Furthermore, their viewpoint was consistent with that of others, inside as well as outside the intelligence community, who looked back with dismay at the Bay of Pigs, and asked what had gone wrong. Whatever one's view of the Missouri Gang, the people behind the CIG invite sympathetic reappraisal.

Notes

1. Editor's note: This chapter is a shortened version of Danny Deane Jansen's dissertation, 'The people behind CIG,' submitted for the degree of M.Sc. in history at the University of Edinburgh in 1989. Danny Jansen died shortly after learning that he had been awarded the degree. In modifying the thesis for publication, I have paraphrased and condensed the author's introductory and concluding observations.

Except for further condensations needed to fit editorial requirements, the majority of the prose is unmodified. Throughout the chapter, the interpretation is Danny Jansen's. RJ-J.

2. See Corey Ford's supportive *Donovan of OSS* (Boston, Mass.: Little, Brown, 1970), and Thomas F. Troy's declassified official history, *Donovan and the CIA: A history of the establishment of the Central Intelligence Agency* (Frederick, Md: University Publications of America, 1981).

3. Truman was conscious of the geographic shift in emphasis: 'The reconstituted Cabinet resulted in an unprecedented situation in that five members were from west of the Mississippi': Harry S. Truman, *Memoirs*, 2 vols. I *Year of Decisions* (Garden City, NY: Doubleday, 1955), p. 326. J. C. Goulden noted in *The Best Years* (New York: Antheneum, 1976), pp. 213–4 that the term 'Missouri Gang' was an invention of Truman's critics who wished to suggest that his appointees were reminiscent of the notorious 'Ohio Gang', the corrupt confederates of President Warren G. Harding. These critics tended to label Truman's appointees as members of the 'Gang', even if they did not come from Missouri. But Truman did appoint some fellow-Missourians: his old poker pal Harry Vaughan as a military adviser, Robert E. Hannegan as Postmaster-General, John W. Snyder as head of the Office of War Mobilization and Reconversion, and, as we shall see below, Sidney W. Souers.

4. See Richard M. Freeland, *The Truman Doctrine and the Origins of McCarthyism: Foreign policy, domestic politics, and internal security 1946–1948* (New York: Schocken, 1974).

5. John Ranelagh, the author of a detailed history of the CIA, wrote dismissively: 'Souers did not have a clear policy function to perform', but acknowledged his 'friendship with Truman', and the fact that he worked 'easily' in the White House: *The Agency: The rise and decline of the CIA, from Wild Bill Donovan to William Casey* (New York: Simon & Schuster, 1986), p. 103.

6. Editor's note: See Chapter 1 for a discussion of the CIA's official histories. The first volume in Montague's 726-page, five-volume study in the DCI Historical Series, 'General Walter Bedell Smith as Director of Central Intelligence, October 1950–February 1953' was on 'The Essential Background'. Montague therefore asked Truman and Souers questions about the whole span of the Truman presidency, and Truman commented on drafts of Montague's work.

7. Gratitude is due to the staff at the Harry S. Truman Library, and in particular to Mr Emil Miller, for making available some documentary treasure troves.

8. Ford, *Donovan*, pp. 200–202.

9. Letter, Harry Truman to Clark Clifford, 14 July, 1956, Clifford folder, Box 16, Post Presidential Files. In common with all the other collections cited in this chapter, the Post Presidential Files are located in the Harry S. Truman Library, Independence, Missouri.

10. Memorandum, Leahy to Truman, 16 May, 1945, OSS folder, Box 4, Security Files.

11. Editor's note: The Jedburgh teams were teams of British and American specialists who parachuted behind enemy lines to help the French resistance movement.

12. Ford, *Donovan*, p. 176.

13. Letter, Souers to Lee Montague, 11 April, 1964, Montague folder, Box 2, Souers Papers.
14. Ford, *Donovan*, p.76
15. Memorandum, Donovan to Truman, 21 April, 1945, Donovan folder, Box 18, Security Files.
16. Letter, Truman to Charles Ross, 16 Oct. 1947, Intelligence folder, Box 249, President's Secretary's Files. Ross was in the same class as Truman in Independence High School, Missouri. They founded a magazine together. Ross graduated above Truman, and went on to win a Pulitzer prize for journalism.
17. Letter, Souers to Montague, 29 June, 1964, Montague folder, Box 2, Souers Papers.
18. Note, Truman to Donovan, 20 Sept. 1945, Intelligence folder, Box 249, President's Secretary's Files.
19. Letter, Lawrence Houston to Souers, 2 March, 1956, Houston folder, Box 6, Souers Papers. Houston was general counsel to both the CIG and the CIA.
20. See William Cox, 'Harry Truman in Missouri politics' (Ph.D. dissertation, University of Kansas, 1967).
21. Letter, Souers to Montague, 14 Feb. 1965, Montague folder, Box 2, Souers Papers.
22. Letter, Souers to Calvin L. Christman, 22 Dec. 1970, General Correspondence, 1953–1972, Souers Papers. Calvin Christman was a Ph.D. candidate at Ohio State University writing his dissertation on the career of Ferdinand Eberstadt.
23. Robert Ferrell, *Off the Record: The private papers of Harry S. Truman* (New York: Harper and Row, 1980), p. 408.
24. Unidentified newspaper clipping, Personal folder, Box 6, Souers Papers.
25. Letter, Souers to Montague, 17 June, 1964, Montague folder, Box 2, Souers Papers.
26. Letter, Souers to Clark Clifford, 16 July, 1962, Correspondence folder 3, Box 6, Souers Papers.
27. Letter, Souers to Montague, 28 June, 1964, Montague folder, Box 2, Souers Papers.
28. Letter, Souers to Montague, 3 Aug. 1964, Montague folder, Box 2, Souers Papers.
29. Letter, Souers to Houston, 12 Oct. 1949, Correspondence file 2, Box 6, Souers Papers.
30. Letter, Souers to Montague, 2 July, 1964, Montague folder, Box 2, Souers Papers.
31. Souers oral history transcript, 15 Dec. 1954, Memoirs, interviews with associates, Box 2, Post-Presidential Files.
32. Draft directive, Vandenberg to NIA, 16 June, 1946, CIG folder, Box 1582, Official Files.
33. Souers oral history, cited above
34. Letter, Souers to Christman, 22 Dec. 1970, General Correspondence, 1953–1972, Souers Papers.
35. Letter, Truman to Senator Wayne Morse, 14 March, 1963, Correspondence folder, Box 121, Post-Presidential Files.
36. This text is taken from the *Evansville Courier*, 21 Dec. 1963. The article appeared in the *Washington Post* on the following day.
37. Ranelagh, *Agency*, p. 18n. The information and both quotations are

from the same note. Ranelagh is an Irish aristocrat who has worked for the Conservative Party in England, and for British television.

38. Letter, Souers to 'Boss' [i.e. Truman], 27 Dec. 1963, Correspondence, Harry S. Truman, Box 1, Souers Papers.

39. Letter, Souers to Montague, 3 Aug. 1964, Montague folder, Box 2, Souers Papers.

40. Letter, Souers to Montague, 19 July, 1971, General Correspondence, 1953–1972, Souers Papers. [Ed.: Eisenhower had inherited the Dulles team from the 1948 Republican presidential candidate, Thomas E. Dewey. He did on occasion feel obliged to restrain John Foster Dulles, for example when the Secretary of State wanted to help the French on the eve of their defeat by Vietnamese communists at the battle of Dien Bien Phu (1954): see Peter G. Boyle, ed., *The Churchill–Eisenhower Correspondence, 1953–55* (Chapel Hill, NC: Univ. of North Carolina Press, 1990), p.135.]

41. Letter, Souers to 'Boss' [i.e. Truman], 27 Dec. 1963, Correspondence, Harry S. Truman, Box 1, Souers Papers.

42. Handwritten note, signed 'HST', on the first page of Souers oral history transcript, 15 Dec. 1954, Memoirs, interviews with associates, Box 2, Post-Presidential Files.

7

British McCarthyism

KAREN POTTER

Numerous books have been published on McCarthyism in America, exploring the man and the movement, recording the victims and attempting to explain the anti-communist hysteria that marked the period after the end of the Second World War. However, there has been an incomplete accounting for Britain during that time. More spy scandals of the late 1940s and 1950s occurred in Britain than in the United States. Yet the United States reacted much more radically to the perceived communist threat. This essay attempts to trace the sources and manifestations of anti-communism in Britain during the cold war years, and to offer contrasts between the responses of Great Britain and the United States.

It is, of course, perilous to offer generalisations about opinion on such a controversial issue. Its complexities are of a subjective nature, and are beyond the scope of even the most professional of quantitative opinion pollsters. Newspaper opinion is more helpful. To be sure, one must be careful about equating press opinion with public opinion. In America, papers are regional and may not represent 'national' opinion. This is less problematic in Britain, a centralised nation-state. But the situation in Britain is different from that in America in a further important respect. The left–right spectrum of opinion in America is not so wide as it is in Europe, and the press, uniformly to the right of centre by European standards, is not glaringly unrepresentative of what the American people think. But in present-day Britain, no major newspaper represents the socialist viewpoint, in spite of the Labour Party's leading status.

In the late 1940s and early 1950s, though, while the conservative press did predominate in Britain, there was a minority left-wing press which represented the views of the socialist electoral majority of that time. It is therefore possible to sample a cross-section of press opinion ranging from left to right, from the *Tribune* through the *Reynolds News*, the *Daily Herald*, the *Manchester Guardian* and *The Times* to the *Daily Mail*.[1] This device is not foolproof: the democratic left is not necessarily more respectful of civil liberties than the democratic right. But it is perhaps one of the least unsatisfactory ways of investigating a sensitive problem.

While there was little unbridled panic in Britain, there were fears of communist infiltration, some of them legitimate. There was certainly a British counterpart to President Truman's loyalty programme, launched in 1947 with the object of eliminating disloyal elements in the civil service and described by one historian as 'the most sinister and destructive departure in postwar [American] politics'.[2] In the same year Clement Attlee, the first Prime Minister to visit MI5 headquarters, authorised a secret cabinet committee to weed out communists and fascists from sensitive government jobs.[3]

Only eleven people had been moved from their British civil service posts by 1949. Yet some campaigners have pointed to more widespread, informal discrimination – notably, the blacklists compiled and supplied to potential employers by the right-wing Economic League, founded in 1919 and rejuvenated in 1950 at the height of McCarthyism. These campaigners believe that there existed in Britain a 'silent McCarthyism' that was never openly proclaimed and therefore never publicly rejected.[4] There were, it is true, purges of communists and suspected sympathisers in several spheres of British society, including the trade unions, the civil service, the universities, the Church and the British Broadcasting Corporation (BBC). If to a lesser degree than in the United States, a few British victims were discredited without the chance to respond.

But could the British boast an equivalent of the notorious Senator Joseph McCarthy? One candidate might be the Conservative Member of Parliament, Sir Waldron Smithers, who has indeed been described as 'an English version of' McCarthy. But Smithers' repeated calls for a 'Committee on Un-British Activities' to shadow the investigations of its US counterpart met with crushing dismissals from Attlee and Churchill.[5] My contention is that a more credible candidate loomed in the figure of the veteran opponent of Nazism and appeasement, former Permanent Under-Secretary of State for Foreign Affairs, Lord Vansittart. Vansittart, when he took his case to the House of Lords in 1950 in the twilight of his career, appears to have been motivated more by genuine fears than by the political opportunism that activated McCarthy in the same year – but, in spite of this and other significant differences between the two men, the parallel is still worth pursuing.[6]

An examination of the way Vansittart and McCarthy were received in their homelands offers a window to the different political landscapes in Britain and the United States. At the same time that America's McCarthy was declaring to a women's group in Wheeling, West Virginia, that he possessed the names of communists in the US government, Vansittart was preparing for a similar announcement to the House of Lords. Vansittart's words on 29 March 1950 were eerily reminiscent of those McCarthy had uttered a month earlier, on 9 February, words that came crashing in on much of the United States for a decade. 'I have full particulars of sixteen Communists and 100 percent fellow travellers who have got themselves into good jobs in the Department of Inland Revenue,'Vansittart said in an address to the House of Lords. 'Again, I am not talking from gossip or hearsay. In some cases, I have actually seen the Communist Party cards.'[7]

Vansittart went on at length to accuse the BBC of promoting communist candidates by giving them broadcast time during the election. He claimed that two thousand teachers were active communists, and that Birmingham University had an active communist clique. He claimed that the Church was infested, and that communists had infiltrated all manner of government offices including the War Office, Education and Health.

However, no hysteria followed Vansittart's pronouncement. If Vansittart is remembered in Britain today, it is not as a would-be McCarthy, but as an opponent of pre-Second World War appeasement in the Chamberlain government. Vansittart was not heralded or followed as a leader against communism in Britain. The press ridiculed him. The *Reynolds News* weekly dubbed him 'Lord Van-Witchhunt'.[8] Vansittart wished not to be compared to McCarthy. 'The Motion [by Vansittart requesting public security precautions] before your Lordships' House this afternoon has nothing in common with the shy-making ballyhoo of Senator McCarthy – the very way not to handle the matters of this kind', Vansittart said. 'What I shall set before you this afternoon is fully documented, fair and factual.'[9]

Even these assurances did not satisfy their lordships, who were yet more determined than Vansittart to avoid the excesses of the American commoner. The House almost censured Vansittart on 2 May for committing libels against the people he accused. During his defence, Vansittart imprudently insisted he must name names.

'After all we are fighting for our lives,' he said. 'You cannot possibly make a political omelette without breaking some bad eggs.'[10] Only his gentlemanly aplomb and elegant defence saved him from the ignominy of censure, and he was left a broken man to wonder why no one ever listened to him.

It is notable, nevertheless, that continuing cold war tensions meant that Vansittart's warnings could be taken seriously as late as the 1970s. The respected biographer Norman Rose remarked in his 1978 book *Vansittart: Study of a diplomat* that Vansittart's performance before the House of Lords was a skilful demonstration of parliamentary tactics, and that his efforts were not hollow:

> It would be a simple exercise to dismiss Van's immediate anti-Communist rhetoric; to regard him as an antiquated, pre-historic survival of a bygone age out of touch with the post-1945 era . . . He adamantly refused to take Communist prot-estations of peace at their face value. It is too early to judge whether Van's fears were fully justified. The discussion is in full swing.[11]

Rose thought that Vansittart and McCarthy came to their anti-communist platforms with different motives; still, 'the timing and contents of their respective campaigns left these two vastly contrast-ing characters as strange bedfellows'.[12] The peers' dismissal of Van-sittart does not mean that his relationship to McCarthyism should be ignored. The comparison between Vansittart and McCarthy is still illuminating, as is the comparison between the reactions they engendered in their respective countries.

Vansittart and McCarthy were very different in approach and character. McCarthy played the carnival showman; Vansittart acted the stage dramatist. The ageing Vansittart (sixty-nine in 1950) was aggrieved by his lack of a future; the upstart McCarthy (forty-one) was aggrieved by his lack of a past. However, their methods were similar. Both, for example, had connections in the security services – the one in MI5, the other in the FBI.[13] Both found 'evidence' in waste-paper baskets. The *Manchester Guardian* explored the similarities between the two men and their respective countries in a leader of 31 March, 1950:

> We should hate to see Lord Vansittart becoming another Sen. McCarthy, although naturally he would do his smearing with much more artistry and wit . . . We have somehow to keep

our heads and avoid the American hysteria as well as the French laxity.[14]

In the end, the climates of the two nations had much to do with why McCarthy was listened to and Vansittart ignored. While Americans felt very threatened, the British were accustomed to the communists, and the Labour government felt a philosophical kinship. While British leaders were full of concern for individual liberties when a mild purge of the civil service was announced in 1948, the Americans were quicker to flinch at signs of infiltration by their Soviet opponents in the superpower struggle, quicker to listen to people like McCarthy and quicker to sacrifice civil rights. As the Lord Chancellor, Viscount Jowitt, noted in his rebuke of Vansittart: 'In trying to deal with the evil . . . we must not fall into the error of adopting those very methods which we condemn in totalitarian countries . . . You cannot cast out Satan by means of Beelzebub.'[15] Jowitt was to remain convinced that Americans over-reacted to spy cases, and in 1953 he would publish a book on the celebrated US trial or, as he saw it, mis-trial, which had ignited the McCarthyist fuse – *The Strange Case of Alger Hiss*. Such mistreatment of high-ranking officials should not and, he was convinced, could not occur under the British legal system.[16]

Government leaders in the United States found it to their advantage politically to galvanise support by exploiting the enemy within. But the British response was neither opportunist nor rash. Speaking in the House of Lords on 29 March 1950, Jowitt said: 'There is no complacency, no panic, no hysteria. Don't let anybody think that this country is riddled with Communism, because I suspect that of all countries in the world, this country is more free from Communism than any other. With that mixture of imperial pride and cool-headed control the Lord Chancellor assured the House of Lords and the bellowing Vansittart that Britain remained a fortress against an international communist threat. He had consoled them even after the arrest and confession as a communist spy of British atomic scientist Klaus Fuchs nearly two months earlier. That arrest had shown the world that the British scientific community too had spies and might even be more vulnerable than some, but Jowitt dismissed his case as a fluke.

In the same way, most of the instances of espionage involving treachery by British citizens and the Soviets during the post-war period were explained away as aberrations, or were, in a few cases, covered up from public view. While some Americans seized on every fragment of evidence of infiltration or disloyalty, real or imagined, as proof of a 'communist conspiracy', the British, full of hopes of a continuing accord with the Soviet Union, and of a stillpre-eminent role in the world, were slow to recognise that the country might need to brace itself against an internal threat.[18]

It was with reluctance that purges were made within the civil service, the Labour Party and the trade unions. (Those three areas accounted for most of the scrutiny, though the BBC dismissed at least three employees in 1948, and University College, London, dismissed history assistant lecturer R.H. Beevers in 1950.)[19] The purges were conducted by the organisations themselves to a large extent. The issue of communist infiltration, shrouded in secrecy, was not generally considered an affair for public discussion or, worse still, political exploitation, as it was in the United States. Communists were seen as addled half-brothers who detracted from the family, who must be disinherited and shipped away quietly. There was no need or desire for a scene in public, or for heated rhetoric. The Conservatives, who were anti-communist and anti-socialist both, realised this after an unsuccessful attempt in 1954 to discredit Harold Laski by picturing him as a sinister totalitarian. In the words of the contemporary observer Leon Epstein: 'It was a matter of keeping in step with the public's apparent receptivity to what it stigmatized as "Red-baiting".[20]

The British were more tolerant of the communist threat and less fearful. In Epstein's words again:

> The idea that there was an advantage, in anti-Communist results, sufficient to justify open attacks on a variety of sus-pects was something the British rejected because of their greater tolerance of Communism, in particular, as well as because of an intellectual tolerance in general. This tolerance cannot be assumed to have prevented responsible authorities from removing Communists from critical positions, but such removals were likely to have been accomplished quietly and without public pressure.[21]

On the one hand, Epstein evidently scented the existence of what later critics dubbed 'silent McCarthyism'. On the other hand, he seemed to believe that British tolerance – or intolerance of American intolerance – could be taken to excess, as in the press furore over Charlie Chaplin's expulsion from America.

The numbers of those purged in Britain paled next to the American experience, as a look at the civil service demonstrates. In 1954 Financial Secretary Henry Brooke announced that 124 British civil servants had been removed and ten thousand screened since 1948.[22] Meanwhile, in the United States, four million civil servants had been screened, and more than four thousand had quit or resigned: 570 were dismissed, 1,935 resigned after the FBI began investigations and 1,848 left when charges were made to loyalty boards.[23]

In Britain, as great a concern as ridding vital organisations of communists was the accomplishment of that goal in a legal and ethical manner. Foremost in nearly every government debate was respect for liberty and individual rights. Some said there was too much emphasis on individual freedom and too little questioning of individuals' backgrounds and beliefs for the good of the state. But the number of civil liberties violations is insignificant compared to the number that took place in the United States.

To understand how the British reacted to what was eventually perceived as the 'communist threat', it is necessary to delve into the British attitude toward the Soviet Union at the close of the Second World War. Every coloration of political opinion in Britain was hopeful of continuing some form of friendship with the Soviets from the end of the war.[24] The nation felt indebted to the Soviet Union for bearing the brunt of the German attack in 1941 and 1942. And in a time when a resurgence of aggression by the Germans was feared, co-operation with the USSR meant protection and was therefore greatly desired.[25]

With the pro-Soviet attitude came a wariness of alliance with the United States. The US was seen in 'imperialistic, capitalistic' terms by the left especially, and was viewed with envy by the masses as a prosperous nation which had entered the war late and which continued to enjoy the fruits of plenty while rationing continued in Britain. The British considered themselves betrayed by the Americans at the sudden halt of lend-lease aid in 1945, and saw the Anglo-American agreement of 1945–6 as a compact based on commerce rather than comradeship, a case of the British being forced to accept conditions imposed by the United States.[26]

When Winston Churchill delivered his 'Iron Curtain' speech in Fulton, Missouri, on 5 March, 1946, the American press seized on its anti-communist dimension. But the popular press in Britain only reluctantly admitted that the USSR might become a threat, and that alliance with the United States might be necessary. Coverage of the speech in Britain focused mainly on the Anglo-American alliance he proposed, and played down Churchill's warnings on

Russia. Most papers were conscious of the dangers of appeasement in the face of the Soviets' sprawling empire in Eastern Europe, but they were equally fearful of becoming an American economic satellite.

The press and the public were still wary when the Truman Doctrine was announced in March 1947. *The Times* was a case in point. Though more sympathetic to left-wing ideas than it would be in later years, it was a pillar of the British establishment and did give a generally favourable verdict on the initiative by Britain's main ally. But *The Times* could not divest itself of a residual distrust of things American, and was afraid that blind anti-communism might guide US actions:

> The potency of the new policy will depend upon the manner and mood in which it is applied. The danger that it may yet be perverted into a barren and restrictive anti-Communist crusade cannot be ignored; a 'red scare' is already in full swing against Communist 'fellow-travellers' in the American Administration and the Labour movement.[27]

The Marshall Plan, when announced 11 June, 1947, was seen by all shades of political opinion as a return to sanity by America, and was heralded as a genuine peace programme. In the meantime, away from the public eye, irritations with the Soviets were finally being voiced in 1947 by the Foreign Office. Symptomatically, Anthony Eden, wrote after the signing of a twenty year alliance in 1947: 'We have to make an effort to put our relations with the Soviets on a better footing. Even if the fault is all theirs, this is still necessary.'[28]

As the British attitude towards the Soviet Union was slowly hardening, incidents of spying began coming to light. Once again, the British were slow to panic. News broke in February 1946 of a Canadian spy ring perpetrated by the Russians and designed to obtain atomic secrets. This news prompted a dual reaction in Britain: relief that the spies were appearing only in Canada and the United States, and incredulity at the Soviet transgressions. Prime Minister Attlee set the tone when he refused to discuss the disclosures beyond assuring the House of Commons on 19 February that he had no knowledge of the spy ring.[29] On 22 February, the *Manchester Guardian* greeted with relief President Truman's restrained response to the spy scandal: 'It is obvious enough that the danger of 'spy scare' with all its endless possible repercussions, is clearly seen and is reflected in the extreme caution with which the President and the Secretary of State face the press.[30]

It took the more popular *Daily Herald* to report, on 6 March, that Britain was discussing repercussions of the Canadian ring. Its report was that three separate but interlocked government departments were carrying out investigations in London and the provinces into 'alleged leakage of atom bomb secrets'.[31] There was no official comment that might confirm this until 19 March when the Canadian premier, Mackenzie King, said that he had made secret journeys to London and Washington to inform Attlee and Truman that information 'of great and grave concern to the United States and Britain was sought by Russia from Canadian sources. What was being created in Canada was a fifth column. I felt it my duty to inform the United States and the United Kingdom.'[32] Even as the *Herald* announced the investigations, it assured its readers that all of the scientists had been checked on and their contacts quietly examined. So, while daily reports of the disclosures in Canada were detailed enough, the British connection was little mentioned by the press. The appearance of 'all is well' in Britain was maintained.

As the first account of the scope of the Canadian scandal was being announced on 5 March, 1946, the first of the British links to the Canada atomic spy ring, Alan Nunn May, was introduced to the reading public in *The Times* – in a relatively obscure two-paragraph notice headed 'London scientist arrested',[33] at the bottom of the page. Subsequent trial proceedings were relegated, in the major papers, to positions near rugby results or to supplementary news pages. The *Daily Herald* seized on the case only because it contained human-interest potential – May's students, who had seen him lecture the day before, were back to see him again . . . only this time in court.[34] The full accounts of the evidence that at last appeared in *The Times* and the *Guardian* still fell short of fulsome condemnation. For example, the *Guardian* noted the question that defence attorney Gerald Gardiner put to character witness Sir Wallace Akers, an Imperial Chemical Industries board member who supervised May's nuclear research: 'Is there strong feeling among many scientists, rightly or wrongly, that contributions like atomic research should not be kept to one country?' and Sir Wallace's answer to it: 'There is strong feeling.'[35] Sharing his atomic knowledge did not seem like such a bad thing for May to do, and there was no fulmination in the press on this point. Nor was there significant editorial comment, unless one counts a little ditty by the *Daily Herald*'s worldly-wise Scorpio:

Sing a song of spy rings. Spies are in the news
All the States have secrets other states can use
Espionage disclosures come as no surprise
Why become excited when it's headlines for the spies
Everybody's doing it
Spies are all around
Lurking under cover, working underground
British Secret Service, Yankee FBI
Every Foreign Office gives a passport for a spy

Secret forts and weapons
Formulas and maps
If countries shared their secrets
Spy rings would collapse
Why not open dealing?
Bid the spies good-bye
While nations make a secret, the Secret makes a spy.[36]

The critic and novelist Rebecca West, in *The New Meaning of Treason*, noted the government's clumsy response to the Canadian scare.

It is one of the oddest manifestations of our governmental failure to cope with the giant inconvenience of Communism that for a full year, after the publication of the Canadian Blue Book on the spy ring, it was impossible to obtain it in England.[37]

Meanwhile in the United States, an anti-communist hysteria was growing. Richard Freeland, in his book *The Truman Doctrine and the Origins of McCarthyism*, argues that Truman was responsible for whipping up anti-Red sentiment in an effort to muster support for the Truman Doctrine and Marshall Plan.[38] While external factors may help explain the reactions to communist spies in both nations, there appears to have been more of an internal political incentive in the United States. The United States had traditionally been more wary of the Soviets and of foreign ideologies. Many political careers – not only McCarthy's – were made in crusading against the communist threat. As one M.J. Rossant wrote in the *Tribune* on 2 January 1948, the cold war anti-communist hysteria in the US was reminiscent of the Red Scare of 1919–20: 'The same forces that operate today – Congress, the press, big business led the attack.

Along with the witch hunt, familiar forms of intolerance, such as anti-Semitism, anti-Negroism were intensified, and the KKK began its dirty work'.[39] Rossant further refers to the US' anti-intellectual tradition: 'Part of the trouble is due to widespread ignorance and self-righteous faith in American democracy. In a recent Gallup poll, for example, one-third of those interviewed believed that Socialist Britain was not a democracy'.[40] Having prevailed against the enemies of the Second World War, the United States focused on fighting internal enemies. The fear permeated every aspect of American culture, even, if one authority is to be believed, down to the automobile:

> Throughout the early 1950s, the faces of cars tended toward hostility and defensiveness, especially on the big cars, but also on the Chevrolets and Plymouths. The chrome was thick. The teeth were large, the bumpers suggested armour. One is tempted to find the countenance of Sen. Joseph McCarthy glaring out defensively from their front ends. The pugnacious grilles provided a mobile image of an American obsessed with finding and fighting.[41]

The event that ultimately changed the minds of the British public about Soviet intentions did not involve spy disclosures or threats to British security. It was that most blatant show of Soviet post-war power and intimidation, the late February 1948 coup of in Czechoslovakia. As the last democracy in Eastern Europe, Czechoslovakia had stood as a symbol of British hopes for the future. The press and the politicians alike were therefore dismayed at the democracy's fall. Michael Foot on 27 February called the week of the coup the most tragic since the end of the war. The future Labour Party leader declared:

> Cooperation with the Communists leads only to one end. They are ready to intrigue, to negotiate, but their aim is total victory and the total subservience of their allies . . . A bridge between the East and the West has been shattered.[42]

By mid-1948, nearly all segments of British opinion acknowledged a Soviet threat, belatedly realising that the Soviets would not and never had lived up to their image as honourable partners with the Western world.[43] Against this background of disappointment, British purges of communists began with regret. With a few exceptions, there never was much zeal behind the call for curbing communists. Characteristic British desire for restraint and secrecy, as well as unwavering devotion to the principle of liberty, marked the purges, which never reached deep. Witch-hunts would never be tolerated, it was said again and again. As Edmund Burke once put it:

> Liberty, too, must be limited in order to be possessed. The degree of restraint is impossible in any case to settle precisely. But it ought to be the constant aim of every wise public counsel to find out by cautious experiments, and rational, cool endeavours, with how little, not how much, of this restraint the community can subsist.[44]

The need for a careful balance between liberty and security, it seemed, was obvious.

Within the constraints of such beliefs some steps were taken of course, and they were not confined to government. The trade union movement, whose leaders saw communist organisation within its ranks more as competition than as an evil plot by the Soviets, started the earliest of the anti-communist campaigns. Despite initial attempts to work with the communist unions through international congresses in 1943–5, good feeling soon waned, and the Communists were blamed as instigators of the 1946 squatters' movement in London, in which unattended properties were occupied. By December 1947 Morgan Phillips, General Secretary of the Labour Party, was calling for a campaign against communist infiltration in the trade unions, warning that the Reds would attempt to inspire discontent: 'We can therefore expect that a campaign of sabotage against the Labour government will be carried out by the Communists and their fellow-travellers during the coming months.'[45]

In spite of such attitudes, the British approach to attacking communism remained controlled and even genteel. Concern for the rights of those under suspicion was paramount, and spared Britain the excesses and embarrassments that resulted from American fervour. At the same time, it may well be that purges and dismissals did take place, but were shielded from the public eye in the British tradition of secrecy – a procedure that would curb public hysteria but, at the same time, make it more difficult for victims to seek redress against a McCarthyism nobody was prepared to admit existed.

The British approach to anti-communism during the cold war

was not without faults, one of which was an excessive dislike of excesses. But the British example is illuminating. The caution and concern for liberty displayed by the British, if transferred to America, would have prevented many heartbreaks and injustices in the United States during the 1950s. And it could still serve as a guide for rationality, should the world order shift to revive cold-war style distrust and should espionage once more threaten nations' security.

Notes

1. In the wake of the 1961 Royal Commission on the Press, the *Economist* (vol. 200, 9 Sept. 1961, p. 949) supplied the following figures for 1950:

Reynolds News (Sundays)	705,000
Daily Herald	2,083,000
Manchester Guardian(daily)	
	138,000
The Times (daily)	246,000
Daily Mail	2,083,000

   In 1962 the British journalist Anthony Sampson wrote: 'The British press has the biggest circulations in the world . . . And the British (although total circulations have fallen by about 9 per cent since 1950), still read more newspapers per head than any other people: they read nearly twice as many newspapers as the Americans.'
      Sampson noted that advertisers could influence the fate of newspapers, and the *Daily Herald* was suffering accordingly. See Sampson, *Anatomy of Britain* (London: Hodder & Stoughton, 1962), chapter 8, 'Press', pp. 12–31, and pp. 112–14.
2. David Caute, The Great Fear: *The anti-communist purge under Truman and Eisenhower* (London: Secker & Warburg, 1978), p. 269.
3. Christopher Andrew, *Secret Service: The making of the British intelligence community* (London: Heinemann, 1985), p.490; Bernard Porter, *Plots and Paranoia: A history of political espionage in Britain 1790–1988* (London: Unwin Hyman, 1989), p. 187; Peter Hennessy and Gail Brownfeld, 'Britain's cold war security purge: the origins of positive vetting', *Historical Journal*, 25 (1982), 965–73. Following a reorganisation in 1916, the British Security Service (with responsibility for counter-espionage) came to be known as MI5, meaning Military Intelligence, section five.
4. Mark Hollingsworth and Charles Tremayne, *The Economic League: The silent McCarthyism* (London: National Council for Civil Liberties, 1989).
5. Mark Hollingsworth and Richard Norton-Taylor, *Blacklist: The inside story of political vetting* (London: Hogarth, 1988), p. 10.
6. The progression from genuine anti-fascism to genuine anti-communism was clearly exclusive to neither side of the Atlantic, and may even have been the product of confusion, in the public mind, between the two ideologies. See Les K. Adler and Thomas G. Paterson, 'Red fascism: the merger of Nazi Germany and Soviet Russia in the American image of totalitarianism, 1930's–1950's'. *American Historical Review*, 75 (April 1970), 1046–64.

7. Lord Vansittart's address in *Hansard*, Vol. 166, 29 March 1950, pp. 627–8.
8. *Reynolds News* quoted in *The Times*, 3 May 1950, p. 4.
9. *Hansard*, vol. 166, 29 March 1950, p. 608.
10. *Hansard*, vol. 167, 2 May 1950, p. 29.
11. Norman Rose, *Vansittart: Study of a diplomat* (London: Heinemann, 1978), p. 284.
12. *ibid*.p. 284.
13. On Vansittart's MI5 and other governmental and private secret intelligence connections, see Andrew, *Secret Service*, pp. 383–4.
14. *Manchester Guardian*, 31 March 1950, p. 6. According to the French authors Roget Faligot and Pascal Krop, France was not guilty of laxity in security matters. They suggest that stories of laxity were the product of CIA disinformation: Faligot and Krop, *La Piscine: The French Secret Service since 1944*, transl. W.D. Halls (Oxford: Basil Blackwell, 1989), p.61.
15. Lord Chancellor's reply in debate with Lord Vansittart in *Hansard*, vol. 166, 29 March 1950, pp. 649–50.
16. See John Chabot Smith, *Alger Hiss: The true story* (New York: Holt, Rinehart & Winston, 1976), p.435.
17. *Hansard*, vol. 166, 29 March 1950, p. 659.
18. *Manchester Guardian*, 29 March 1948, p. 5.
19. Information on the Beevers dismissal is from Dr Jeffreys-Jones' interviews with people familiar with the case.
20. Leon D. Epstein, *Britain: Uneasy ally*, (Chicago, Ill. University of Chicago Press, 1954), p. 182.
21. *ibid.*, p. 29.
22. *Keesing's Contemporary Archives, Weekly Diary of World Affairs*, IX (1952–54), p. 13, 942.
23. *Keesing's Contemporary Archives*, VIII (1950–52), p. 11, 980.
24. Epstein, *Britain*, throughout.
25. Victor Rothwell, *Britain and the Cold War, 1941–47*, (London: Jonathan Cape, 1982), introduction.
26. Epstein, *Britain*, p. 34. For a broad-ranging discussion of this theme, see D. Cameron Watt, *Succeeding John Bull: America in Britain's place 1900–1975* (Cambridge: Cambridge Univ. Press, 1984), p. 162 and passim.
27. *The Times*, n.d., quoted in Epstein, *Britain*, p. 161.
28. Rothwell, *Britain and Cold War*, p. 98.
29. *Manchester Guardian* leader, 22 Feb. 1946, p. 4.
30. *Manchester Guardian* leader, 5 March 1946, p. 4.
31. *Daily Herald*, 6 March 1946.
32. *Daily Herald*, 20 March 1946.
33. *The Times*, 6 March 1946, p. 2. See also *Manchester Guardian*, 6 March 1946.
34. *Daily Herald*, 6 March 1946, p. 3.
35. *Manchester Guardian*, 20 March 1946, p. 6.
36. *Daily Herald*, 28 March 1946, p. 2.
37. Rebecca West, *The New Meaning of Treason* (New York: Viking, 1964), p. 167.
38. Richard M. Freeland, *The Truman Doctrine and the Origins of McCarthyism: Foreign policy, domestic politics, and internal security 1946–48* (New York: Schocken, 1974).

39. *Tribune*, 2 January 1948, p. 8.
40. *Ibid.*
41. Thomas Hine, *Populuxe* (New York: Knopf, 1987), p. 96.
42. Michael Foot in *Daily Herald*, 27 Feb. 1948, p. 2.
43. Articles on Soviet mindset, numerous at the time in scholarly and political journals.
44. Robert K. Carr, *The House Committee on Un-American Activities 1945–1950*, preface.
45. *Keesing's Contemporary Archives*, V, (1946–8), p. 9, 035.

8

The birth of the Defense Intelligence Agency

PATRICK MESCALL

The need for an effective intelligence apparatus in the second half of the twentieth century has resulted in an acute dilemma for American policy-makers. Efficient collection, analysis and dissemination of the vast amount of information which flows through the American intelligence machine demands a certain amount of centralisation. Only through centralisation can order and coherence be imposed upon the disparate elements and activities of the intelligence community. Centralisation facilitates greater co-ordination and aids in the orderly flow of data. It minimises the duplication of effort often present among the competing intelligence agencies, and allows these agencies to remain responsive to the changing needs of policymakers.

However, centralisation is often viewed as anathema to American values. It is equated with obese, corrupt bureaucracies. It is frequently thought to be against the democratic principle of pluralism: opposed to competition, division of powers and checks and balances. From a structural perspective, centralisation often results in suppression of dissent, a decline in quality of product, and a rigid hierarchy which stifles innovation and limits responsiveness. Additionally, it has long been feared that a consolidated intelligence organisation might acquire a disproportionate amount of power and so threaten the American democratic system. Thus the challenge to post-war policy-makers has been to construct an effective intelligence community which is centralised in structure, yet retains many of the characteristics and benefits of pluralism. The dilemma is to find a working compromise within this dichotomy – to plot a course between Scylla and Charybdis. The Defense Intelligence

Agency (DIA) represents but one attempt to navigate this dire strait.

The DIA is one of the most criticised, yet least understood, organisations in the American intelligence community. It was established in 1961 by Secretary of Defense Robert S. McNamara to unify the intelligence efforts of the Department of Defense, while allowing the intelligence components of the armed services to retain some autonomy. Since its creation, the DIA has been widely condemned for a multitude of failures. Most investigations of the agency, particularly government-sponsored studies such as the 1970 Fitzhugh report and the 1976 reports of the Church and Pike Committees, have censured the organisation for being ineffective in its efforts to integrate military intelligence. Additionally, many analysts have focused on the failure of the agency to increase efficiency within the Pentagons intelligence activities and to eliminate the duplication of effort among the armed services' intelligence components.

Despite such widespread criticism, there has been little scholarly research into the formation of the DIA. While historians have carefully catalogued the symptoms, they have neglected the cause. This chapter is an attempt to redress the balance, to stimulate new questions about the establishment of the DIA. I will show that the agency was neither an anomaly nor a response to a specific incident. Rather, it was the product of an organisational progression towards centralisation which was occurring within the Department of Defense (DOD) as a whole. Moreover, I will shed new light on the motives and actions of the principal agencies involved in the creation of the DIA, the Office of the Secretary of Defense (OSD) and the Joint Staff. I will argue that the compromise which resulted in the creation of the DIA represented the triumph of the parochial interests of the Joint Staff and the military services over the national interests of the OSD and civilian policy-makers.

A review of the literature on the DIA will illuminate the nature of the task ahead. We shall see that there has been a developing awareness of the link between the DIAs provenance and its later failures. Yet, there has been a remarkable lack of curiosity about the nature of that link. It is, in fact, notable that previous writers have tended to treat the creation of the DIA in a piecemeal manner. They often claim that the agency was a response to a specific incident (typically the 'missile gap' or the Bay of Pigs). They generally fail to examine the establishment of the DIA in the broader historical context of the increasing centralisation of the DOD as a whole. The work of Thomas Ross and David Wise typifies such an approach. In their 1964 book *The Invisible Government*, one of the earliest writings on the agency, the two authors conclude that the formation of the DIA was a direct response to the 'missile gaps'.

But Wise and Ross also performed a useful task in being amongst the first to identify the problems which were to afflict the DIA over the years, and to speculate about the agencys origins. The authors noted that an important bureaucratic conflict had been central to the formation of the agency: the disagreement between Director of Central Intelligence (DCI) Allen Dulles and Secretary of Defense Robert S. McNamara over military representation on the United States Intelligence Board (USIB).[1] This dispute had significant influence within the bureaucracy during the struggle over the organisation of the new agency. It isolated Robert McNamara – leaving him without allies in his battle to structure the DIA in accordance with the needs of the OSD.

A key actor in the birth of the DIA, Lyman Kirkpatrick, Jr, wrote about his experiences in 1968. Kirkpatrick has a claim to having been the 'father of the DIA' due to his position as chairman of the Joint Study Group on the Foreign Intelligence Activities of the United States: an interdepartmental study group established late in the Eisenhower administration which had recommended a series of intelligence reforms that served as a catalyst for the creation of the DIA. In his book *The Real CIA*, Kirkpatrick provides unparalleled insight into the formation, deliberations and recommendations of the Joint Study Group. Of particular significance is his claim that the recommendation for the consolidation of military intelligence activities was not a novel idea, but rather a innovation consistent with the centralising reforms of the 1958 Defense Reorganisation Act.[2]

Widespread dissatisfaction with the agency, and indeed the entire military intelligence community, occurred in the later years of the Vietnam conflict. It was a result not only of the poor performance of the agency in South-East Asia (particularly with its faulty intelligence estimates), but also of its inability to reduce duplication within the military intelligence effort. From 1961 to 1970, no fewer than six major studies were commissioned by the federal government to probe redundancy within the military intelligence community. All concluded that, despite the establishment of the DIA, the defense intelligence community performed neither effectively nor efficiently.[3] The most infamous of these studies, the 1970 Report to the President and the Secretary of Defense on the Department of Defense by the Blue Ribbon Defense Panel (the Fitzhugh report), was commissioned by President Richard Nixon due to the concern of individuals within his administration (including Secretary of Defense Melvin Laird) that Pentagon intelligence programmes were expanding uncontrolled. The report was extremely critical of the DIA, stating that, while the agency was created to consolidate the intelligence activities of the three armed services, it had in fact resulted in the growth of the individual service intelligence operations. The report concluded: 'The principal problems of the DIA can be summarized as too many jobs and too many masters.'⁴ Thus, it focused upon the conflict between the two primary consumers of DIA products: the OSD and the Joint Staff. The needs of both consumers are dissimilar. The OSD requires national intelligence while the Joint Staff demands battlefield intelligence. The DIA is caught in the middle: it lacks the resources to satisfy both sets of demands fully and the authority to compel the armed services intelligence components to assist it.

The Fitzhugh report also focused on the inability of the DIA to eliminate redundancy within the military intelligence effort. The report seemed to conclude that the agency was inherently flawed, for it recommended radical reorganisation of the agency along functional lines (separating collection and production activities into two agencies). Yet, the Fitzhugh report did not enquire into historical causation. It for this reason neglected the key role that threat assessments played – and still play – in deliberations over optimal ways of organising the intelligence community.

This role was finally examined in the 1970s. In 1973, Major General Daniel Graham, formerly chief of estimates at the DIA, publicly acknowledged the disenchantment with the agencys estimate product, stating: 'To put it bluntly, there is a considerable body of opinion among decision-makers, in and out of the DOD, which regards threat estimates prepared by the military as being self-serving, budget-oriented, and generally inflated.'⁵ This admission added to the growing list of failures of the agency. It also drew attention to a hitherto unexamined facet of the DIAs operations: the preparation of threat assessments. Exploration of this activity would be taken up by later analysts.

Among the first were John Marks and Victor Marchetti. In 1974, the duo accused the DIA of failing to co-ordinate and consolidate intelligence efforts. Moreover, they asserted that the agency had failed to minimise the parochial influences of the armed services in the formulation of the threat assessments. They saw this as a direct result of the establishment of the DIA as an agency subordinate to the JCS. This had forced the agency to respond primarily to the needs of the JCS rather than the Secretary of Defense, making the agency, in effect, the intelligence arm of the Joint Staff. Consequently, the intelligence products of DIA embodied the parochial views of the services rather than the national views of the Secretary of Defense. Although the establishment of the agency under the authority of the JCS had been noted and analysed in the past, Marks and Marchetti were the first to note the impact of this move on intelligence product.[6]

Arnold Kanter carries this argument a step forward. He asserts that threat assessment had been of primary importance to Robert McNamara and his principal concern in pushing for the establishment of the agency. In order to obtain these assessments, Kanter claims that McNamara was forced to grant major concessions to the JCS to gain their support.[7] Consequently, the establishment of the DIA directly under the JCS – the critical mistake so lamented by past analysts – was not accidental. It was a direct concession to the JCS. Kanter states:

> McNamara, who was more concerned about having to deal with conflicting intelligence reports – none of which he trusted – than with improving the quality of military intelligence – which he despaired of – gave control of the DIA to the Chiefs [JCS], and then proceeded to virtually ignore it.[8]

The 1976 report of the Church Committee was the first official government study to embrace the views of Marks and Marchetti and to tie the creation of the DIA to its later failures. In examining both the birth of the agency and its failures, the committee concluded that they were interlinked: 'In retrospect, a strong case can be made that the DIA never really had a chance. Strongly resisted by the military services, the Agency has been a creature of compromise from the outset.'[9] The report also identified the dissimilar concepts which Secretary of Defense Robert McNamara and the JCS originally held concerning the proposed agency. While it noted that the final form of the agency was a result of the bitter bureaucratic struggle, it did not attempt to ascertain whether the compromise favoured the interests of the OSD or the Joint Staff, as did Kanter.

The counterpart of the Church Committee, the House of Representatives' Pike Committee, was not loath to make such controversial judgements and issued a report which was far more critical of the DIA. It concluded that the compromise upon which the DIA was founded had resulted in its failure. The report stated:

> The three independent branches of the military resist any attempt which might curb their authority to direct programming and allocate resources. They undermine the concept on which DIA was founded, by overriding its authority and preventing it from obtaining qualified manpower.[10]

William Corson came to the defence of the agency in 1977. In his book *The Armies of Ignorance* he claimed that most criticism of the agency is unfair: that the agency is charged with near-impossible tasks and does its best to fulfil its missions. Like Ross and Wise, Corson believes that the roots of the DIA are to be found in the 'missile gaps' and the launching of Sputnik. However, he asserted that the principal catalyst for the creation of the agency was the failed Bay of Pigs operation. He concluded that, despite the fierce bureaucratic struggle over the agency, the DIA was established in accordance with the original recommendations of the Joint Study Group.[11]

Finally, both Lawrence Freedman and John Prados have contributed invaluable studies of the role of the DIA in the formation of National Intelligence Estimates. Both believe that the main role of the agency is co-ordinating and consolidating threat assessments. Freedman concludes that the DIA was a result of the 'missile gaps' and thus that the resolution of conflicting service estimates was the Kennedy administration's primary motive in its establishment. He highlights the conflict between the motive of the administration and the motive of the military leaders – preserving the autonomy of the service intelligence components. Freedman believes that the DIA is the flawed compromise which resulted from these dissimilar motives, and claims that the agency was doomed to failure from its creation.[12]

Prados elaborates on these points, while bringing some broader considerations into discussion of establishment of the DIA, including the role of the U-2 affair and the recommendations of the Joint Study Group. To his credit, Prados is one of the few writers to assert that the Bay of Pigs was not a causal factor in the creation of the agency. The strength of his work lies in discussion of the failure of the DIA to fulfil its primary mission of the reduction of the military's role in the formulation of threat assessments, which

Prados views as the original aim of the recommendations of the
Joint Study Group. On this issue his analysis is direct conflict with
that of Corson.[13]

In this chapter, I shall focus upon the role of National Intelligence
Estimates, due to my belief that they were of central importance
in the birth of the agency. I will not explore the other functions
of the agency, such as management reorganisation and collection
requirement reform due to my conviction that they were of peripheral importance. Nor will I document the early years of the agency,
as I am bound by editorial considerations.

My essay is divided into four sections. The first examines the
establishment of the post-war Department of Defense, tracing the
progression towards the centralisation of the activities and functions
of the armed services within the Office of the Secretary of Defense.
Noting the resistance of the military intelligence community to this
trend, the first section explores the failures of military intelligence
during the 1950s and concludes that some consolidation of the
service intelligence elements was inevitable. The second section
examines the key actors in the creation of the agency – Secretary
of Defense McNamara and the Joint Chiefs of Staff – and ponders
their goals and motives. Consequently, the significance of National
Intelligence Estimates in the formation of the DIA is investigated.
The third section explores the effect of the Bay of Pigs on the
deliberations over the agency and probes the events leading up to
the official establishment of the agency on 1 August, 1961. It highlights the failure of the DIA to rise above parochial military
interests. The final section aims to explain the mistakes of 1961 and
weighs their consequences.

The seeds of the postwar intelligence community are to be found
in the ashes of Pearl Harbor. In the aftermath of the Second World
War, the bombing of Pearl Harbor was perceived to be emblematic
of the pre-war failures of American intelligence. It was believed,
that had there been better co-ordination and communication
between the disparate and largely autonomous government agencies involved in the national intelligence effort, the disaster could
have been prevented. This led President Truman to establish the
Central Intelligence Group in 1946 – a small interim agency composed of an interdepartmental staff charged with co-ordinating the
national intelligence effort. However, the hardening of the cold war
and increased tensions in Europe reinforced the conviction of many
American policy-makers that a permanent central intelligence body

needed to be established to counter the nascent 'Soviet threat'. It was apparent to many in Washington that the Central Intelligence Group was unsuited for such a role.[14] While there was broad agreement among civilian policymakers over the need for greater centralisation in intelligence, there was considerable disagreement over the degree of consolidation necessary to improve efficacy. Moreover, the military, particularly the navy, opposed almost all proposals to effect reform, often advanced as some form of consolidation of the military services, desiring to preserve their considerable autonomy. They argued that, although centralisation is desirable in some realms, it is undesirable in intelligence, for it would ultimately result in an unwieldy bureaucracy which would be unresponsive to the differing tactical intelligence needs of each service.[15] Many civilians dissented, arguing that centralisation was essential in order to facilitate improved communication and greater coordination between the disparate members of the American intelligence community.

Eventually a compromise was fashioned, embodied in the National Security Act of 1947. The Act was an attempt to balance the interests of the contending sides: it strengthened and consolidated civilian authority over the military services by bringing the War, Navy and newly formed Air Force Departments together under a single Secretary of Defense – placating many advocates of military centralisation; yet the separate identities of the services were preserved and strengthened – a clear concession to military leaders. Although theoretically the Secretary of Defense was directed to exercise '*general* direction, authority, and control' over the military departments, and to take appropriate steps to eliminate duplication and overlapping, in reality he lacked the means to do so. He had little statutory power to compel services to follow his lead. In fact, the services still retained considerable autonomy. As a result, a form of loose federalism prevailed in the embryonic Department of Defense, with a weak Secretary of Defense exercising 'general authority' over the stronger military services.[16]

The weakness of the National Security Act of 1947 was immediately apparent. Lacking clear authority to run the fledgling Department of Defense, the Secretary of Defense was dependent upon the goodwill of the services. Often this goodwill was not forthcoming. In the absence of central authority, the services became mired in petty bureaucratic infighting, each subordinating the national interest to organisational self-interest.[17] Confronting this rampant parochialism, Congress and the Truman administration sought to strengthen the authority of the Secretary of Defense *vis-à-vis* the military services by enacting the 1949 amendment to the National Security Act. The three military departments were eliminated as executive departments, and the Department of Defense was created to envelop the services. Although the services continued to be administered by their respective Secretaries, they were now made directly responsible to the direction, authority and control of the Secretary of Defense.

Further reforms effected greater centralisation in military activities and expedited the consolidation of power within the DOD into the Office of the Secretary of Defense. In 1953 the DOD was reorganised by President Eisenhower (with congressional approval) with the intention of directing the focus of the Joint Chiefs of Staff away from their respective parent services, towards their national responsibilities. In all, the 1953 reorganisation abetted the trend towards the centralisation of power and authority in the Office of the Secretary of Defense.[18]

None the less the 1953 reorganisation failed to appease many critics of the DOD. They believed that the OSD required still greater power: it should possess comprehensive and indisputable authority over the leviathan named the DOD. Moreover, in a department saturated with waste and duplication, they claimed that the Secretary of Defense must be allowed to take active measures to promote efficiency and eliminate duplication.[19] For a time these critics were ignored. Yet the launching of Sputnik on 4 October, 1957, fortified these arguments and served as a catalyst for the reforms of 1958.

As Sputnik shocked the American scientific and intellectual communities, so to did it cause great upheaval in Washington and at the Pentagon. At the behest of President Truman, Congress passed a new amendment to the National Security Act of 1947 known as the 1958 Reorganisation Act. Among other things, the Act gave the Secretary of Defense greater authority to delve into traditional service activities in order to direct military research and development. It also called for the establishment of 'unified' and 'specified' military commands, and removed the individual military departments from the chain of command over operational forces. Overall, the 1958 Reorganisation Act further shifted the balance of power at the Pentagon away from the services, towards the Office of the Secretary of Defense and the collective Joint Chiefs of Staff.[20]

The most significant and controversial provision of the 1958 Reorganisation Act was the McCormack–Curtis Amendment, which is section 202(c)(6) of the National Security Act (as amended). It states:

> (6) Whenever the Secretary of Defense determines it will be advantageous to the Government in terms of effectiveness, economy, or efficiency, he shall provide for the carrying out of any supply or service activity common to more than one military department by a single agency or each other organisational entities as he deems appropriate.[21]

The amendment was adopted by the House of Representatives during floor action on the 1958 Reorganisation Act on 12 June, 1958. One of its co-sponsors, John W. McCormack (Speaker of the House of Representatives) explained, prior to the amendments approval, that it was intended expressly to include:

> procurement, warehousing, distribution, cataloging, and other supply activities, surplus, disposal, financial management, budgeting, disbursing, accounting, and so forth, medical and hospital services, transportation – land, sea, and air – *intelligence*, legal, public relations, recruiting, military police, training, liaison activities, and so forth [Italics added][22]

The amendment was intended to give the Secretary of Defense the necessary authority to fulfil his legal responsibilities, as stated in Section 202(c)(1) of the National Security Act (as amended), 'to take appropriate steps (including the transfer, reassignment, abolition, and consolidation of service functions) to provide in the Department of Defense for more effective, efficient, and economical administration and operation, and to eliminate duplication.'[23] It allows the Secretary of Defense to effect further centralisation by consolidating common service functions and placing them under the direct control of the OSD rather than the individual services. However, it is important to note that such consolidation could only be implemented in the name of greater efficiency and/or the elimination of duplication.

Historically, Congress had resisted a unilateral defence concept and insisted that the services not be merged.[24] Thus it was wary of any proposal which might endow the Secretary of Defense with the power to fuse the services. The amendment was passed only after extensive debate in which many members of Congress were persuaded to endorse the proposal due to their impression that it would bring about substantial savings in the procurement of common-use military items.[25] Yet future Secretaries of Defense would interpret the amendment broadly (as its sponsors had), employing the amendment to justify further centralisation within the DOD in the name of 'greater efficiency' and the 'elimination of duplication'. By the 1970s, successive Secretaries of Defense would use this amendment to sanction the transfer of most of the service activities to eight unified commands and ten 'superagencies'. The military services would eventually retain only training and logistic capabilities.[26]

From 1947 to the present, therefore, the trend within the DOD has been toward increasing centralisation. The power and authority of the Secretary of Defense has repeatedly been strengthened *vis-à-vis* the military services, and the focus of the JCS has been turned towards joint responsibilities. The successive reorganisations, culminating in the 1958 Reorganisation Act, gave the OSD almost complete control over the DOD. Since the 'support' and 'command' lines ran directly to the Secretary of Defense, he was able to exert direct supervision over almost all military functions.

Yet in 1958, military intelligence still escaped his grasp. Regardless of the centralisation which was occurring within the DOD as a whole, throughout the 1940s and 1950s military intelligence remained autarchic. While the National Security Act of 1947 consolidated American civilian intelligence efforts under the aegis of the Central Intelligence Agency (CIA), the military services were allowed to maintain control of their individual intelligence components by citing their need for specialised tactical intelligence. The creation of the CIA was facilitated by the absence of pre-existing vested interests among the civilian intelligence components of the magnitude of the military agencies. Although the 1947 Act did create the Joint Intelligence Group (JIG), a small interdepartmental body housed within the Joint Staff, ostensibly to provide greater military intelligence co-ordination, its limited size and lack of clear authority caused it to be largely ineffective. Parochial interests continued to prevail. William Corson notes:

> The JIG represented the military's acceptance of an armistice-type organisation in which the various intelligence services would agree to discuss problems of common interest *without surrendering any of their perquisites*, and cooperate with each other beyond the strict criteria of self-interest [emphasis added].[27]

During this era the military services jealously guarded their individual intelligence components. The result was a military intelligence community composed of fiercely independent bureaucratic entities which looked to their parent service for guidance rather than to the Secretary of Defense or the DCI. One former military intelligence officer noted that the system most closely resembled a 'tribal federation'.[28] Each service separately collected, produced and distributed intelligence for its own use. Each service was also responsible for supplying its intelligence products to the OSD and other involved government entities. The result was a military intelligence system which was inefficient and duplicatory. Moreover, the system fostered an 'extremely parochial approach in each services analyses of enemy capabilities'.[29] This, in turn, prevented the formulation of unified military intelligence estimates (or threat assessments) – a commodity increasingly demanded by Washington policy-makers.[30]

By 1950 the failure of the JIG to obtain greater co-operation between the military intelligence elements was manifest. The JIG lacked the size and, more importantly, the authority to compel the services to co-operate more efficiently. Furthermore, the JIG was in the impossible position of having to serve two masters – the OSD and the JCS. The needs of these two agencies were dissimilar: the JCS tended to be more concerned with battlefield (tactical) intelligence, while the OSD required national (strategic) intelligence. The JIG simply lacked the necessary manpower and statutory authority to satisfy the requirements of both groups.

The 1953 reorganisation of the DOD sought to remedy this situation by creating the Office of Special Operations (OSO) within the OSD. This office was headed by an Assistant Secretary of Defense for Special Operations, who sat on the National Security Council and was responsible for providing intelligence staff support to the OSD. It was intended that the OSO would replace the JIG in serving the intelligence needs of the Secretary of Defense, thus allowing the JIG to concentrate on the tactical intelligence requirements of the JCS. Additionally, the OSO was charged to serve as a point of co-ordination for Defense intelligence activities and a liaison with civilian intelligence agencies. Yet the OSO found itself in much the same position as the JIG: it was dependent upon the services for raw intelligence, but lacked a clear mandate and therefore the power to impel the services to provide this intelligence and co-operate in joint projects. Thus, its effort to gain the collaboration of the services in formulating unified national intelligence estimates for civilian policy-makers was largely a failure.

This failure was evident in the 1950s. The decade was dominated by bickering within the American intelligence community over the 'bomber gap', and later the 'missile gap'. At heart, the 'gaps' were a dispute between the military intelligence elements over Soviet strategic capabilities. Attempts to estimate the quantity and the quality of Soviet long-range bombers, and later inter-continental ballistic missiles (ICBMs), provided the intelligence agencies with what defence analyst Lawrence Freedman termed a 'traumatic and critical experience which affects attitudes . . . to this day' [1977].[31] The air force's exaggeration of Soviet strategic capabilities and of the 'gaps' between them and those of the USA highlighted the divisions and lack of leadership within the intelligence community. Freedman notes: 'There seems little doubt that the Air Force from the start was determined to prove the existence of a Soviet [strategic] programme of massive proportions, whatever violence the arguments employed did to evidence or logic.'[32]

The air force, which controlled both the US bomber and ICBM arsenal, was the obvious beneficiary of its own exaggerated Soviet bomber and missile estimates. The acceptance of the air force's assertions of a huge Soviet strategic build-up by Washington policy-makers compelled them to reciprocate with an American counter-build-up, resulting in increased funding (hence, increased power and prestige) to the air force and its strategic programmes. It was apparent to many observers that the air force was using its intelligence agencies to engage in 'profiteering'.[33]

To make matters worse, army and navy intelligence were issuing estimates which confused matters in that they tended to play down the Soviet build-up, primarily not because of differing empirical evidence, but 'because of a general inclination to disagree with the Air Force on almost any issue.'[34] The dispute was exacerbated by the fact that it was made public in 1956, during congressional hearings on the fiscal 1957 budget. Thus, the quarrel within the intelligence community was to acquire political dimensions. In all, the conflict would emphasise the divergent goals and viewpoints within the loose confederation of semi-autonomous military intelligence agencies. Conversely, the CIA estimates were fairly accurate and reflected favourably upon the centralised civilian component of the intelligence community.[35]

The 1958 Reorganisation Act did little to redress the failures of military intelligence. The JIG became the J-2 of the Joint Staff: a change in name only. Its manpower and mandate were not substantially altered, and thus it still was unable to force the intelligence community to concur on a much-needed product: unified national intelligence estimates. In all, the 1958 reforms of military intelligence were largely cosmetic. Once again, military intelligence was able to evade the tides of centralisation which swept through the DOD.

Ultimately, the 'missile gap' debate ended when 'hard' intelligence provided by the Soviet mole Oleg Penkovsky (and confirmed by U-2 overflights) conclusively proved that the Soviet Union was engaged only in a modest strategic build-up.[36] Not surprisingly, in the last years of the Eisenhower administration there was widespread discontent with military intelligence. The deliberations of the United States Intelligence Board (USIB), an interdepartmental working group whose main tasks were issuing National Intelligence Estimates (finished intelligence products which were intended to reflect the judgement of the whole of the American intelligence community on important national security issues) and setting intelligence collection requirements and priorities, were marked by long and bitter controversies over the conflicting bomber and missile estimates. The resolution of these conflicting estimates into a single National Intelligence Estimate (NIE) was arduous at best. Often, in order to gain the approval of all agencies involved on the entire estimate, it was necessary to allow individual agencies to file footnotes in the body of the estimate. Consequently, the finished estimates were often filled with myriad dissenting footnotes, which served to undercut the strength of the documents conclusion, hence reducing its utility to policy-makers. This resulted in extensive disillusionment among senior administration officials with the effectiveness of the JIG with regard to co-ordinating military input to threat assessments.[37]

This disenchantment prompted President Eisenhower to propose a review of the entire American intelligence effort in 1959. At his behest, the Bureau of the Budget (BOB) reviewed with greater rigour than before the size and the scope of US intelligence activities. Moreover, the BOB proposed two studies designed to evaluate thoroughly the effectiveness of the present intelligence system. However, resolute opposition of the military to these studies resulted in their postponement and eventual cancellation.[38]

Yet, the U-2 affair of May 1960 finally shattered resistance to investigative studies of military intelligence and set in motion a chain of events which would culminate in the establishment of the

DIA. The downing of a secret American U-2 reconnaissance aircraft over the Soviet Union and the subsequent capture of its pilot Francis Powers resulted in widespread criticism of US covert surveillance activities. Moreover, the failure of the intelligence agencies to make the 'cover story' credible and thereby validate 'plausible deniability' convinced the Eisenhower administration that the time had come to examine the possibility of consolidating the services' general intelligence (defined rather clumsily as all non-SIGINT, non-overhead, non-organic activities) to facilitate the formulation of NIEs and improve coordination in order to prevent a recurrence of the U-2 incident.[39] By now, a good number of senior officials believed that the consolidation of military intelligence was long overdue: that intelligence, like the command and support functions, should be removed from the service domains and made more responsive to the authority of the OSD.[40]

Therefore an interagency study group was established, named the Joint Study Group on the Foreign Intelligence Activities of the United States. It operated under the auspices of the Director of Central Intelligence and was chaired by the CIA Inspector-General, Lyman Kirkpatrick, Jr. It was composed of representatives from the State Department, the White House, the DOD, the BOB and the CIA.[41] The group examined US intelligence activities throughout the summer and autumn of 1960, paying particular attention to military intelligence because its terms of reference directed it to explore: 'The present military intelligence coordination machinery and its relationship to the intelligence community – with particular attention to possibilities for closer integration under the authority of the DOD Reorganization Act of 1958.[42]

By now, a debate was occurring within the Eisenhower administration concerning the most effective approach to centralising the intelligence community. As early as mid-October 1960, the Joint Study Group had indicated to the administration that they believed that they could make some helpful recommendations for improving military intelligence, 'including greater integration of intelligence activities and the elimination of unnecessary duplication'.[43] Within the administration the issue in contention became the best means by which to effect the coming recommendations. Eisenhower personally believed that the answer was to create a large military central intelligence agency within the Joint Staff. This belief was based on his conviction that the JCS should be given more power with which to focus on their joint 'national' responsibilities. Eisenhower hoped that this would serve to minimise their service

interests. Yet he acknowledged that military intelligence reform
would be difficult, asserting that 'the hardest thing to destroy in
this world is entrenched bureaucracy and [the] intelligence agencies
are among the worst.'[44] Two alternative proposals were considered
by the administration: to vest co-ordinating responsibility of *all*
intelligence activities (including DOD) in the DCI, or to situate
co-ordinating responsibility for the DOD in a new government
agency or official. Additionally, there was also considerable debate
over whether new legislation would be required to implement
these alternatives, or whether the existing legislation (the National
Security Act, as amended) was sufficient.[45]

Significantly, a DOD memorandum in October, 1960, concluded
that the role of the DCI to 'exercise strong, centralised direction'
within the DOD was limited to national (strategic) intelligence.
Since the DCI had no statutory authority over departmental intelligence, he had no authority over the service intelligence efforts.
However, the memorandum did observe:

> Under the Defense Reorganization Act of 1958, the Secretary
> of Defense is empowered to take the necessary steps (other
> than a merger of the services) to provide for efficient adminis-
> tration and '*to eliminate duplication*' within Defense [Empha-
> sis in original document].[46]

Note the emphasis on the elimination of duplication. In effect, the
memorandum suggests that the Secretary of Defense is legally
empowered to enact any reform provided that the ostensible justification is to 'eliminate duplication'. In fact, Secretary of Defense
Thomas Gates had used used this provision of the National Security
Act, complemented by the McCormack–Curtis Amendment, to
establish the Defense Communications Agency (DCA) on 12 May,
1960. The DCA was charged with reporting to the OSD *through
the JCS*, and was authorised to act as the single manager for all
DOD long-haul, point-to-point government communications.[47] Surprisingly, there was little congressional or military resistance to its
creation. No doubt the implication of this consolidation was not lost
on civilians in OSD – that the military could be further reorganised
and centralised under the existing legislation. The above memorandum is significant in that it illustrates the shift in consensus that
was occurring among senior officials in the Eisenhower administration: that the authority for further reorganisation need not come
from outside the DOD (i.e. Congress), but that it could come from

within (i.e. the Secretary of Defense). Whereas in 1958 the OSD had turned to Congress for the legislative authority to enact DOD reorganisation, now, in late 1960, the OSD believed that it had the necessary authority to enact reform on its own. This was an important shift, for the new administration would inherit this belief.

Ironically, an advisory committee set up by President-elect Kennedy immediately after his election to examine the prospects for further DOD reorganisation, the Kennedy Committee on the Defense Establishment, would conclude the opposite. In its on 5 December report to the President-elect, the committee asserted that previous legislation had failed to give the OSD the executive power needed to exercise the necessary control over the DOD. It confronted the issue head-on: noting that some analysts believed that the existing legislation gives ample basis for the Secretary of Defense to exert complete authority while others believed the contrary, the committee sided with the latter, stating: 'It is the conclusion of this Committee that the doctrine of civilian control will be compromised as long as any doubts exist on this vital point.'[48] The committee censured the current DOD, firmly placing the blame for lack of efficacy on the services. It asserted: 'the present multiple layers of control and overlapping among military programs and operations [are] caused by steadily increasing inter-service rivalry'.[49] Thus, it concluded: 'In short, there is a clear need for defense interest rather than particular service interest.'[50] It recommended the passage of radical new legislation to effect the elimination of the separate armed services and to reinforce the powers of OSD 'to make the Secretary of Defense the civilian official in the DOD with unquestioned authority and control over *all elements* of the DOD at *all levels.*' (Emphasis in original document).[51] The Kennedy Committee on the Defense Establishment rejected the pluralistic bureaucratic organisation of the contemporary DOD, instead espousing a single manager concept. The President-elect was strongly influenced by the report of the committee – in his search for a Secretary of Defense he would seek (and find) a strong executive to implement this new management concept within the DOD.

On 15 December, 1960 the report of the Joint Study Group (also called the Kirkpatrick report, after its chairman) was submitted to the Eisenhower administration. The National Security Council endorsed it on 18 January, 1961, and called for the implementation of its forty-eight recommendations as swiftly as possible. As expected, the report was extremely critical of the military intelligence system, branding it 'duplicatory and cumbersome'. It noted the failure of the JIG to serve as a 'focal point' for the Secretary of Defense and to effectively co-ordinate National Intelligence Estimates.[52] The thrust of its recommendations was aimed at centralising the military intelligence effort. Due to its concern over the possibility of military domination of the USIB (of the six members on the current USIB, four represented the military), the Joint Study Group recommended limiting the armed services to observer status and creating a co-ordinating agency which would represent the armed services as a voting member. The chairman of the Joint Study Group, Lyman Kirkatrick, Jr, has noted:

> The report had not specifically, in so many words, recommended the creation of the Defense Intelligence Agency, but had made recommendations directed toward streamlining the military intelligence system in order to reorganize it, as the Defense Reorganization Act of 1958 had streamlined and modernized the command and operations system.[53]

Kirkpatrick correctly places the report of the Joint Study Group in historical perspective: it was not an anomaly, but rather it represented the latest in a long series of attempts to effect greater centralisation within the DOD. The military intelligence components had managed to escape past consolidations, not due to negligence, but due to the resolute bureaucratic resistance of the services to any attempt to encroach upon their sacrosanct intelligence elements. They were motivated by neither pride nor contempt, but by simple organisational self-interest. Yet in early 1961, it appeared that they could resist the winds of change no longer. Secretary of Defense Gates had given the JCS a copy of the Joint Study Group report in January and asked the military leaders to consider ways and means of consolidating their intelligence functions, particularly in the strategic field.[54] However, the JCS were not able to complete their evaluation of the report before the Kennedy administration entered office on 20 January, 1961, thus leaving the future of the Joint Study Group's recommendations in doubt. Would the new administration endorse the report? The military was uncertain, yet it prepared for the worst. As the new administration replaced the old, the Pentagon readied itself to battle for the most jealously guarded military fiefdom: that of intelligence.

The eighth Secretary of Defense of the United States of America would be Robert S. McNamara – the supremely rational technocrat. In 1960 McNamara was the foremost practitioner of the new management technique of systems control; applying its methodology with spectacular success first at the air force during the Second World War under Charles Thornton, and later at the Ford Motor Company. His achievement at Ford was unparalleled: he and his fellow disciples of modern analytical methods (who would eventually become known as the 'Whiz Kids') transformed Ford from an ageing, inefficient dinosaur into a streamlined, competitive giant in the automobile industry. In the process, McNamara emerged as the pre-eminent Whiz Kid and rose quickly within Ford, eventually becoming the president. He relinquished this position after a mere month to accept the post offered to him by the President-elect: the Office of the Secretary of Defense.

The Herculean task which now confronted McNamara was that of converting the DOD from the paradigm of waste and inefficiency into an efficient and cost-effective department. McNamara had accepted the office on the conditions that he be allowed to choose his own men to staff the DOD and, further, that he be allowed after studying the controversial report of the Kennedy Committee on the Defense Establishment to decide personally whether the radical reorganisation of the DOD it recommended was necessary. Kennedy agreed and gave his new Secretary of Defense a single directive: 'to determine and provide what we needed to safeguard our security without arbitrary budget limits, but to do so as economically as possible'.[55] This directive was a consequence of Kennedy's campaign strategy. During the election Kennedy had harshly criticised the Eisenhower administrations defence policies, utilising the 'missile gaps' to support his claims that America had lost its strategic superiority and that Eisenhower had 'gone soft' on communism. Thus, upon winning the election, Kennedy was pledged to overhaul the DOD and restore America's strategic superiority. McNamara was charged with fulfilling this pledge.

McNamara seized the initiative. After accepting the office from Kennedy in late 1960, he immediately consulted defence experts and former DOD officials on the current state of the Pentagon. Outgoing Secretary of Defense Thomas Gates advised his successor to ponder both the recommendations of the Joint Study Group and a Pentagon study entitled the Air University Black Book of Reorganisation Papers. The latter, representing the views of many senior officials late in the Eisenhower administration, concluded that the Secretary of Defense had extensive authority under the

National Security Act, but had failed to wield it.[56] The combined effect of the two documents was to persuade the new Secretary of Defense not to seek new legislation for reorganisation of the DOD. McNamara would later state:

> From the beginning in January, 1961, it seemed to me that the principal problem in efficient management of the Department's resources was not the lack of management authority. The National Security Act provides the Secretary of Defense a full measure of power. The problem was rather the absence of the essential management tools needed to make sound decisions on the really crucial issues of national security.[57]

By the time that McNamara was officially sworn into office, he had already identified many of the problems which plagued the DOD, and had created working groups of civilian specialists to examine these problems. To centre these working groups McNamara established the Office for Management Planning and Organizational Studies (OMPOS) and appointed Solis Horwitz as its director. By creating OMPOS, McNamara hoped to bypass the entrenched bureaucracy at the Pentagon and sought fresh approaches in solving the old problems which infected the DOD.

McNamara brought a new form of leadership to the Pentagon. His 'active management' technique was a radical departure from the traditionally cloistered, bureaucratic, bargaining method of policy formulation which had long reigned in the DOD. McNamara rejected the traditional method as cumbersome and inefficient. Instead he espoused a centralised, administrative, single-manager concept. Order would be imposed from the top down, with power and authority being concentrated in the OSD. Through the use of systems analysis, McNamara and his 'Whiz Kids' applied the strict standards of cost-effectiveness to Pentagon programs. In its simplest terms, cost effectiveness seeks to determine whether a specific programme need be implemented and, if so, how best to do it. McNamara's management strategy was the fitting conclusion to the decade of congressional and executive attempts to strengthen the power of the Secretary of Defense. McNamara was symbolic of the first generation of rational (as opposed to political) public policymakers. As one analyst notes:

> It is clear that while a creative, reinforcing tension between military and civilian professionalism is indispensable to

national security policy, the thrust of the new management
has been to neutralize such pluralism. The new management
is, in a word, apolitical.[58]

After officially assuming office, McNamara immediately set out
to examine and remedy the 'missile gap' and to discern what needed
to be done to restore American strategic superiority. He soon discovered that the allegations of the Eisenhower administration had
been accurate: the 'missile gap' did not exist – it was a fond illusion
concocted by air force intelligence. McNamara first publicly
revealed his disillusionment with the 'missile gap' to reporters at
an off-the-record session at the Pentagon on 6 February, 1961.[59]
His rejection of the 'missile gap' theory caused quite a stir in
Washington, particularly since it had been a major election issue.

McNamara's examination of the 'missile gap' and the state of
military intelligence left him disturbed.[60] He felt that the military
had allowed political (particularly budgetary) influences to cloud
their objectivity – resulting in biased intelligence estimates by the
armed services. In his view, intelligence was essentially a quantifi-
able matter, ideally limited to a careful compilation of the numbers
of weapons and equipment on each side. He was sceptical of any
efforts by the intelligence agencies to go beyond this base and into
predictive dimensions, such as judging weapon effectiveness and
enemy intentions. To McNamara, intelligence of the latter sort
was simply conjecture. Thus he became convinced of the need to
eliminate service bias from the threat assessments, for they had
played a prominent role in advancing the myth of the 'missile
gap'. McNamara believed that current military intelligence was too
loaded with political implications – it seemed consistently to play
a role in arguments over the size of the American military establishment.[61] He was convinced that it was essential for senior policymakers to be provided with objective intelligence free of political and
organisational bias. To accomplish this it would be necessary to
remove the evaluative capabilities from the services, leaving them
only with collection functions. Consequently, the services would
handle only raw intelligence. Evaluation would occur at a higher
level in the DOD – within the OSD. In this way, decision making
would be removed from the armed services and kept confined to
the highest levels of government. Thus, it is not surprising that
McNamara endorsed the recommendations of the Joint Study
Group.

On 8 February, 1961 the JCS presented McNamara with the

draft proposal for the consolidation of the service intelligence efforts called for by the Joint Study Group and requested by his predecessor, Thomas Gates. Their proposal called for the creation of a central military intelligence agency.[62] Under the JCS plan, this agency would function as a co-ordinating and integrating body for military intelligence. The individual service intelligence elements would, of course, retain partial autonomy, to ensure responsiveness to the tactical needs of the parent service. Predictably, the JCS recommended that the agency be made subordinate to them, rather than to the OSD. They also recommended that the agency be established slowly, in an evolutionary manner, to avoid disruption in the service intelligence efforts. Though the proposed agency would be a voting member of the USIB, it would first be answerable to a military intelligence board which would effectively safeguard the organisational interests of the JCS.[63]

Essentially the JCS proposal was an enhanced version of the current J-2 (formerly the JIG). Like its predecessor, the military intelligence agency was designed to have little statutory authority over the services; thus it would lack the power to effect any true consolidation. The JCS proposal was, in fact, a paper tiger: the reforms were largely superficial, designed to preserve the autonomy of the service intelligence elements. This type of self-serving proposal was characteristic of the JCS. Although the members of the JCS are charged with dual roles – each is responsible for the supervision of his parent service and for his collective duties as a member of the Joint Staff – the former role tends to prevail. The prevalence of parochialism among the JCS prompted the Rockefeller report of 1958 to refer to the JCS as 'a committee of partisan adversaries'. Yet despite such parochialism, they coalesced to battle a common enemy – McNamara – to safeguard a common asset – their intelligence components.

McNamara did not view this proposal favourably. Experienced in bureaucratic politics, he recognised organisational protectionism. He desired a greater level of consolidation in the military intelligence effort. The OMPOS had examined the DOD intelligence activities at McNamara's request and had concluded that a centralising military intelligence agency should be established directly under the OSD to improve the responsiveness of the agency to the demands of senior policy-makers.[64] This was in accord with McNamara's personal convictions concerning intelligence, as previously noted. Moreover, McNamara sought a means to resolve the conflicting service estimates. His ability to overhaul strategic thinking within the Pentagon was dependent to a large extent upon his ability to attain unified NIEs. He saw a central military intelligence agency as an opportunity to remove the evaluative capabilities from the service components (which would reduce service bias), and to replace the three oft-feuding service representatives with a single representative from the agency. This would make it easier to achieve a consensus at USIB meetings, and this, in turn, would facilitate the formulation of NIEs. This was Robert McNamara's *primary objective* in establishing the Defense Intelligence Agency: the consolidation of conflicting service estimates. He would later write: 'I believed that removing the preparation of intelligence estimates from the *control* of the military services would reduce the *risk* that service biases – *unconscious* though they might be – would color the estimates' (emphasis his own).[65]

To understand why NIEs were so important to McNamara, one must examine the broad reforms that the Kennedy administration sought to achieve within the DOD. In the context of American strategic doctrine, the administration sought to alter radically the foundation of the US nuclear deterrence concept. Prior to the Kennedy administration, America had relied upon a single rigid concept of nuclear deterrence: that of massive retaliation. Consequently, this predilection to rely on nuclear weapons for universal deterrence contributed to a decline in American conventional forces. To McNamara and the administration, the DOD's 'all or nothing' approach to nuclear deterrence was foolish: they believed that a more diversified force structure was desirable to cope with the wide range of possible nuclear and non-nuclear conflicts, and so provide Washington policy-makers with a broader choice of options.[66]

Upon entering office, McNamara embarked upon 'a general reassessment of our military forces in relation to our national security policies and objectives'.[67] This was nothing less than a wholesale re-examination of American strategic thinking. As a result, McNamara decided that it was necessary to rebuild conventional forces and upgrade nuclear forces to improve their alert status and reduce vulnerability. National Intelligence Estimates played a crucial role in McNamara's reassessment and, consequently, the reforms he would advocate. These threat assessments represent the judgement of the US intelligence community as to the quantitative and qualitative strategic capabilities and political intentions of the Soviet Union and other national entities. NIEs combine analysis of past and current intelligence data with evaluative judgements on the consequences and efficacy of proposed policies. While a full discussion of the role that NIEs play in influencing American strategic policies is beyond the scope of this dissertation, it is necessary to emphasise that NIEs essentially frame the terms of debate as to the appropriate American response. It can be illustrated simply. If an NIE reports that the Soviet Union is ready to deploy a new generation of ICBMs, American policy-makers and military planners must respond to the NIE and debate the most effective US counter-measure to the Soviet ICBMs. It is important to note that the NIE is the catalyst for the debate and provides the data base for subsequent discussion.

The Kennedy administration entered office committed to altering American nuclear deterrence policy. Its policy of 'flexible response' sought to give American policy-makers more options in response to enemy aggression. Yet when the Kennedy administration sought to introduce their new policy they encountered a major obstacle: the intelligence agencies were having difficulty agreeing on NIEs. Each agency involved tended to advance self-serving lines in the formulation of the threat appraisals. As previously noted, this resulted in discord among the service intelligence components on the USIB, and impaired the formulation of consensus threat assessments. Without agreement on these critical intelligence estimates there could be no foundation for meaningful discussion on the new flexible-response policy which McNamara and the administration so desperately wanted to implement. The situation was analogous to attempting to win a debate by employing valid logical reasoning when there is still broad disagreement over the basic premises: it is an exercise in futility. Caught in this dilemma, McNamara turned to the Joint Study Group's recommendation to establish a central military intelligence agency (i.e. the DIA) as a solution. By taking away from the individual services the preparation of estimates, he hoped to neutralise parochialism and force military intelligence to agree to a unified NIE. These putative threat assessments could then be used to establish a firm foundation (or data base) upon which he could push the administration's new policy of flexible response. The elimination of service dissent within NIEs was crucial to the Kennedy administration's reassessment of American nuclear policy and the thoroughgoing reforms it would enact as a consequence.

Additionally, in the context of the increasing centralisation of DOD activities, the DIA seemed the next logical step in the consolidation of military activities. The OSD had been poorly served by both the JIG and the J-2, and therefore McNamara must have been attracted to the concept of a DIA subservient to the Secretary of Defense. Historically, the Secretary of Defense had been in the paradoxical position of being responsible for the bulk of US intelligence collection but lacking any effective means of co-ordination. The DIA appeared to be the solution to this problem. By establishing the DIA under the OSD, McNamara could ensure that it would above all be responsive to the national intelligence needs of the Secretary of Defense rather than the tactical needs of the JCS. Furthermore, the creation of the DIA under the direct authority of McNamara was consistent with his determination to 'utilize better the service assets to support policymakers and force planners, and to achieve management economies'.[68] As originally conceived by McNamara, the DIA would serve the national interest rather than the narrow interests of the armed services.

It was also intended that the DIA would eliminate, or at least drastically reduce, duplication within the military intelligence effort. Yet, as will be shown, McNamara was increasingly forced to sacrifice this aim in order to gain the support of the JCS for his primary objective and the overall establishment of the DIA. Yet the 'elimination of duplication' would still dominate Pentagon statements and documents on the proposed agency, leading many to believe, incorrectly, that the elimination of duplication was the *primary* aim of the DIA. These public statements were specious: NIEs were of primary import, not duplication or inefficiency.

By mid-February 1961 the bureaucratic battle lines had been drawn over the DIA. McNamara and the JCS each wanted a different DIA, created to conform to their individual needs. The JCS realised that some form of centralisation of their coveted intelligence components was inevitable; yet they were determined to limit the extent and effectiveness of the consolidation as much as possible. McNamara wanted to establish an agency which would be responsive to the intelligence needs of the Secretary of Defense, yet he recognised that military opposition to such a move ran deep. It appeared to many in Washington that a compromise would necessarily ensue. As both sides mobilised bureaucratic allies for the dispute, DCI Allen Dulles, long an adversary of the military, placed his considerable reputation behind the JCS proposal. He feared, correctly, that McNamara wanted to remove the service intelligence components from the USIB and replace them with a single DIA representative.[69]

This idea made Dulles and senior CIA officials apprehensive

because they feared that such a move would result in the CIA no longer having direct access to raw military intelligence, leaving civilians dependent solely on the judgement of the DIA.[70] Although the USIB meetings were often tumultuous, the frequent open disagreement between the services allowed the CIA and civilian officials to see the divisions within the military intelligence community on raw data and its interpretation. The establishment of the DIA changed all this. The consolidated military posture created by a single DIA representative would, in effect, suppress dissent within the military intelligence community. Civilians on the USIB would be forced to accept DIA estimates unquestioningly, since they would have no other military sources for data. As one former State Department official noted: 'It was desirable to maintain enough service tension to flush out service interests.'[71] Furthermore, a unified military intelligence community could also threaten traditional areas of civilian dominance. In private, civilian officials complained that the establishment of the DIA would prevent the State Department and CIA from playing the services against one another as they had in the past: the strategy of 'divide and conquer' would become ineffective against their military rivals.[72] Thus Dulles, a most unlikely ally, would support the JCS position that the military service representatives should not be merged into a single DIA representative.

The merits of both the McNamara and the JCS proposals were hotly debated in the Pentagon, where the bureaucratic infighting was exceptionally fierce.[73] Upon reviewing this struggle, one respected policy-maker concluded: 'Powerful interests in the military opposed, and continue to oppose, more centralised management of intelligence activities.'[74] This was certainly true in the spring of 1961. The conflict over the DIA raged into April: a month which held the Bay of Pigs and the compromise which would eventually result in the establishment of the Defense Intelligence Agency.

The relationship of the Bay of Pigs to the formation of the DIA is a contentious issue among historians. While many believe that the disaster was critical to the creation of the DIA, few agree on how. None the less, it is certain that the timing of the failed invasion of Cuba was portentous: it occurred in the midst of the furious debate within the Pentagon over military centralisation in April 1961. The Bay of Pigs, like the U-2 affair which preceded it, publicly exposed the fragmentation within the American intelligence community.

The plan for the invasion originated in the Directorate of Plans of the CIA late in the Eisenhower administration. By the time the Kennedy administration entered office, the planned invasion had developed considerable bureaucratic momentum and was forcefully presented to the new President by Deputy Director for Plans Richard Bissell and covert action chief Tracy Barnes. Desiring to win the approval of their political masters, these senior CIA officers presented the new administration with optimistic appraisals of the chances of success for the mission. Due to the CIA's monopoly on access to senior policy-makers, the President and his advisers were not exposed to the dissenting opinion which was prevalent in the intelligence community. Hence, the President was unaware of vital Office of Naval Intelligence reports which cast grave doubts on the possibility of a spontaneous uprising of the Cuban people – an event deemed critical to the success of the operation. Likewise, Bissell and Barnes shut out the opinions of the JCS, the State Department and even senior CIA officials that were sceptical of the plan.[75]

Although the CIA officials dominated discussions over the proposed mission, the JCS seemed to assent to the plan – or at least they did not voice active opposition. In retrospect, it was discovered that the JCS never formally approved the plan, yet their silence gave the White House the impression of their acquiescence. McNamara, still struggling to gain control over the Pentagon, had accepted the judgement of the JCS without exploration.[76] Hence, when the operation failed, Kennedy was particularly angry with the military. He felt that they should have made their private objections to the mission known to him. Kennedy's adviser Arthur M. Schlesinger, Jr, noted that, while the CIA shared in much of the blame: 'My impression is that, among these advisors, the Joint Chiefs had disappointed him [President Kennedy] most for their cursory review of the military plans.[77]

General Maxwell Taylor, Army Chief of Staff during the Eisenhower administration, was called back from retirement to lead a committee of inquiry into the failure of the operation. The committee was composed of DCI Allen Dulles, Chief of Naval Operations Admiral Arleigh Burke, and Attorney-General Robert F. Kennedy. Oddly, Dulles and Burke were, in effect, investigating themselves, leading Schlesinger to conclude:

> Their real function was to preserve the CIA and JCS from feelings of persecution. The Attorney General was guarding

the presidential interest. Taylor, as chairman and draftsman, concentrated on securing a unanimous report. 'I was far more critical . . . of the military', Robert Kennedy said later, 'than perhaps Maxwell Taylor wanted to be.' For his part, Taylor, caught in a crossfire, had, he said later, 'more difficulty with the Chiefs than with the others'.[78]

The Taylor Committee concluded that from the military perspective the operation was inadequate and that the JCS had served the President poorly.[79] The CIA shared in the blame. Yet while the CIA was subsequently reorganised and senior officials such as Barnes and Dulles were forced into retirement, the military did not suffer any negative consequences. In excusing the failures of the JCS in the Bay of Pigs, the Kennedy administration missed an ideal chance to reform military intelligence. In hindsight, the Bay of Pigs appears to have been the perfect justification for introducing centralising reforms into the military and for strengthening civilian control over the DOD (i.e. establishing the DIA to McNamara's original specifications). But the Kennedy administration let this chance slip by. The JCS received only a mild reprimand from the White House. Consequently, the Bay of Pigs had little influence on the formation of the DIA.

It has been stated that the creation of the DIA was a result of the failure of the Bay of Pigs operation.[80] This is simply untrue. The trend towards increasing centralisation within the DOD of which the DIA was a natural product has been documented earlier in this chapter. Moreover, it has been suggested that the failed invasion played a vital role in determining the final shape of the DIA – by giving either McNamara or the JCS the upper hand in deliberations over the the the final form of the agency.[81] The author of this suggestion has found no evidence to support his view. In fact, an analysis of documents cited in the final report of the 1970s congressional inquiry by the Church Committee indicates that memoranda between the JCS and McNamara concerning the DIA had ended on 13 April, 1961, suggesting that the struggle over the final structuring of the DIA was decided just *prior* to the Bay of Pigs operation.[82] The event was neither the catalyst for the creation of the DIA nor the decisive influence on the shape of its organisation. The significance of the Bay of Pigs is overrated – its political implications simply were not that serious. 'A brick through the window' McGeorge Bundy, the Special Assistant to the President for National Security Affairs, would later refer to it among friends, implying that the damage was easily repaired.[83]

If anything, the Bay of Pigs appeared to reaffirm the compromise already reached on the DIA: that it report to the Secretary of Defense *through* the JCS. In the aftermath of the incident, the Taylor Committee had concluded that the CIA was poorly suited for handling large-scale paramilitary operations like the Bay of Pigs invasion, and recommended that such future operations be carried out by the Pentagon. Subsequently, in June 1961, Kennedy signed National Security Action Memoranda 55 and 57, which transferred large-scale paramilitary operations from the CIA to the DOD and gave the chairman of the JCS full responsibility for these operations, (including the forceful presentation of objections to the President).[84] Since the DOD was now responsible for large paramilitary operations, it follows that it would need some form of central intelligence apparatus to integrate and co-ordinate any proposed missions. Ideally, this central intelligence apparatus would be established under the JCS rather than the OSD, for the former had responsibility for the paramilitary operations and therefore required greater responsiveness from the new agency. Thus the recommendation of the Taylor Committee to transfer paramilitary operations to the DOD would seem to have reinforced the earlier decision to establish the DIA under the JCS.

Although the official record is vague and incomplete, it appears that the decision to establish the DIA under the JCS was the result of a compromise made in mid-April 1961. After internecine strife between the military and civilians, McNamara finally agreed to the military proposal to let the DIA report to the Secretary of Defense through the JCS, rather than report directly to the OSD. Why McNamara agreed to this arrangement is unclear. Being a shrewd bureaucratic player, McNamara must have realised that this move would make the DIA more responsive to the JCS than to himself – thus dulling its effectiveness as a management tool of the Secretary of Defense. This was why he had originally proposed and fought for the DIA to be established under his OSD. Yet he abandoned this position in mid-April, for reasons known only to himself. Perhaps McNamara, seeing the weight of the bureaucracy side with the military, sensed that this was one issue on which he could not prevail. Maybe he was reluctant to force a major battle over military intelligence at a time when American military intervention seemed likely in Laos and senior administration officials were urging a deepening of the American commitment to Vietnam.[85] Perhaps

McNamara viewed the concession as necessary in order to safeguard his primary objective of unified NIEs. Whatever his motive, the JCS viewed the compromise as a victory. They realised that, by establishing the DIA under them in the chain of command, they were ensuring, above all, that the DIA would be primarily responsive to the JCS.

Even in the face of this major concession, there was still considerable opposition within the military to the creation of the DIA. The army fought its formation to the very end. The navy initially resisted the agency, but appears to have been persuaded by the JCS that it was a necessary evil. Only the air force – always seeking new ways to expand its power and influence – would truly support the establishment of the DIA, quickly realising the opportunities it presented for the young service to enhance its prestige *vis-à-vis* the older services. Consequently, in the beginning most of the top management positions in the DIA went to the air force.[86]

To placate still further military concerns over the DIA, McNamara allowed the services to collaborate in setting up the organisational structure of the agency. Each service was asked to nominate an officer to represent it. These representatives were to supervise an interdepartmental staff in establishing an organisational structure and activation plan for the DIA.[87] After being nominated by the respective services, these officers were recommended to the Secretary of Defense by the JCS; the former eventually appointed them to their posts. The air force chose as its representative Lt.-Gen. Joseph Carroll, and McNamara appointed this air force officer as the first director of the DIA. Carroll had begun his intelligence career with the FBI and had become a leading assistant to J. Edgar Hoover. When the Second World War broke out he was transferred to the air force and in 1947 he set up its first investigation and counter-intelligence section. Prior to his appointment as DIA director, he had been the inspector-general of the air force. Lt.-Gen. William W. Quinn of the army was appointed his deputy director, and Rear Admiral Samuel B. Frankel was appointed as chief of staff.[88]

These officers were all named to posts that at the time did not exist. They were charged with turning the DIA from concept into functional reality. Carroll began by going separately to each service and requesting their input concerning the form of the DIA. His staff then drafted a detailed *joint* plan for transferring the armed services, intelligence responsibilities and capabilities to the DIA. It is important to note that the services were consulted during every step towards the creation of the DIA: thus they were able to preserve their vested interests and pay lip service to the planned consolidation through superficial reform. Significantly, the Secretary of Defense had no representative on the DIA planning staff to ensure that his interests were preserved. The agreed plan for the establishment of the agency as formulated by the service representatives was submitted to the JCS, who, in turn, endorsed the plan and presented it to McNamara for his final approval.[89] McNamara formally approved the plan in June 1961, thus confirming the shape of the agency which would be so bitterly castigated for its parochialism and bureaucracy.

If the plan was a compromise between the JCS and McNamara, then it certainly was a lopsided one. The 'compromise' was little more than a slightly altered version of the original JCS proposal of February 1961. True to the original JCS proposal, the DIA was established directly under the authority of the JCS. The staff was largely composed of military men who did not expect to make their careers within the DIA (this would have been to risk severing the link between the intelligence officer and his parent service, allowing him to 'go native'), but were engaged instead on rotational tours of duty (thus reinforcing service loyalties); the services were allowed to maintain full autonomy in field operations and preserve their monopoly over collection capabilities and raw intelligence; and the DIA was given little real power to command or discipline the service intelligence components. Aside from several management, largely budgetary, concessions, the only proposals that McNamara would preserve from his original concept of the DIA were the transference of the evaluative capabilities from the services to the DIA and the consolidation of the service representatives on the USIB into a single DIA representative. The fact that McNamara chose to preserve only these proposals – proposals which were integral to the consolidation of conflicting service estimates – confirms the earlier assertion that McNamara's primary purpose in establishing the DIA was to facilitate the formulation of consensus NIEs. It appears that, so long as McNamara received his unified estimates, he was content to let the Chiefs have the DIA.

On 30 June, 1961 McNamara presented the final proposal for the DIA to the President's Board of Consultants on Foreign Intelligence Activities, an Eisenhower creation resurrected by Kennedy after the Bay of Pigs to monitor the intelligence community. The board was impressed with the proposal and recommended its early implementation. In a memorandum to the President on 6 July,

McNamara outlined the plan for the establishment of the DIA. It is notable that this memorandum dwells on the failure of the Pentagon to co-ordinate unified estimates:

> Today, the military departments develop separate intelligence estimates which exert a substantial influence on the identification and justification of their own force requirements. *This process may well mean that the estimates and requirements statements of the separate Services do not provide the optimum basis for developing the total military posture of the United States* [emphasis added].[90]

This memorandum encapsulates McNamara's thinking at the time. He was still primarily concerned less with improved efficiency than with estimates and the need to reconcile them with the American force structure. He does put the agency in its proper historical perspective: 'Moreover, this solution [the DIA] is consistent with the expressed intent of Congress in adopting the McCormack Amendment of the 1958 Defense Reorganization Act.'[91] It is true, also, that he mentions the DIA's role in the elimination of duplication and points out that centralisation of the military intelligence effort is desirable for the sake of efficiency. But he does not note exactly how the DIA will achieve these gains. What duplication will be abolished? McNamara never specifies.

Throughout the summer of 1961, Carroll and his staff worked on the activation plan for the DIA. True to the original JCS proposal, they decided that the DIA would be activated in an 'evolutionary' manner: service functions and manpower would be slowly transferred to the DIA over a period of three years.[92] The ostensible justification for this action was to minimise the disruptive effects of organisational change on the flow of intelligence information.[93] Yet, more subtly and insidiously, it allowed the services to ensure that their protected interests were not threatened, for they were allowed carefully to approve and monitor all changes. Moreover, as a result of this gradual implementation, the DIA never achieved and profited from the organisational impetus that other newborn agencies enjoyed. One former official stated: 'DIA was born old. McNamara just gathered the drones and put them all in one building'.[94]

After securing the agreement of the service, in September Carroll presented the completed activation plan to the JCS, who quickly approved it and forwarded it to the OSD. McNamara formally endorsed the plan on 29 September, and two days later, on 1

October, the DIA was activated.[95] The Defense Intelligence Agency was created by Defense Department Directive 5105.21 issued by Secretary of Defense Robert S. McNamara in accordance with the powers given to him under the National Security Act, as amended. The accompanying press release emphasised that the purpose of the agency was to achieve a more 'efficient allocation of critical intelligence resources and the elimination of duplicating facilities.[96] Subsequently, the OSO and the J-2 were abolished (on 31 October, 1961 and 1 July, 1963, respectively), for the DIA was intended to meet the intelligence needs of both the OSD and the JCS. It would take over three years for the agency to become fully operational in all assigned functional areas. These formative years were critical to the success of the DIA – its relationship to the services, both functional and institutional, developed and matured during this time. If the DIA was to succeed in its challenge to and subordination of the services, it needed to impress in its early years.

In a congressional appearance six days after the formal establishment of the DIA, McNamara stressed that the new agency would 'achieve a more efficient allocation of intelligence resources, more effective management of all Department of Defense intelligence activities, and the elimination of duplicating intelligence facilities, organisation, and tasks'.[97] Noting the historic opposition of the armed services to all efforts at centralisation, one Congressman asked the Secretary of Defense if an earlier claim that the JCS 'wholeheartedly' supported the new agency was true. McNamara replied: 'Yes. One of the reasons, of course, is that we propose that this new agency operate under the direction of the Joint Chiefs of Staff so *they will have full opportunity to shape its operation* (emphasis added)[98] At no time is the agreement between McNamara and the JCS stated more explicitly: military support in exchange for control of the DIA.

In mid-1962, amid growing congressional fears of over-centralisation within the DOD, the House of Representatives Armed Services Committee, long a staunch ally of the military leaders, created a Special Subcommittee on Defense Agencies which held hearings to inquire into agencies that had been created or were being contemplated by the OSD. This included the National Security Agency, the Defense Communications Agency, the DIA and the Defense Supply Agency (the latter having been established on 6 November 1961 by McNamara to co-ordinate military supply and service functions). The House Armed Services Committee had been a strong supporter of military services, insisting that they not be merged and that each department be separately organised. The hearings were called because the House was concerned that increased centralisation was moving the DOD toward a 'single defense concept' – an idea which they opposed. Thus, they moved to investigate.

The principal task of the special subcommittee was to determine if the agencies created by the Secretary of Defense had sufficient statutory basis. Since all were created under the authority of the National Security Act, specifically the McCormack–Curtis Amendment, the subcommittee, in effect, was trying to determine whether the agencies truly increased efficiency and eliminated duplication; thus making them legal under the terms of the Act.[99] McNamara, senior DOD officials and General Carroll and his staff testified before the subcommittee. The hearings and final report of the subcommittee provide considerable insight into the development of the DIA in its formative years, and therefore will be examined in some detail here.

McNamara's appearances before the subcommittee were marked by the disagreement between the Secretary of Defense and subcommittee members over the correct interpretation of the McCormack–Curtis Amendment. Whereas McNamara and the OSD preferred to interpret the amendment as broadly as possible, allowing for the consolidation of nearly all service functions except training, the subcommittee, citing the floor debate over the amendment, chose to view it narrowly as justifying only those reforms intended to bring about substantial savings on common-use items.[100] They correctly noted that the OSD interpretation allowed the Secretary of Defense to enact virtually any reform, for any reason, by simply claiming, truthfully or not, that it would bring about more efficient administration and/or the elimination of duplication.[101] McNamara failed to address this assertion adequately, repeatedly digressing and deferring to his legal counsel. Furthermore, when questioned closely about the specific reforms which would result in greater efficiency, his answers were vague.[102]

Thus the subcommittee members questioned General Carroll carefully about the same matter. Carroll conceded that the new agency would not reduce the overall manpower of the military intelligence effort, nor would it reduce the number of service personnel assigned to intelligence duties. Where would the gains in efficiency come from? asked the subcommittee. Carroll digressed. Still the subcommittee pressed. Finally, Carroll was forced to state directly that he was not prepared at the time to state where the increase in efficiency would come from.[103] This was a sombre and startling announcement by the DIA's top official. Although he had personally drafted the organisational agenda for the DIA, an agenda allegedly committed to greater efficiency and the elimination of duplication, he would stand before Congress in 1962 and state that he could not reveal the exact manner in which the agency would discharge its principal purpose. Intimations of greater efficiency and streamlining became an increasingly thin reed on which to rest the DIA's claim to legitimacy. In reality, there was little truth to these claims. The services had deliberately created the DIA in a manner that would protect the autonomy of their intelligence components. Thus, they sought to preserve duplication, not, as they claimed, to eliminate it. Likewise, they sabotaged efforts aimed at greater efficiency because they sought to preserve their self-serving bureaucracies. By entrusting the development of the DIA to the services, organisations opposed to the very reforms that the agency was charged with enacting, McNamara had doomed the DIA to failure.

Not surprisingly, the one reform which was frequently cited by both military and civilian officials was the transference of the ability of evaluate raw data from the services to the DIA.[104] McNamara repeatedly referred to the creation of a single intelligence estimate as the primary benefit of the establishment of the agency.[105] Indeed, my argument is that it was McNamara's primary purpose in creating the DIA. For legal reasons, he would hide this objective behind secondary aims – greater efficiency and the elimination of duplication. Yet his actions confirm the thesis: while he would eventually abandon his drive for enhanced efficiency in military intelligence, McNamara continued to battle for putative threat assessments.

Let us now consider more carefully the proposition that McNamara may have succeeded in his main, disguised objective, the improvement and control of threat evaluation. It is surely significant that during the course of the hearings both McNamara and senior DIA officials frequently stressed that the DIA was *directly responsible* to the JCS.[106] There was little question as to who would be the master of the agency: it was the Joint Chiefs, not the Secretary of Defense. By answering directly to the JCS, the DIA was doomed to repeat the experience of the JIG (later, the J-2): being more responsive to the tactical needs of the Chiefs, it would poorly serve the national needs of the Secretary of Defense. Surely, the lesson of history was not lost on the Chiefs. Furthermore, the DIA was given no real power or authority over the services. Congressman William H. Bates prompted this exchange with General Carroll:

MR BATES: Well, you [the DIA] supervise, but you don't really mean supervise, I guess, do you? You take a look at something. But you can't tell them [the services] to do anything. You can't tell them to change a thing. All you might do is write a memorandum upstairs and have somebody maybe –

GEN. CARROLL: If that should be necessary, that certainly would be done.

MR BLANDSFORD: General Carroll, isn't this basically, however, what the Army, Navy, and Air Force have historically had?[107]

Congressman Blandsford astutely located the crucial flaw in the DIA. It really would change nothing. The DIA, being a creature of the services, would have little authority over them. It is impossible to envision the weak agency forcing the powerful services to relinquish control of their most prized assets: their intelligence components. This, of course, was the point. The military had deliberately created a weak DIA to preserve their organisational interests. Simply because it lacked the power and authority to do so, the agency would never truly be able to fulfil its much heralded mission of consolidating the service intelligence efforts. General Carroll never responded to Congressman Blandsford's question, but it was apparent that the answer was yes.

In the end, the subcommittee concluded that they could find no faults in the DIA. They did, however, object to its establishment under the authority of the McCormack–Curtis Amendment. This was consistent with their traditional apprehension of any measure which might allow the services to be consolidated against the will of Congress. Ironically, they did object to the only true reform that DOD officials continually referred to – a single intelligence estimate. The subcommittee, like Allen Dulles and senior CIA officials, simply feared that this reform might result in the suppression of dissent from policy-makers.[108] Thus, the military found another ally for its future struggle to resist the only measure left from McNamara's original DIA proposal – that for which he had fought so hard and given so much to preserve – the consolidation of the preparation of threat estimates.

Testifying before Congress in 1964, McNamara would concede that little had changed in two years. The question of whether the DIA would truly provide a more effective intelligence capacity was still unanswered. McNamara noted that there were 'divergent

views' within the intelligence community over the efficiency benefits of the DIA, but he insisted that in the 'long run' greater efficacy
would result. He also told the Congress that the 'capability within
the individual services for preparing detailed intelligence reports
has, of course, been transferred to the DIA' and that the service
representatives were being removed from the USIB.[109] It is entirely
indicative of his willingness to give way on principle that the latter
development never took place.

It would be the final irony in this tale of the DIA that McNamara
would never truly achieve that which he desired, that which he
sacrificed so much for: a single NIE. McNamara had always
intended that the DIA would eventually replace the services and
represent the entire intelligence community on the USIB. Yet the
JCS continually delayed the implementation of this change. Finally,
in late 1963 Allen Dulles' successor, DCI John McCone, recommended to the NSC that the DIA be included in the USIB as
of January 1964. The military vigorously resisted this proposal,
arguing that the increasing American commitment to Vietnam
strongly supported their case that the services needed to retain
their evaluative capabilities in order to ensure that they were provided with tactical intelligence and enemy 'order of battle' information. Implementation was again delayed. It was only when President Kennedys successor personally intervened to support McCone
and McNamara on 4 February, 1964 that the proposal was finally
pushed forward despite the opposition of the JCS. Yet in a final
compromise, perhaps influenced by the deteriorating situation in
Vietnam and the possibility of direct American military involvement, the military services were allowed to sit on the USIB as
observers while retaining many of their former privileges. As John
Prados notes:

> the services were 'invited and encouraged to sit as observers'
> without distinction to subject. The services were also assured
> that they would retain full privileges on all USIB subcommit-
> tees, on which 'no immediate changes will be made'. No
> changes were ever made. The military intelligence branches
> kept their place in the working apparatus of the intelligence
> community and retained their right to dissent on NIEs as well.
> As a result there was no effective reduction of the military
> role in intelligence, which had been the original aim of the
> Kirkpatrick Report.[110]

In the end, one question remains: why did McNamara grant significant concessions to the JCS on the organisation of the DIA that ultimately undermined its effectiveness? The questions can also be posed: why did McNamara not fight harder to establish the agency to his original specifications? why did he surrender his objectives? McNamara himself provides no answer. Perhaps the answer lay in the times. The year 1961 was a tumultuous one for the Kennedy administration. Successive crises challenged the new policy-makers: Laos, Cuba, Berlin, then Vietnam. The demands on the new Secretary of Defense were enormous. Already burdened by foreign crisis management, he was fighting the Pentagon bureaucracy on many fronts: pushing his Planning–Programming–Budgeting–System (PPBS), flexible response, systems control, and other organisational and management initiatives simultaneously. Time was of the essence. The administration strove to implement the new policies quickly in an attempt to capitalise on the presidential 'honeymoon' – the first hundred days of an administration when the President's power to influence both Congress and the federal bureaucracy is at its zenith. There was so much to do – no effort could be wasted. Given this environment, it is possible that McNamara, realising the strength of the military opposition to the centralisation of the service intelligence efforts, simply decided that this issue was not worth the fight. Employing cost–benefit analysis (as was his wont), perhaps he concluded that the stakes were too high: that despite expending considerable time and prestige, his view was not likely to prevail. Besides, he had other, more pressing concerns. His goal was to revolutionise the Pentagon: to introduce modern management controls, making it more efficient and more responsive to policy-makers. Military intelligence reform was only a small facet of a much larger goal. At the time, it seemed a small battle in a large war. It was a battle that McNamara, to his cost, chose not to fight.

'I've got to think precisely,' McNamara once told an interviewer. 'The cost of being wrong is very, very high.'[111] In the case of the DIA, the cost of failure would be high indeed. Although the policy-makers who had created the agency were aware that it might evolve into simply another layer in the intelligence bureaucracy, and cautioned the military against thinking of it as such, a decade after its establishment the Fitzhugh report would condemn the DIA for perpetuating the very faults that it had been designed to remedy – duplication and layering.[112] Moreover, in a final irony, McNamara's failure to press for the implementation of the principal objective of the DIA – the co-ordination of threat assessments – would play no small role in his downfall. Biased military intelligence estimates, underestimating the strength and determination of the Vietcong, repeatedly influenced many of the decisions on military involvement and escalation in the Vietnam conflict. McNamara, at first a strong supporter of the military estimates, increasingly became sceptical of the accuracy and objectivity of the military intelligence reports being processed by the DIA. Eventually, in 1966, this growing scepticism would cause him to abandon the DIA which he had created and turn to the CIA for objective intelligence on Vietnam. Of course, by then it was too late. The crucial decisions had already been made, based largely on prejudiced intelligence. America was caught in the quagmire of Vietnam. In the end, Vietnam would stain not only the integrity of the nation, but the tenure of Robert McNamara as well. David Halberstam wrote:

> For McNamara, the great dream had been of controlling the Pentagon and the arms race, but the war had ruined all that. War Secretaries do not limit the power of the military, and to a large degree he had lost control. The war absorbed so much of his time, his energy, his credibility, that he had little to give to the kinds of control that he had wanted. It was not by accident that his name would come more to symbolise the idea of technical warfare than it would civilian control of the military.[113]

Some might claim that this chapter is too hard on Robert McNamara; that the failure of the agency was not his fault alone; that others were also involved. Yet it holds McNamara primarily responsible for the failures of the DIA for this reason: on an issue of such contention, where the bureaucracy was so polarised, only the personal intervention of the Secretary of Defense can ensure that the solution which results will be in the best interests of the nation. In this situation, there is no effective substitute for the leadership of the Secretary of Defense. He alone must ensure that the broad interests of the United States of America prevail over the limited interests of the Joint Chiefs of Staff and the armed services. This is the purpose of the National Security Act of 1947 and the modern Department of Defense: vigorous civilian control over the military. McNamara himself believed that the Secretary's role consists of active, imaginative, and *decisive* leadership of the [military] establishment at large, and not the passive practice of simply refereeing the disputes of traditional and partisan factions. (emphasis added)[114] He would later state: 'For my mistaken decisions, I stand alone', and, further 'every hour of every day the Secretary is confronted by a conflict between the national interest and the parochial interests of particular industries, individual services, or local areas.'[115] With respect to the founding of the DIA, it may be said that, by his own definition, McNamara failed in his duty to the national interest.

Notes

1. Thomas Ross and David Wise, *The Invisible Government* (New York: Vintage, 1964), pp. 212–17. Any objective analysis of modern American intelligence tends to be problematic, and this work was no exception. The veil of secrecy which cloaks the Defense Intelligence Agency has proved to be exceptionably durable. Analysts outside the US intelligence community face very real limitations on the quantity and quality of information which they are able to obtain. One must attempt to assemble the puzzle while missing many of the pieces. In all, a topic such as this presents the historian innumerable dilemmas, particularly with regard to research schemes and source material. For this work, I have utilised both public-domain and request-declassified documents to verify and enhance a large body of primary and secondary sources. Additionally, private correspondence with one of the principals involved in the birth of the DIA, the former Secretary of Defense Robert S. McNamara, was of great help in resolving several contradictions and ambiguities. None the less, upon the completion of my research some areas of the tale remained opaque, simply due to the lack of reliable source material (a problem exacerbated by the intelligence communitys refusal to make key memoranda concerning the establishment of the agency available to outside researchers). In these areas, I was forced to rely on my judgement to draw reasonable conclusions from the source material at hand. In several of these instances, where the source material was particularly sparse, I have pointed out these inferences to the reader. I acknowledge the possibility of error in these areas, despite my attempts to minimise it.
2. Lyman Kirkpatrick, Jr, *The Real CIA* (New York: Macmillan, 1968), pp. 205–67.
3. United States Congressional Document (hereinafter USC). Ninety-fourth Congress, Second Session. Senate: Select Committee to Study Governmental Operations with Respect to Intelligence Activities (hereinafter cited as the Church Committee). *Final Report: Book I.* Washington: GPO, 1976, p. 341. (Hereinafter congressional sessions will be specified number of Congress/number of session (e.g. 86/1), the originating committee and the title.)
4. Morton Halperin and Arnold Kanter, eds., *Readings in American Foreign Policy* (Boston: Little & Brown, 1973), p. 374.
5. Victor Marchetti and John Marks, *The CIA and the Cult of Intelligence* (Hodder & Stoughton: Coronet, 1974), p. 334.
6. *ibid.*, p. 117.
7. Arnold Kanter, Defense Politics: A budgetary perspective (Chicago, Ill. Univ. of Chicago Press, 1975), p. 49.

8. *ibid.*, p 53–4.
9. Church Committee (I), p. 350.
10. *CIA: The Pike report* (Nottingham: Spokesman, 1977), p. 83. Although both committees acknowledged that the failures of the DIA stem from its creation, they offered radically different solutions concerning reform. The Church Committee recommended a host of minor, largely superficial, reforms including the exemption of civilian DIA officials from civil service requirements, an increase in the management authority of the agency and improved communication between the service intelligence components. Yet none of these really addressed the true issue, which was structural in nature. Minor, cosmetic reforms could not solve the critical problem of the DIA: that it was wholly a creature of the military services, and thus unresponsive to the demands and needs of national policy-makers. The Church Committee touched upon this, yet never did grasp it in its entirety, as the Pike Committee did. Realising that the agency was fundamentally flawed, the Pike Committee simply recommended that the DIA be abolished and that its functions be transferred to the Assistant Secretary of Defense for Intelligence and the Central Intelligence Agency.
11. William Corson, *Armies of Ignorance: The rise of the American intelligence empire* (New York: Dial, 1977), pp. 386–31.
12. Lawrence Freedman, *US Intelligence and the Soviet Strategic Threat* (London: Macmillan, 1977), pp. 23–5.
13. John Prados, *The Soviet Estimate: US intelligence analysis and Russian military strength* (Princeton, NJ Princeton Univ. Press, 1982), pp.122–8.
14. Allen Dulles, *The Craft of Intelligence* (New York: Harper & Row, 1963), pp. 220–5.
15. Henry L. Trewhitt, *McNamara* (New York: Harper & Row, 1971), pp. 59–60.
16. James R. Roherty, *The Decisions of Robert S. McNamara* (Coral Gables, Fla Univ. of Miami Press, 1970), p. 27.
17. Trewhitt, *McNamara*, p. 65.
18. Keith C. Clark and Lawrence J. Legere, *The President and the Management of National Security* (New York: Praeger, 1969), p. 175.
19. Trewhitt, *McNamara*, p. 74.
20. Clark and Legere, *Management*, p. 175.
21. USC (87/2) House Armed Services *Report: Special Subcommittee on Defense Appropriations*. Washington, DC GPO, 1962, p. 6609.
22. *ibid.*, p. 6597.
23. *ibid.*, p. 6597.
24. USC (87/2) House Armed Services, *Hearings: To inquire into agencies that had been created or were being contemplated by the Office of the Secretary of Defense*, Washington, DC GPO, 1962, p. 6683.
25. USC (87/2) House Armed Services. Report. p. 6611.
26. Lawrence J. Korb, *The Joint Chiefs of Staff: The first twenty-five years* (Bloomington, Ind. Indiana Univ. Press), 1976, p. 17.
27. Corson, *Armies of Ignorance*, pp.386–7.
28. Marchetti and Marks, *Cult of Intelligence*, p. 109.
29. *ibid.*, p. 116.
30. Defense Intelligence Agency, *History of the Defense Intelligence Agency* (1985), no page numbers.

31. Freedman, *US Intelligence and Soviet Threat*, p. 67.
32. *ibid.*, p. 79.
33. Prados, *Soviet Estimate*, p. 32.
34. Freedman, *US Intelligence and Soviet Threat*, p. 80.
35. *ibid.*, p 68.
36. Prados, *Soviet Estimate*, p. 116.
37. *ibid.*,p. 122.
38. Kirkpatrick, *Real CIA*, p. 205–6.
39. Church Committee (I) pp. 325.
40. Prados, *Soviet Estimate*, p. 123.
41. Kirkpatrick, *Real CIA*, p.(216.
42. Joint Study Group, 'Terms of reference', 12 July 1960 (no declassification date), p. 3. Declassified Documents Reference Service (hereinafter DDRS): 1980–341–a. The DDRS is a microfiche collection first issued in 1975. It is organised in a retrospective series and subsequent annual series. In citations the year of the series is given, followed by a card number and, where applicable, by an alphabetic document identifier.
43. National Security Council, 'Considerations and objectives involved in achieving closer integration of foreign intelligence activities within the Department of Defense', 21 Oct. 1960 (declassified 29 April, 1988), p. 10. DDRS: 1988–2274.
44. Goodpaster,'Memorandum of conference with the President', 11 Oct. 1960 (Declassified 18 December, 1978), p. 3. DDRS: 1979–168–a.
45. NSC, 'Considerations and objectives', pp. 9–10.
46. National Security Council, 'Closer integration of foreign intelligence activities within the Department of Defense', 25 Oct. 1960 (declassified 29 April, 1988), pp. 2–3. DDRS: 1988–2775.
47. USC (87/2) House Armed Services, *Report*. p. 6598.
48. United States Senate, Committee on the Defense Establishment (Symington Committee), *Report to Senator Kennedy on the Defense Establishment*, 5 Dec. 1960 Washington, GPO, 1960, p. 4.
49. *ibid.*, p. 7.
50. *ibid.*, p. 6.
51. *ibid.*, p. 8.
52. Prados, *The Soviet Estimate*, p. 123.
53. Kirkpatrick, *Real CIA*, p. 225.
54. USC (87/2) House Armed Services, *Hearings*, p. 6814.
55. Robert S. McNamara, *The Essence of Security* (New York: Harper & Row, 1968), p. 87.
56. Douglas Kinnard, *The Secretary of Defense* (Lexington, Ky Univ. of Kentucky Press, 1980), p. 86.
57. McNamara, *Essence of Security*, p. 88.
58. Roherty, *Decisions of McNamara*, p. 21.
59. Prados, *Soviet Estimate*, p. 114.
60. Trewhitt, *McNamara*, p. 21.
61. Ernest Volkman, *Warriors of the Night: Spies, soldiers, and American intelligence* (New York: Morrow, 1985), p. 113.
62. Church Committee (I), p. 325.
63. USC (87/2) House Armed Services, *Hearings*, pp. 6814–15.
64. C. W. Borklund, *Men of the Pentagon: From Forrestal to McNamara*, (New York: Praeger, 1966), p. 214.
65. Personal correspondence with author, 16 Feb. 1990.

66. McNamara, *Essence of Security*, pp. 70–71.
67. *ibid.*, p. 71.
68. Church Committee (I), p. 325.
69. Marchetti and Marks, *Cult of Intelligence*, p. 117.
70. Ross and Wise, *Invisible Government*, p. 214.
71. Freedman, *US Intelligence and Soviet Threat*, p. 22.
72. Thomas Powers, *The Man Who Kept the Secrets: Richard Helms and the CIA* (London: Weidenfeld & Nicolson, 1979), p. 160.
73. Corson, *Armies of Ignorance*, p. 387–8.
74. Church Committee, (I) pp. 351.
75. Rhodri Jeffreys-Jones, *The CIA and American Democracy* (New Haven: Yale Univ. Press, 1989), p. 122.
76. Arthur M. Schlesinger, Jr, *A Thousand Days: John F. Kennedy in the White House* (Boston, Mass. Houghton-Mifflin, 1965), p. 250.
77. *ibid.*, p. 295.
78. Arthur M. Schlesinger, Jr, *Robert Kennedy and His Times* (Boston: Houghton-Mifflin, 1978), p. 448.
79. Roger Hilsman, *To Move a Nation: The politics of foreign policy in the administration of John F. Kennedy* (New York: Delta, 1967), p. 79.
80. Corson, *Armies of Ignorance*, p. 388.
81. Jeffreys-Jones, *CIA and American Democracy*, p. 123.
82. Church Committee (I), p. 325.
83. David Halberstam, *The Best and the Brightest* (New York: Random House, 1969), p. 86.
84. Trumbull Higgins, *The Perfect Failure: Kennedy, Eisenhower, and the CIA at the Bay of Pigs* (New York: W. W. Norton, 1987), p. 87.
85. *The Pentagon Papers*, as published by the *New York Times*, written by Neil Sheenan, Hedrick Smith, E. W. Kenworthy and Fox Butterfield (New York:Bantam, 1971), pp. 90–5.
86. Halperin and Kanter, eds., *Readings*, p.320.
87. USC (87/2) House Armed Services, *Hearings*. p. 6763.
88. Ross and Wise, *Invisible Government*, p. 215.
89. USC (87/2) House Armed Services, *Hearings*, p. 6670.
90. Office of the Secretary of Defense, 'Memorandum for the President: the establishment of a Defense Intelligence Agency (DIA)' 6 July 1961 (declassified 3 March, 1985), pp. 1–2. DDRS: 1986–85'
91. *ibid.*, p. 2.
92. Defense Intelligence Agency, *History*, no pagination.
93. USC (87/2) House Armed Services. *Hearings*, p. 6814.
94. Prados, *Soviet Estimate*, p. 179.
95. USC (87/2) House Armed Services, *Hearings*, p. 6768.
96. Church Committee (I), p. 349.
97. USC (87/1) Senate Government Operations, *Hearings: National policy machinery Washington, DC GPO*, 1961, p. 1187.
98. *ibid.*, p. 1123.
99. USC (87/2) House Armed Services, *Hearings*, p. 6683.
100. USC (87/2) House Armed Services, *Report*, p. 6611.
101. *ibid.*, p. 6613.
102. *ibid.*, p. 6699.
103. USC (87/2) House Armed Services, *Hearings*, p. 6773.
104. *ibid.*, pp. 6777–813.
105. *ibid.*, p. 6710.

106. *ibid.*, pp. 6763, 6767, 6814.
107. *ibid.*, pp. 6784–5.
108. USC (87/2) House Armed Services, *Report*, p. 6622.
109. USC (88/1) House Armed Services, *Hearings*, Washington: GPO, 1964, p. 221.
110. Prados, *Soviet Estimate*, p. 180.
111. Trewhitt, *McNamara*, p. 296.
112. Church Committee (I), p. 349.
113. Halberstam, *Best and Brightest*, p. 798.
114. McNamara, *Essence of Security*, p. x.
115. *ibid.*, pp. xi, 103–4.

9

The Bold Easterners revisited: the myth of the CIA élite

ROBERT E. SPEARS, JR

For reasons that will become evident, this essay is not about the actual composition of the CIA élite. Instead, it is concerned with perceptions of that élite. On one level, the perception has been of an exclusive organisation, given to recruiting its leadership from the ranks of privileged white men. On a supposedly better-informed level, some authorities have suggested that the CIA was exclusive to begin with, but became more democratic from the 1960s onwards. For my own purpose, however, it is the nature of the perceptions themselves which is of special interest, as is the way in which they changed over time.

Let me state, at the outset, my belief that the CIA was probably not the master of its own destiny in the matter of recruitment. It is simplistic to say that a wholesale recruitment conspiracy on the part of the CIA made the early agency élitist. Members of the American élite flocked to the CIA of their own volition. In fact, the CIA never did recruit in an attitudinal void. Of course, the agency did adjust its recruitment goals periodically. But it appealed to élitist applicants in varying degrees over time for reasons that were largely independent of its own recruitment policy.

Does this mean – the CIA having been 'cleared', as it were, of discriminatory practices – that the whole issue of how its leadership is perceived can be laid to rest? Far from it. One of the recurring themes of this essay is that the agency's leadership and its perform-ance have been judged according to shifting criteria. Apologists and critics alike have been affected by subjective considerations. This has had an effect, as we shall see, on hiring and firing policy, and has probably influenced in other respects the nature and quality of the CIA's work.

My reasons for holding these views will become clearer in the course of a chronological review of changing perceptions of the CIA's élite from the 1950s to the 1980s. But I would like to anticipate that review with a preliminary definition of what some influential commentators meant by an élitist CIA, and with a caution about the limitations of prosopographical methodology.

William Colby had an exceptionally high profile as director of the CIA in the 1970s and for this reason ranks as an influential commentator. In his autobiography, he remarked:

> Hard as it may be to imagine nowadays, considering the attacks on the agency in recent years, joining the CIA back in 1950 was a highly esteemed, indeed rather glamorous and fashionable and certainly the most patriotic thing to do. In those days the agency was considered the vanguard . . . it attracted what nowadays we would call the best and the brightest, the politically liberal young men and women from the finest Ivy League campuses and the most impeccable social and establishment backgrounds.[1]

This nostalgic statement by William Colby illustrates the changes in the reputation of the CIA from the 1950s to the 1970s. Colby was unabashedly portraying the CIA of the 1950s as employing the cream of American society, people from the right families and schools. Inherent in this idea of the 'golden era' at the CIA is the tacit assertion that, by the 1970s, the CIA was no longer made up of the 'best and the brightest'. The connection between the Ivy League and the CIA has existed as much in rhetoric as in reality since the inception of the CIA in 1947. Indeed, the question of this special relationship has taken on a life of its own.

Colby's perception is not an isolated one. In all periods of the CIA's history, commentators have associated it, benevolently or malevolently, with a specially defined group of people who held power in the United States. Roger Halberstam described this group in *The Best and the Brightest*, the famous 1973 book whose biting irony seems to have been lost on the CIA director (according to Halberstam, 'the best and the brightest' were too arrogant to doubt their own judgement, and got the United States into the Vietnam mess). Halberstam defined 'the best and the brightest' as those who came from the best families and attended eastern prep. schools and then an Ivy League university.[2] Halberstam's subjects generally had matured and completed college before or during the Second World War, placing them in careers during the 1950s and 1960s. The quintessential example of this stereotype would have attended Harvard, Yale or Princeton, those universities being the élite of the élite in both educational and social terms. These people, more precisely these men in light of the fact that women were not admitted to these universities before the 1960s, then sought to enter powerful institutions. These powerful institutions were mainly in the eastern United States, especially in New York and Washington, DC. They were either private, such as a Wall Street law firm or brokerage house, or in the federal government.

My contention will be that the Central Intelligence Agency appealed to this type of person during the 1950s and early 1960s, because it was then that Washington held the agency in high esteem. The reasons for the high esteem are not hard to identify. At the height of the cold war, the CIA executed various covert operations, prestigious at the time even if later condemned by congressional inquiries, to foil perceived Soviet advances in Europe and the Third World. The coups in Iran and Guatemala in 1953 and 1954 respectively seemed to be tangible examples of the CIA exercising power in a way that protected the interests of the United States. Even more impressively, the CIA was charged with assessing the threat posed to the United States by the Soviet Union. Though the CIA is not the sole organisation analysing the state of American national security, its director is the co-ordinator of all intelligence estimates to the President. More importantly, the CIA was expected to formulate a comprehensive analysis of the capabilities of the USSR's economic, political and military situation, thus making the CIA's opinion the broadest interpretation of the threat to the United States. Both missions, the operations and estimates of Soviet capabilities and intentions, gave the CIA an authoritative voice and image in the government in the 1950s.[3] Similar considerations governed the CIA's attractiveness to potential applicants after the 'golden' 1950s. The amount of power held by the CIA was to vary with the success and accuracy of its activities as well as with the perceptions held by Presidents concerning the biases and performance of the agency. Hence, the attractiveness of the CIA to 'the best and the brightest' fluctuated.

While we now have the outline of a hypothesis based on Colby's perceptions and Halberstam's definition, the notion of the Ivy League 'best and brightest' is still a vague one. To some degree it must remain so, for we are discussing a largely mythical beast. But we should recite one more perception before departing the realm of definition. This has to do with the people who chose to exercise power, for there were two inherent characteristics of the stereotypical Ivy Leaguer: profound intellectual sophistication, and an understanding of power. The conjectured connection with the Ivy League institutions concerning scholastic aptitude is easily understood – by and large, they had high academic standards. The second aspect, the association between Ivy League alumni and power, is somewhat more nebulous and imprecise.

The relationship could be inverted: the Ivy Leaguers did not appropriate power but created it, as power is the creation of the intelligent and dissolves in the hands of the stupid. But the question remains – why might some Ivy Leaguers have been particularly attracted to the wielding of power through the CIA? Not all intelligent people are attracted to, or wish to create, power. Self-evidently, not all intelligent Ivy League graduates came to hold economic or political power. What was the distinguishing characteristic of those who did?

One attempt to define it is an earlier book, Stewart Alsop's *The Center* (1968). Alsop, whose brother served in the CIA, conjured up the label 'the Bold Easterner'.[4] The Bold Easterner was the Ivy Leaguer who was interested in power. Alsop felt the Bold Easterner, with his intensity and drive, was the key to the CIA's effective performance of its mission. Even if they contained an element of tautology, Alsop's perceptions were to prove influential. In his 1974 biography of Howard Hunt, for example, Tad Szulc elaborated on the Bold Easterner stereotype by contending that 'there was something almost British about them', serving to emphasise these élitist and almost sentimentally imperialistic view of the world.[5] Such stereotyping, it must be admitted, was not universal. When Richard Nixon described the CIA as a group of 'Ivy League liberals' the image was one of inactivity and passivity.[6] Typically, though, the CIA Ivy Leaguer was perceived to be 'bold' – or, in the eyes of his critics, dangerously adventurist.

It would therefore appear that, in addition to the question of the incidence and possible preponderance of Ivy League graduates in the CIA, one must ask if the disposition and outlook of Ivy League graduates changed as well. If the 1950s was a period in which the Ivy League was heavily represented at the CIA, as Colby contends, was it because the Ivy League graduates were generally Bold Easterners in that decade? How did the Ivy League influence become so strong in the agency? Additionally, was there an identifiable point or period in the history of the CIA when the number of Ivy League graduates decreased, and for what reasons did this occur? Did the Bold Easterner come close to extinction during the Vietnam War when the bold or interventionist tendency of this mentality was discredited? Conversely, did the CIA lose its attractiveness to this type of person over time because of changes in the agency? Most importantly, if there were fluctuations in the numbers of the Ivy League element, did these fluctuations have an impact on the performance of the CIA?

At first glance, the best way to assess these questions might seem to be the compilation and analysis of a collective biography of the upper-level employees of the CIA. This method of inquiry, known as prosopography, would hopefully reveal the educational backgrounds of personnel, as well as their social status. From this, one might extrapolate biases and trends in the group. Prosopography was, for example, the method used by Charles A. Beard in his celebrated book, *An Economic Interpretation of the Constitution of the United States* – where he examined the economic interests of the framers of the United States Constitution. Another great historian, Sir Lewis Namier, further developed prosopographical methods in his examination of voting records, kinship, business affiliations and political favours in England's Parliament.[7]

But, for a prosopographical study to be methodologically sound, several requirements must be met. The group to be examined must be well documented, so that its members are identifiable, and so that enough facts about their lives are available to identify trends with strong statistical reliability. In the course of the academic year 1989–90, I availed myself of the rights available to American citizens under freedom-of-information legislation, and applied for information relevant to my research.[8] The following became evident. The Central Intelligence Agency releases no information concerning its employees, past or present. This obviously limits the amount of data available to the researcher. The CIA does not even release the number of people it employs, making it impractical to assess the strength of the Ivy League group in the context of the whole agency. The US Office of Personnel Management does not provide information concerning CIA employees either. It is therefore not feasible to gather information relatiing to the educational backgrounds of CIA employees which covers the entire history of the agency.

A second consideration in prosopography is that, if information is available for only a small number of the group, it is possible that the sample for which one has data may be atypical.[9] The unavailability of information from official government sources means that there must be a question about the precision of unquantified generalisations such as that made by William Colby. An additional consideration further identifies the seriousness of the problem. This is that the verifiable data available to the public concern only the upper-level personnel at the CIA, thus making a comparison of the CIA élite with its rank and file impossible. The problems are, in fact, legion. To mention yet another complication, if one were to insist on working with the small amount of information that is available, one would discover that even that amount dries to a trickle as one approaches the present, making comparisons over time unviable.

Finally, the prosopographer makes the assumption that similar interests or experiences among his subjects create associations and sympathies among those people. For example, there is the assumption that Ivy Leaguers who entered the CIA were 'Bold Easterners'. In the absence of a proper definition of the term, let alone adequate information, how can one possibly prove or disprove that? Were the officers who patiently laboured on National Intelligence Estimates really 'bold' in the sense implied by Alsop? Sherman Kent, who for many years directed the activities of the CIA's Office of National Estimates, remarked to a Wellesley College student: 'People who know about spy systems do not write about them. People who do not know about them, or fancy that they know about them, do do some writing'.[10]

The actual composition of the CIA élite is, as our review of prosopographic methodology shows, an intractable problem. Yet, just because they cannot be counted, historical phenomena do not cease to exist. Much can be gleaned from a review of changing perceptions and images of the CIA's élite – indeed, in some ways, the composition of the élite pales into insignificance, compared with the mythology of its composition. On this more encouraging note, it is now time to start our chronological review.

The composition of the Office of Strategic Services (OSS), the CIA's forerunner, contributed to the notion that there was an association between the intelligence community and Ivy League universities. Professors as well as recent graduates from the Ivy League universities did enter the OSS in appreciable numbers to perform intelligence analysis, gather information and execute field operations. After the CIA was founded in 1947, a number of Ivy League

OSS veterans joined the agency. Other Ivy Leaguers who returned to academia provided an informal recruiting network for the CIA by identifying promising students to colleagues in the CIA. If the Ivy League–CIA network was a myth, that myth drew at least some sustenance from reality.[11]

Yet it should be noted that universities and colleges not in the Ivy League were also involved in the post-war network. By 1948–9, seventy-seven universities and colleges were represented among the employees of the CIA. This figure does not, of course, indicate the level of influence or departmental distribution of schools. But the conspicuous presence of Ivy League professors in the OSS, and the importance of the 'P' source ('P' meaning professor in CIA jargon) in post-war intelligence, lent plausibility to claims of a high incidence of Ivy Leaguers. Yale University's alumni seemed to provide an example of the trend. Out of the Yale class of 1943, forty two men entered the OSS and most were later employed by the CIA.[12]

In 1954 the presidentially commissioned Doolittle Commission reported on the effectiveness of the CIA's personnel. It found that some segments of the agency were blighted by a bloated bureaucracy and by incompetent employees. It criticised the recruiting process for not attracting qualified people.[13] The discrepancy between the gloomy Doolittle findings and later, more flattering recollections on behalf of the Ivy League network may be explainable by a difference in emphasis – or bias. The Doolittle report complained of the CIA's inability to attract technically trained people, whereas the 'P' source cherished by later apologists consisted of liberal arts graduates.[14] Here, it should be noted that the Doolittle report, one of the very few repositories of concrete evidence on CIA personnel, was limited in the scope of its enquiry. It gave data concerning the level of education of a group of employees. Of that sample, 47 per cent had BA degrees and 24 per cent had postgraduate degrees.[15] But the group was of unspecified composition and size, and there is no mention or helpful information in the report concerning Ivy League influence.

Despite inconclusive evidence in the Doolittle report, intelligence veterans as well as other authors persisted in portraying the CIA of the 1950s as having been permeated by Ivy League graduates in the Bold Easterner mould. Some of these portrayals merit closer examination. In his book *The Craft of Intelligence*, Allen Dulles, Director of Central Intelligence from 1952 to 1961, did not try to portray the CIA as an Ivy League dominated institution, stating that among the top one hundred officials in the CIA sixty-one universities were represented. However, he also noted that 'Harvard, Yale, Cornell and Princeton lead the list' of universities which have the most alumni employed at the CIA'. It was this observation that fascinated outsiders. For example, one reviewer of Dulles's book fastened on to the point, even though it is only mentioned in one paragraph on page 77.[16] Despite Dulles's attempt to moderate the perception of the CIA as an exclusive club, Ivy League domination became a retrospective myth that widely-read authors helped to popularise – whether they were friend or foe of the agency. To Alsop, the agency of the 1950s was felicitously '. . . riddled with old Grotonians (Groton being an élite eastern prep school that fed graduates into Ivy League universities).[17] The journalists David Wise and Thomas B. Ross were more critical of the CIA. But they too claimed that, although the CIA was not entirely composed of Ivy Leaguers during the 1950s, the top twenty or so people were invariably from those schools.[18]

Perhaps such writers were influenced less by the words of Allen Dulles, than by the spectacle of Allen Dulles the man. For Dulles was the quintessential Bold Easterner Ivy League graduate. He came from a well-placed Eastern family with a tradition of service in the federal government. He was in the Princeton University class of 1914 and took an MA from the same university. He was an intelligence officer in the First World War, after which he joined his brother, John Foster Dulles, on Wall Street. In the Second World War, Dulles ran the American spy network in Switzerland, where he gained a reputation for being a master of espionage. He entered the CIA in 1951 as deputy director of intelligence before succeeding General Walter Bedell Smith to the directorship. For most of the time that Dulles was head of the CIA, his brother and Wall Street partner was Secretary of State, creating an unusual link between the two government organisations. Dulles did emphasise innovation and action, with clandestine operations being of special interest to him.

Impossible though it may be to quantify, it is at least plausible that Dulles had a magnetic effect. The author of a recent study of the CIA in John F. Kennedy's presidency believes that it was Dulles who was in many ways responsible for attracting 'Ivy League types' to the CIA.[19] For various reasons, the Ivy League connection probably did grow in the 1950s. Dulles actively utilised the existing 'P' source and also recruited additional professors. In this connection, it is significant that he created a haven from McCarthyist attacks in the CIA by refusing to allow employees to appear before the inquisitorial Senator's committee. The Eastern élite was an important target for McCarthy. Because of Dulles's non-co-operation with McCarthy, the Bold Easterners could work in the well-defended CIA without fear of attack or slander.

Whatever the statistical shortcomings of assumptions about Ivy League tenure of top CIA jobs, the foregoing considerations convinced some people, whose opinions were in themselves a factor in the politics of secret intelligence, that the CIA had succeeded in attracting the best. The historian and White House aide A.M. Schlesinger, Jr, suggested this in a memorandum to President Kennedy in the wake of the Bay of Pigs disaster: McCarthy's assault on the State Department had aided the CIA in that it had reduced State's reputation and power in Washington, creating a void in foreign affairs; highly qualified persons interested in international relations found the CIA attractive because of its increased power and its relative safety.[20] A few years later, Robert Kennedy put it this way: 'During the 1950s . . . many of the liberals who were forced out of other departments found a sanctuary, an enclave, in the CIA. So some of the best people in Washington, and around the country, began to collect there.[21]

It may be conjectured that at least some of the Ivy League recruits relished their escape from McCarthyism to such a degree that they became enthusiastic fugitives from any kind of control. Dulles's appreciation of and affection for covert action would have been an encouragement to such people, who would have thrived in a cold war atmosphere which inhibited close scrutiny of their anti-communist activities. There is some evidence to identify this covert activism with the earlier years of the CIA. For example, when in the 1970s covert action brought the agency into disrepute and the government responded with restrictions and personnel cuts, the most strenuous complaints reportedly came from a specific quarter. Admiral Stansfield Turner, Director of Central Intelligence under President Jimmy Carter, commented that, after stricter congressional oversight had been established over the CIA, many of the 'old boys' in the agency had expressed resentment.[22] 'Old boys' is a phrase that suggests a link with the Dulles era.

The Kennedy administration marked a turning point in the fortunes of the CIA – and, which was suggestive of a causal link, in its Ivy League image. The agency was heavily involved in the planning of the Bay of Pigs invasion and received blistering criticism for its failure. At the start of his term Kennedy looked upon the

CIA as an example of his 'New Fronteerism', countering communist influence in the world. He valued the expertise at the agency and its reputation for employing the best personnel. This changed with his loss of face over the Bay of Pigs. Though Kennedy took public responsibility for the failure, the CIA became the whipping-boy within the government. Allen Dulles was eventually forced to resign and Kennedy placed less stock in the CIA. John McCone, a ship-building mogul and staunch Republican from California, replaced Dulles and instituted a different management style. Where Dulles had been a loose manager who took an active role in the analysis of topics, McCone saw his job as running the CIA efficiently and producing the best possible product for the President. This corporate mentality was, reportedly, anathema to the individualistic Bold Easterners brought into the agency under Dulles. Though McCone attempted to improve morale at a CIA demoralised by the Bay of Pigs, there were those who complained that he was not one of the 'band of brothers' associated with Dulles and the Ivy League.[23] He replaced an extremely popular director who, a number of upper-echelon employees felt, had been railroaded out of the CIA by a President playing politics. Hence, his credibility was impaired in influential circles, and disenchantment remained.

The Bold Easterners among the Ivy Leaguers also held deeper resentment based on the feeling at the CIA that they had taken the fall for the Bay of Pigs when bad political decisions were really to blame. The CIA had not been subject to this type of public ridicule during the 1950s, nor had it been made to take the responsibility for failed operations. Its fall from grace was all the more dramatic in view of the fact that, during the 1950s, the CIA had been a young agency where Ivy League alumni could essentially create the policy and rules by which they operated. Parts of the CIA had run like university faculties, with emphasis placed on innovation and new ideas as opposed to accountability. The repercussions of the Bay of Pigs altered this environment at the CIA.[24] In a survey of Yale alumni who had worked at CIA at the time of the Bay of Pigs, most of the two hundred respondents expressed resentment the beating the agency took over the incident and the changes it sparked.[25]

The rest of the 1960s saw a continued decline in the reputation and standing of the CIA, and a simultaneous decline in the abundance and power of the Ivy Leaguers. The appointment of Admiral William Raborn to replace McCone as DCI in 1965 was a signal of this in several ways. Congressional attacks on the CIA and President

Lyndon Johnson's non-defence of the agency were indicative of the loss of respect for the CIA. Raborn had no previous experience in intelligence work, and further could not claim the managerial experience of McCone. A navy man from Texas, he was even further removed from the Ivy League scene than McCone. Raborn was not a director who pushed innovation at the CIA, nor was he a highly respected member of the foreign-policy-making group at the White House. As morale at the CIA declined, employees joked that 'Dulles ran a happy ship, McCone ran a tight ship and Raborn runs a sinking ship'.[26] Johnson did not look to the CIA for guidance as he pondered policy formulation. Rather, he expected unwavering loyalty from the agency over the Vietnam Wwar. Daily intelligence memoranda were scaled down and played a minor role in Johnson's decision-making process.[27] All of these factors, together, perhaps, with the equal-rights expectations of the 1960s, could well have spurred the actual as well as the conjectured departure of Ivy League Bold Easterners.[28]

In the place of the Bold Easterners, according to Alsop, came the 'Prudent Professionals': men who sought out to create or alter programmes, but rather to manage what was already in place. The CIA had changed in the further respect that procedures and methods had become institutionalised. During the 1950s, the CIA was still establishing its chain of command, methods and organisation. By the late 1960s, all of these were set and a bureaucracy had taken hold of the agency. Old-timers complained that there were 'too many memos' and that the new CIA headquarters in Langley, Virginia, was a 'mausoleum' in which the agency had become entombed. Alsop insisted that the CIA had become conservative with its institutionalisation, in a way which repelled the Bold Easterner.[29]

But this is to look at just one side of the equation, for the position of the Bold Easterner, if such a person could be defined, was deteriorating in his very breeding ground, the Ivy League school. For one thing, a critical breeze was blowing. Dissatisfaction over the Vietnam War affected the Ivy League schools. Students at Harvard or Princeton no longer accepted the righteousness of opposing communism on all fronts, as had the members of the classes from the 1930s, 1940s, and early 1950s. The critical new generation began to associate the CIA with an invisible government which had usurped power from the American people and entangled the country in an unjust war.

Another factor is also important. In the absence of data, we do not know whether 1960s equal-rights legislation affected the CIA. But we do know that it affected the universities. Students in Ivy League schools began to come from a wider cross-section of the population. The social status of the Ivy League diminished as a result. Indeed, the Ivy League, Bold Easterner type became unfashionable. The CIA could no longer recruit the Bold Easterner even it wanted to, because he had ceased to exist even as a figment of the approving imagination. Those Ivy Leaguers who still worked at the CIA were fully aware of the changes in college attitudes and social composition. We can see this from a second survey of Yale alumni employed at the CIA, which addressed the split and enmity that developed between universities and the agency. Most of the respondents cited felt that the universities had come to view the CIA with distrust and moral reprehension.[30]

But the nadir for the CIA was in the early 1970s. This was the period of its exclusion from the policy-making process in the Nixon administration. President Nixon consciously sought to exclude the CIA from power because he felt thatit was 'staffed by Ivy League liberals who behind the facade of analytic objectivity were usually pushing their own preferences'. Richard Helms, DCI at that time, was excluded from cabinet meetings for a period and played no major role once he was invited back.[31]

Nixon viewed the CIA as at best an ineffective organisation and at worst a fifth column that would subvert his policies if given the chance. Much of this hostility was based on Nixon's resentment towards those who had tried to keep him from power, a group which he identified with the Ivy League universities. But the universities themselves were nowhere near a reconciliation with the intelligence community. Nor was the immediate post-Nixon climate any more conducive to a change of heart. The investigations by the Otis Pike and Frank Church committees, in the House of Representatives and Senate respectively, damaged the standing of the CIA by exposing past operations that had been illegal or immoral. Universities in general distanced themselves even further from the CIA for these reasons.[32]

In the late 1970s, attitudes to the CIA and to its composition once again began to change. A group of intellectuals – small in number but instrumental in creating the climate of opinion that secured the election to the presidency of Ronald Reagan – raised the question of the competence of the CIA, and of its ability to assess the Soviet threat to the United States. One of the most vocal critics was Richard Pipes, a Harvard professor of Russian history who claimed that the CIA's analyses failed to take into account the *intentions* of the Soviet leadership. Pipes argued that the CIA lacked an appreciation for the Soviet mentality. He blamed this on an overreliance on technical data, and on a myopic adherence to *American* perceptions of the arms race. According to Pipes, CIA analysis was based upon the view, held by many American scientists, that mutual assured destruction (MAD) was the basis of Soviet military planning – a view they held for no better reason than the fact that it was the basis for American strategic planning. According to Pipes, Soviet military literature rejected the MAD doctrine.

In Pipes's opinion, the CIA's serious analytical lapse derived from its lack of personnel with a sophisticated understanding of Russian culture and politics. Though Pipes never stated that the CIA should be hiring more Ivy League graduates, he does infer that the root of the problem lay in the increasingly technically oriented nature of its employees.[33] Alsop had argued in 1967 that the Prudent Professionals that replaced the Bold Easterners at the CIA were more specialised in their expertise and less able to synthesise data.[34] In his accentuation of the CIA's technical capability at the expense of human resources, in the late 1970s, Stansfield Turner appeared to be exacerbating the situation. It seemed that the CIA had come to rely upon electronic methods of intelligence gathering to the detriment of its analytical ability. Pipes and his conservative colleagues were apparently calling for a return to the days of the hard-nosed, perceptive generalist.[35]

Perhaps we should ask the question: is, did the Ivy League still produce that type of graduate (if it ever had done), or was that type to be found at more conservative universities? But circumstances and expectations changed in such a way as to make this enquiry irrelevant.. In 1981 William Casey assumed control of the CIA with a mandate from President Reagan to use the CIA to counter the Soviet threat, a promise that had been all-pervasive in Reagan's campaign rhetoric. Though an OSS veteran, Casey was no Ivy Leaguer (he was a Fordham graduate). To meet the Soviet threat effectively, he felt the need to *remove* the 'HYP, Harvard, Yale, Princeton' elements still at the CIA's Operations Directorate.[36] The surprising thing about his view – after the Ivy Leaguers' twenty years in the cold, culminating only recently in numerous dismissals from the Operations Directorate under Turner's aegis – is that there was any HYP element left to prune. We can speculate that this is a case where the myth is more important than the reality –

Casey could have been using the Ivy League label in the same way that Nixon had, for political reasons to make changes at the CIA.

As we have seen, one can question the existence of an Ivy League élite within the CIA. It follows that one should be tentative in advancing ideas to explain its notional decline. In the absence of proper data, one can neither prove nor disprove such theories. But the whole matter is in any case relatively insignificant. To be at all significant, the postulated relationship would need to be one between stable entities. But the real picture is more complex. Several variables changed over time, and therefore related to each other differently in succeeding decades. The Ivy League graduate changed, becoming a different character by the 1970s. The federal government changed – it was no longer so attractive to 'the best and the brightest' after Vietnam, Watergate and the intelligence scandals of the mid-1970s. The same could be said of the CIA, which had seemed a haven for scholars in the 1950s, but which later developed numerous scandals of its own. Finally, the nature of international relations had changed. Whatever one's view of the cold war, it did seem plain in the 1950s that the Soviet Union posed an immediate threat to the United States. Patriotism and the tradition of public service urged some Ivy Leaguers to join the CIA, and perhaps convinced others to believe that even more had done so.

Can one draw a general conclusion from the complex web of changing perceptions? The central point to be addressed is that of the perceived competence of the CIA's employees. Critics have always questioned that competence, and Alsop and Pipes are just two of the commentators who have written of declining standards. But it is clear that the issue of competence has been addressed according to a changing set of values. Its covert actions and instinctive distrust of the Soviet Union endeared the CIA to most Americans in the 1950s, and led people to believe, on no sure evidence, that the agency was well staffed. In a later period, those very same qualities became controversial, leading critics of wide-ranging political persuasions to impute low standards to the CIA, and to explain the problem, though never with the accompaniment of proof, in terms of either a surfeit or a scarcity of Ivy Leaguers. The serious historical study of CIA discriminatory practices must focus not on elusive recruitment figures, but on opinion and prejudice.

Notes

1. *Honourable Men: My life in the CIA* (London : Hutchinson 1978), p. 77.
2. *The Best and the Brightest* (New York: Fawcett Crest 1973).
3. For a recent recollection of the era by a former CIA deputy director for intelligence, see Russell Jack Smith, *The Unknown CIA: My three decades with the agency* (Washington, DC: Pergamon-Brassey, 1989), especially chapter 3.
4. *The Center* (New York: Harper & Row, 1968), pp. 228–9.
5. Tad Szulc, *Compulsive Spy: The strange career of E. Howard Hunt* (New York: Viking, 1974), p. 35.
6. Henry A. Kissinger, *The White House Years* (Weidenfeld & Nicolson, 1977), p. 36
7. Lawrence Stone, 'Prosopography', *Daedalus* (winter 1971), 51.
8. I made several attempts to gather information on employees of the CIA from official sources in the United States government through the Freedom of Information Act (FOIA) of 1974. My first approach was an enquiry to the CIA which included a long list of questions. The CIA's response indicated that they released no information concerning their employees. A second avenue of FOIA investigation was a request to the US Office of Personnel Management. They responded that they did not have information on employees of the CIA. I also pursued avenues of enquiry which did not involve the FOIA mechanism. From the Modern Military Headquarters Branch of the National Archives, I received photocopied pages of the presidentially commissioned 1954 Dolittle report on the CIA, and this did prove beneficial. My other approaches were less fruitful. I asked the Association of Former Intelligence Officers in McLean, Va, if they had any type of directory of members or biographical information on their members. They replied that they did not have any such information. Requests to the various Presidential Libraries and the National Archives brought mixed results. The Truman, Eisenhower, Nixon and Carter Libraries all responded that they had no materials that clearly related to my topic. The Kennedy Library indicated that there was related information in its archives. Hence, I travelled to Boston – but found only a meagre amount of information. The Johnson Library sent me a list of oral histories in its collection. I requested several of these transcripts (Stewart Alsop, Richard Helms, William Colby: many other potentially interesting transcripts were unavailable due to various restrictions on their release), all of which proved to be unhelpful from my point of view. Finally, I contacted the Seeley G. Mudd Library at Princeton University, which houses the Allen W. Dulles papers. They graciously searched the papers reling to the book in which Dulles alludes to CIA personnel, *The Craft of Intelligence* (London: Weidenfeld and Nicolson, 1963), yet responded that there was no relevant information.
9. Stone, 'Prosopography', p. 58.
10. Kent quoted in Robin Winks, *Cloak and Gown 1931–1961: Scholars in the secret war* (New York: Morrow, 1987), p. 449.
11. Winks, *Cloak and Gown*, p. 54.
12. *ibid.*, p. 35.
13. *Report on the Covert Activities of the Central Intelligence Agency* (Doolittle report, 30 Sept. 1954), p. 26.
14. Winks, *Cloak and Gown*, p. 54.

15. Doolittle report, p. 23.
16. Allen W. Dulles,. *The Craft of Intelligence* (London: Weidenfeld & Nicolson, 1963), p. 77; John Barkham, 'Dulles report on CIA lights up dark areas', *New York World Telegram and Sun*, 8 Oct., 1963, p. 27.
17. Alsop, *Center*, p. 229.
18. David Wise and Thomas B. Ross, *The Invisible Government* (London: Jonathan Cape, 1964), p. 229.
19. Peter S. Usowski, 'John F. Kennedy and the CIA: policy and intelligence' (George Washington University Ph.D., 1987), p. 419.
20. Memo Arthur M. Schlesinger Jr, to President Kennedy , 30 June 1961, p. 2, CIA Collection, John F. Kennedy Library, Boston, Mass.
21. Quoted in R. Harris Smith, OSS: *The secret history of America's first central intelligence agency* (New York: Delta, 1973), p. 380.
22. Stansfield Turner, *Secrecy and Democracy: The CIA in transition* (London: Sidgwick & Jackson, 1986), p. 269.
23. Alsop, *Center*, p. 230.
24. Winks, *Cloak and Gown*, p. 448.
25. Winks, *ibid.*, p. 446. Winks's book is a study of Yale alumni in the OSS and the CIA. According to some of his sources, Yale has had a greater impact than any other university on the CIA: p. 16.
26. Alsop, *Center*, p. 237.
27. *ibid.*, p. 246.
28. Unattributable sources claim that the passage of the 1964 Civil Rights Act spurred an egalitarian movement in the hiring practices at the CIA.
29. Alsop, *Center*, p. 250.
30. Winks, *Cloak and Gown*, p. 441.
31. Kissinger, *White House Years*, p. 36.
32. Turner, *Secrecy and Democracy*, p. 105.
33. Richard Pipes, 'Team B: the reality behind the myth', *Commentary* (Oct. 1986), 25–40.
34. Alsop, *Center*, p. 238.
35. The views of American observers like Pipes may be compared with those of the British journalist David Walker, who has written about recruitment problems in MI5 and MI6 in the face of changing threats to national security and questions concerning the competence and ethical conduct of secret-service employees. Walker notes that, during the cold war, the British secret services used 'a network of talent spotters' at top British universities. But then scandals, such as revelations about politically motivated surveillance of Labour Members of Parliament and the abortive attempt to suppress Peter Wright's whistle-blowing book *Spycatcher* (New York: Viking, 1987), created a negative attitude among university graduates towards the secret services. Unable to attract top people, the services fell back, according to Walker, on 'second raters'. Walker, 'If only Bond had been there: a guide to spying in the nineties', *Observer Magazine*, 25 Nov. 1990, 17–21.
36. Paraphrase in Bob Woodward, *Veil: The secret wars of the CIA 1981–1987* (New York: Simon & Schuster, 1987), p. 130.

10

Sense and sensationalism in American spy fiction

KATY FLETCHER

In literary criticism, American spy fiction is relatively new territory. The terms used to describe this fiction have, hitherto, been haphazard. As my object is to distinguish between 'sense' and 'sensationalism' in the spy novel, and as my distinction is related to the concept of 'realism', I shall need to begin by defining the latter term. I shall explore various uses of the concept of realism, and then explain what I mean by it as a prelude to my discussion of varying perceptions of realism by spy novelists.

'Realism' is a word much abused by inconsistent definition and by qualifying adjectives which have tended to obscure its meaning. The term has been applied to a number of distinct areas – art, literature, aesthetics, law and philosophy. In each area, it is supposed to represent a 'real' existence or a relation to it. But in art and literature, the term applies to style as well as to content. The term has further been used to describe a particular movement in the history of art. In some ways it is easier to define what realism is not, rather than strive to explain its meaning. For instance, in literature and art, 'realism' is opposed to 'idealism' in various ways.

A brief review of the varieties of realism will serve a cautionary purpose and will help to identify a chronological peculiarity of the American spy-fiction scene. Realism as an artistic movement originated in France between 1840 and 1880, and soon spread to the rest of Europe and America. Its practitioners reacted against the subjectivity, individualism and historical obsessions of many of the Romantics, and instead adopted a style of art based on a fidelity to nature. Thus the grand heroic subject matter of the Romantic movement was rejected in favour of depicting the details of everyday life. Thus Gustav Courbet (1819–77), generally acknowledged as the initiator of this movement, tried to render the outside world as faithfully as possible in his paintings. He would paint simple village scenes, with peasants and labourers rather than the gods, heroes and biblical characters which were the usual subjects of paintings at this time.

Courbet's painting represented his political beliefs and his wish to show the world as it is, rather than as it should be. The pursuit of realism in his subject matter also influenced his style of painting, and the movement branched into other areas of art such as landscape painting. Camille Corot (1796–1875) painted 'realistic' landscapes directly from nature instead of the idealised landscapes of Romantics such as Nicholas Poussin.

Just as in art, there has been a Realistic movement in literature. Its mid-nineteenth-century pioneers were Honoré de Balzac, 'Gustave Flaubert and George Eliot. European fiction became more representational and attentive to ordinary contemporary life especially as revealed later in the nineteenth century in the novels of Emile Zola and Guy de Maupassant, although some critics may argue that these writers are more accurately described as practitioners of the school of naturalism. Indeed, the volatile state of definitions of realism became increasingly evident with the passage of time. The perception of realism in nineteenth-century literature related to the accuracy of speech and behaviour with which the writer invested his 'low' characters. In the literature of the twentieth century, the focus of realism changed from the accuracy of external detail to the complex workings of the mind. This culminated in the technique of the stream of consciousness as practised by Virginia Woolf and James Joyce, whose fiction keeps faith with the inner psychological processes of the characters.

American literature in the mid-1880s abandoned Edgar Allan Poe's nightmares and the realms of transcendental verse in favour of the realism of democratic scepticism, of a preoccupation with social problems and a concern with ordinary life. From the 'realistic' novels of Mark Twain, Henry James and William Dean Howells, the American novel moved on to the style of naturalism. The playwright Malcolm Bradbury, a leading British critic of American literature, describes this naturalism as 'realism scientized, systematized, taken finally beyond realistic principles of fidelity to common experience or of humanistic exploring of individual lives within the social and moral web of existence.'[1] It was not enough for the realistic novel to adopt a certain style and subject matter; it grew to incorporate a particular philosophy as well. Naturalism was adopted as a native

American philosophy, a way for the novelist to deal with the social, economic and political upheavals that were happening at the time.

This brings us to the chronological peculiarity of the American literary scene. Although the original versions of realism began to decline in Europe in the 1890s, they lasted longer in America. Writers in America had been slower to react to European styles in the nineteenth century, and, while America provided cultural leads in other areas, such as jazz music, it is worth enquiring whether US literary tardiness affected twentieth-century novels too. As we shall see, the tendency of Americans to lag behind is evident in the case of the twentieth-century spy novel – for a considerable period, at least, American writers re-enacted the history of their nineteenth-century for bears.

One must bear in mind the pedigree of the term 'realism' because it supplies an instructive as well as a cautionary tale. My contention is that, in spite of the semantic difficulties, it is useful to look for indications of realism in spy fiction. The search for realism provides a method of assessing the subject matter of the spy novel as well as its treatment, and of comparing the different influences which have affected its development. Spy fiction can be seen as an index to social and political attitudes, an index which reflects the degree of political sophistication and maturity in the intelligence community, in society and, of course, in the authors of the spy novels themselves.

For the purpose of this chapter I have taken the term 'realism' to have three distinct elements, which will act as a guide to distinguish those spy novels described as sensational from those which make sense: that is, those books that are credible and contain political truths. The first element of the realistic spy novel is a verisimilitude of detail derived from observation and documentation. Secondly, the realistic spy novel relies upon the representative rather than the exceptional in plot, setting and character. Thirdly, the realistic spy novel attempts an objective, rather than a subjective or idealistic, view of human nature and experience.

Throughout this chapter I have used the comments of various critics and authors to illustrate a particular point, and these comments reveal different perceptions of realism by the critics and authors concerned. For instance, when the intelligence professionals Douglas S. Blaufarb and Joseph F. Hosey comment on spy novels, their remarks take on a different significance with respect to verisimilitude of detail, in comparison with those of lay critics such as Bruce Merry or James Melville. Just as a historian cannot criticise the subject matter of a spy novel with the same authority as someone who has had experience in intelligence, the lay critic of spy fiction is at the same disadvantage. Similarly, the comments by novelists without any declared first-hand knowledge of the intelligence world, such as W. T. Tyler and Paul Henissart, must be seen above all as the views of professional writers – the novelist in search of verisimilitude cannot visit the spy world as Gaugin visited Tahiti.[2]

In this chapter the subject matter of spy fiction is examined with two criteria in mind – my own definition of realism, and how others perceive realism and its important counterpart in the realm of spy fiction, sensationalism. To this end, the discussion begins with a brief comparison between the detective story and the spy novel, incorporating remarks on the role of the hero. I then discuss the influence of the James Bond hero-type on sensational US fiction in the 1960s. With reference to the books of Edward S. Aarons, E. Howard Hunt and William F. Buckley, I ask whether previous service in an intelligence agency by a particular author materially affects the nature of his fiction. To establish the framework for the next part of my discussion, I delineate the British shift to 'realism' in spy fiction – foreshadowed in the writings of W. Somerset Maugham, and now exemplified in the novels of John le Carré. Here, it is appropriate to ask whether American writers were caught in a time warp. But, when one turns to their 1970s preoccupation with human intelligence, there appear signs of an incipient American genre. At this stage, there is a discussion of the maverick and the analyst as spy hero. Elements of a new literary and political sophistication, even of a creeping new realism, are eventually discernible in the American spy fiction of the 1980s, represented here by the work of W. T. Tyler, David Ignatius and Alan Furst. Finally, I shall speculate about the ways in which the end of the cold war might affect the future development of spy fiction in America.

All forms of literature reflect the social and political attitudes of the author and the culture of the country in which he or she lives. Spy fiction is no exception. Le Carré once wrote that the British secret services were 'microcosms of the British condition, of our social attitudes and vanities'.[3] This observation can also be applied to American spy novels. The background of spy fiction is the real world of politics and international intrigue. More often than not it is the factual world that provides stories and events for the modern spy novel. Whereas the detective novel is limited to an isolated incident, the ramifications of which do not reach beyond the crime, the spy novel has the potential to expand its themes and redefine history as it might have been.

If the spy novel is regarded as a reflection of our times it can also be seen as a valuable historical source, incorporating attitudes towards espionage, politics and society. It can provide insights into a number of contemporary issues, such as terrorism, and seek to explain the political problems of particular areas of the world, such as the Middle East. One of the main attractions of spy fiction is that, unlike an historical survey or a newspaper chapter, it dramatises events and gives us a view of human reactions in a variety of situations. It gives us not only a glimpse of the workings of the secret world, but also a picture which changes with the times and from generation to generation. It is this ability to adapt which ensures its continuation.

Like most literary forms, the detective story has its conventions – it can be divided into different categories such as the police procedural and the mystery. In a similar vein, the spy novel can be put into its sub-genres. The spy story can include elements of adventure, romance, suspense and history, and on occasion all of these elements.

One of the main differences between detective and spy fiction is the setting of the story. The classic detective novel is confined in its location and does not usually expand upon social or political issues, whereas the spy novel has more freedom to involve a larger geographical area, and embrace wider social and political issues which are implicit in the world of espionage. Indeed, the spy novelist has both the opportunity to reflect attitudes and the potential power to influence opinions.

The author's treatment of the hero in the respective genres further distinguishes spy from detective fiction. In the detective story, the plot is centred on the character of the detective: he is the linchpin of the book and can go on until he is retired or killed off. Even then the detective may return, like Sherlock Holmes. However, in the spy story, if the hero is a *spy*, someone who is a foreign national, located abroad, passing information to an intelligence service other than his own, as opposed to an *agent*, who is sent abroad by his own intelligence service to obtain information, then the hero has a very much more precarious existence. Precisely because the fictional emphasis is so often on action, the spy's chances of elimination or discovery are greater.

In a spy novel the hero does not necessarily have to be a spy.

He could be a counter-espionage agent like James Bond, or an intelligence officer directing operations from an office but not spying personally. There are the people who catch spies, there are double and treble agents, hired assassins, *agent provocateurs*, there are those who plant misinformation, like fake defectors, and innocent bystanders used as messengers for secret information, as was Barley Blair in le Carré's *The Russia House*. There are a variety of characters from whose standpoint the author can choose to tell the story, and a range of viewpoints which can be expressed.

Elusive though it may be compared with the detective novel, it is not entirely impossible to discern some of the characteristic features of the spy novel. The story generally involves some kind of political situation; whether this is real or imaginary, it must be credible – creating a reality of its own in which the reader can believe. Spy novelists, as we shall see, employ a variety of techniques to support this 'authenticity'. Yet, one of the rules for the writing of popular fiction is that there must be a good story which encourages the reader to keep turning the pages. One question to be approached in this chapter must therefore be whether the spy novel has to be sensational in order to be entertaining. As spy fiction dramatises events on a world scale it is more prone than most fiction to sensationalism, but does it have to sacrifice political sense in the process? An examination of the cold war spy novel, in particular, should have a fruitful bearing on of these questions.

Attitudes to espionage have changed dramatically in the twentieth century. It was not until these views were modified and the political climate was right that spy fiction became popular. Until the Second World War, spying was seen as an immoral occupation in Britain and America. During the war the excesses of propaganda, including the publicity given to intelligence successes, served to highlight the role of the spy. As Allen Dulles, former director of the CIA, once wrote:

> World War II and the Cold War served to elevate the reputation of spying in the public mind and to make it socially acceptable because a more attractive and more highly motivated type of individual appeared to be engaged in it.[4]

After the war, espionage first came to be regarded as a necessary evil, and later as an expedient in the maintenance of the balance of power between the superpowers. At the same time, the configuration of moral values changed. As portrayed in the American spy novel, these values shifted from the group morality of the large intelligence organisations to the personal morality of the professional agent. To illustrate some of these points, it is now time to turn to some of our writers.

The 1960s saw the beginning of the golden age of spy fiction. The spy hero of the decade was epitomised in Ian Fleming's James Bond, first introduced in *Casino Royale* in 1954. Bond was a superhero – a man of action working for the British Secret Service as a counter-espionage agent. The success of Fleming's creation was enhanced by the many films that were, and still are, made about Bond. These stories were written at the height of the cold war and Bond's enemy in the early books was SMERSH – the Kremlin's 'Death to spies' organisation.

The James Bond stories were written in a different political age and are now regarded as old-fashioned.[5] At present, plans are under way to update the film image of Bond. Sir Fitzroy Maclean, a war hero and one character upon whom Bond was based, recently commented: 'Ian Fleming created a character who was operating 30 years ago. Rather like Sherlock Holmes, Bond is a period piece. If they start re-writing the character, Bond will end up completely different from what Fleming intended.'[6]

It is significant that Fleming's stories had their most lasting influence upon writers and readers in America, where a number of authors adapted or created their spy heroes to fit in with the James Bond image. The appeal of Fleming's books may have lasted longer in America than in Britain because he catered to the American market in his later novels. For instance, he set some of the stories in American cities like Las Vegas and New York, or other locations familiar to Americans, such as the Caribbean. He also introduced an American character who would reappear from time to time. This was Felix Leiter, who worked for the CIA and often provided information or back-up for Bond. Fleming also adopted a certain style in his dialogue which is strongly influenced by the fictional American private eye. All these factors contributed to the popularity of Bond in America: an article in *Life* magazine on 17 March 1961 listed *From Russia With Love* as one of President Kennedy's ten favourite books.

Bond and his American clones were evidently what American readers of popular fiction wanted in the 1960s. The cold war's supplanting of real wars may help to explain the phenomenon. Ronald J. Ambrosetti, an American-based student of spy fiction, observed:

The 'cold war' spy story grew out [of] the isolationalism and international Cold War of the 1950's and early '60s. This formula depicts the peacetime secret agent in his function to *prevent* the final disaster – total global destruction through nuclear proliferation.[7]

In 1973, the date of Ambrosetti's dissertation, it was still possible to regard the US spy-fiction genre as being tied to the cold war.

By this time, the contrast with British fiction was plain. Speaking on the basis of his own experience as a secret agent, Somerset Maugham had once remarked:

The work of an agent in the Intelligence Department is on the whole monotonous. A lot of it is uncommonly useless. The material it offers for stories is scrappy and pointless; the author has himself to make it coherent, dramatic and probable.[8]

One response to this problem is to be inventive, like Fleming. Another is to depict things as they 'really are'. In Britain in the late 1960s, the latter tendency took hold. Authors such as le Carré and Len Deighton became popular. The world of espionage that they presented in their novels was far from glamorous. Their characters were cynical and their violence restrained. If only one could lose sight of the hysteria generated by the Falklands crisis, one might almost believe that British readers had become more mature and sophisticated in their political judgements.

British developments notwithstanding, Bond, or the figure he represented, continued to carry the mantle, previously worn by the private-eye hero, in the sensational sphere of international politics. Authors such as Michael Avallone, Edward S. Aarons, Bill Ballinger, Richard Sapir and Warren Murphy and E. Howard Hunt, developed characters based upon James Bond and sent them on missions against the Soviet Union, and later China, to restore the political balance in the cold war.

In retrospect the spy novel written in this period can be seen as a form of propaganda, even if the views promoted were in large measure a symptom of contemporary feelings, and not their cause. Indirectly, they had the effect of elevating the status of the intelligence operative to that of popular hero, and, by association, these novels have legitimated the function of large espionage organisations like the CIA.

It can be argued that spy fiction as propaganda distorted popular images in a dangerous way in the United States. Influencing opinions, of course, can be a two-edged sword: CIA apostate Victor Marchetti wrote a novel in which he tried to discredit the agency where he worked.[9] By and large, though, American spy fiction of the 1960s contributed to an air of unreality.

A number of literary conventions have made sensational spy fiction inherently unrealistic, in that an element of fantasy pervades the plot and the characters. These devices have influenced how people have perceived the practice of espionage as well as colouring people's perception of the political situation.

The recurring formula of sensational American spy novels is that an attractive hero with special skills is put into a foreign environment, in which he finds himself in a dangerous situation. The hero is described as an agent, a trouble-shooter, and he is American. His function in his intelligence service is usually rather hazy, and because he is so successful his identity is usually known to the enemy, he may have disguises and use false names, but they dissolve easily. He is given an apparently impossible task and plenty of opposition in which to show us his particular abilities, and of course he has only a certain time in which to succeed. Finally, failure to complete his task will mean the destruction of all civilisation as we know it.

Typically, the plots of these stories and the role of the spy hero bear little relation to the real operations, or real employees, of an espionage establishment. No intelligence agency would, in normal circumstances, send one of its own nationals as an agent into enemy territory if there was the slightest chance that his identity, or his connection with an intelligence organisation, was known anywhere in the world. In real life, the agent is usually a foreign national and not an American citizen. In a genuine espionage operation it is often the case that a good agent is someone like Oleg Penkovsky, who has defected in place and has access to important information. So much for glamorous travel to foreign lands. Again, while the question of cover plays a minor role in sensational spy fiction – a lapse that seems less glaring because the hero is so improbable in the first place – cover is essential to the success and survival of the real agent.

Another feature of the cold war spy novel which can be perceived as not true to life, is the behaviour of the agent hero. Literary critic Bruce Merry has written:

the spy story presents an existential contrast in life-style. Agents act *different*. Spy heroes are hard-boiled and they speak in a 'tough' manner: it is useless to object, on the grounds of realism, that spies must be small and inconspicuous, that they must speak very little, and not be heard by their enemies at all. The hard-boiled manner that has apparently become an essential ingredient of the espionage idiom is basically anti-realist.[10]

The non-fictional secret agent's profession is at variance with the lifestyle of the sensationally portrayed hero.

One American spy author who adapted an existing series to fit Fleming's successful formula was Edward S. Aarons. Beginning with *Assignment to Disaster* in 1955, Aarons started a series of books about CIA agent Sam Durell. Like Bond, Durell loved to gamble, indulged in sex with as many females as possible, and had a close relationship with his .38 Special. Durell qualified for missions largely on the tautological basis of his ability to survive. Aarons gives us an idea of his job:

> As a sub-chief for K Section of the Central Intelligence Agency, he had been in the field operations longer than his survival factor permitted. But he would not transfer to a Washington desk, in Synthesis and Analysis, for example to spend his days preparing extrapolative reports for the Joint Chiefs and the White House. He had journeyed too far into the shadows of the secret war, and could never go back to the suburban boxes, commuter schedules, ulcers, and interoffice back-scratching.[11]

While Aarons's novel contains ingredients from the Bond formula, it is in other ways an American product. Its style is reminiscent of the American hard-boiled detective story. The hero expresses his feelings of superiority as an agent in the field, as one might expect, but goes on to reveal his contempt for the analyst and the bureaucrat. This contempt is a constant theme running through the American spy novel of the 1960s. It may well have reflected the inclinations of the covert operators who had seemed to dominate the CIA in the 1950s. It may also have reflected the anti-intellectual tradition in American society.

We turn now to the spy novelist who worked for the CIA and undertook the task of becoming an American Fleming. E. Howard

Hunt was to write a number of spy novels about Peter Ward, his *alter ego*. Hunt had joined the CIA in the late 1940s, and in the twenty-two years he subsequently spent with the CIA, he worked in Paris, Tokyo, Montevideo, Madrid and Mexico City. All this time, however, he worked as a clandestine political operator. He was an officer of the CIA, not an agent like his fictional character Peter Ward.

If his own account is to be believed, Hunt undertook his Ward series with the tacit encouragement of the CIA:

> Victor Weybright, editor in chief of the New American Library and one of the original leaders in the rise of paperback publishing, who had reprinted several of my novels, approached me with the suggestion that I write an American counterpart to the popular James Bond series, which his firm also published. I submitted the idea to Dick Helms, who agreed that certain public-relations advantages would accrue to the CIA if such a series were well received. His sole proviso was that I clear each manuscript in advance with him or his deputy, Tom Karamessines.[12]

Despite the restraints imposed by censorship, Hunt had an opportunity, in light of his own experiences, to present some authentic detail in his spy novels. But, like Fleming, he decided not to use this knowledge to show us the real nature of such operations, nor did he choose to enlighten his readers as to the reasons behind the conflict between the superpowers in the cold war. The job of Peter Ward and other spy heroes of this era was to defend America from attack, and maintain the power balance. Far from being enlightening, these novels merely provided Hunt with a platform for his conservative views and an outlet for his fantasies.[13]

As we have seen in some of the examples taken from Hunt and Aarons, the cold war spy novel, with its emphasis on action and sensationalism, is inherently incorrect in its portrayal of some intelligence personnel. Considered in the context of international spy fiction and of developments in international history, it could be described as a neglected educational opportunity. This, at least, is the opinion of one modern spy-fiction writer. In the words of W.T. Tyler (the pseudonym for Samuel J. Hamrick):

> The spy novel is very much a recitative of popular clichés . . . the post World War II spy novel is a recitative of Cold War

clichés. Ian Fleming, a great favourite of John Kennedy, is probably the best example of that. Spy novelists like Fleming did little to help us better understand ourselves or our times . . . the genre has probably contributed to our gross ignorance of the Soviet Union and heightened our paranoia.[14]

In the cold war spy novel, the literary conventions of the genre cannot easily be separated from the actual content of the stories. That is why the content and style of the sensational spy novel are usually examined together, and why the term 'realism' has been uncritically applied to their literary style as well as the content of their stories. Later, the spy novel matured and attracted better writers who were prepared to include other elements of realism, such as the presentation of complex political issues, as well as more credible characters and plots. But the sensational spy novel of the 1960s certainly sacrificed political sense in its quest for entertainment. Even when the authors themselves had had experience in intelligence, they chose the sensational approach. It was not until the political climate changed and the revelations about CIA methods had such an impact upon American public opinion in the 1970s that spy novelists began to explore different themes and a new maturity appeared.

Later novelists did not always succeed in breaking out of the cold war mould. Though many of William F. Buckley's novels are written in a later period, most are set at the height of the cold war. Like Hunt and other sensational spy novelists, he believes in the maintenance of the political status quo. Buckley is renowned for the ultra-conservative views he expressed for several decades as a political commentator, and it may be that he preferred to perpetuate the hostile atmosphere of the cold war by exaggerating, in his fiction, the threat from the USSR.

Buckley's anti-communism emerges in his 1978 novel *Stained Glass*, in which the hero Blackford Oakes is sent to Germany to keep an eye on Count Axel Wintergrin. The Count has formed a political party whose aim is to reunite East and West Germany. Neither America nor Russia wants this to happen because it would upset the power balance in Europe, from which a third force might evolve to challenge their power bases. To solve the problem, the CIA and the KGB team up to arrange the assassination of the Count should his strength increase before the election.

The political problem as presented by Buckley is a dangerous oversimplification. Since the publication of his novel, of course, the whole political situation has changed – the cold war has ended, the Berlin Wall has been torn down, physically and psychologically, and the two Germanys are now one. These events highlight the degree to which Buckley was out of touch with central European aspirations. Moreover, *Stained Glass* rests on an arrogant assumption, which Buckley shares with other authors, that it is up to the intelligence services to redress this balance. Buckley wrote the novel in the immediate aftermath of presidential and congressional prohibitions on assassination as an instrument of official policy. Buckley nevertheless sees assassination as the solution to the political problem he so dimly perceives, and seems to endorse the right of intelligence agencies to act in this way.

The novels of Charles McCarry, who worked for the CIA for nearly ten years, are more credible than those of Buckley, who spent nine months in the agency. He explores some of the moral ambiguities which arise in espionage. In his 1973 novel *The Miernik Dossier*, for example, he presents a case of fake defection. McCarry makes an effort to create an authentic atmosphere. But according to Douglas S. Blaufarb, an intelligence professional turned spy-fiction critic, he has failed to escape the more sensational aspects of the spy novel:

> Unfortunately, even with a genuine artist like McCarry, the Bondian syndrome seems to be unavoidable. The message left with the reader in the end . . . is that anything is possible inside a secret agency; no flight of imagination can be dismissed as intrinsically unlikely. For the foreseeable future, that seems to be the way the intellectuals and the literary crowd prefer to see the intelligence community.[15]

In this 1977 review of McCarry's novel *The Secret Lovers*, Blaufarb evidently believed that American spy fiction was still caught in its self-destructive time-warp.

Yet, one might argue, at least it can be said that Buckley and McCarry are among a number of spy novelists who have used real historical events to inspire them.[16] Perhaps this inches them nearer the European fold. As John Atkins remarked in his 1984 book on British spy fiction:

> The modern spy writers refer constantly, not only to the sovereign states by name, but to their actual policies, their leaders, their espionage organizations, their successes and

their failures. Sometimes historical personages appear as characters in the novels – spies like Philby particularly, but also Prime Ministers and Presidents. Every effort is made to create an impression of actuality.[17]

However, this is precisely the problem – the introduction of well-known historical data only creates the illusion of reality to convince the reader to believe the story. Historical detail is used to cover the more incredible aspects of the story and unless one has access to such information it is almost impossible to check the facts. The novels which employ such devices can still be sensational in their treatment of the spy hero and the political situations in which he is involved.

In the middle of the 1970s there was a move towards the maverick or 'rogue' agent – someone who has worked for an intelligence organisation, but now works for himself. The rogue agent can be found in Brian Garfield's *Hopscotch*, and in Howard Hunt's *The Hargrave Deception, The Berlin Ending* and *The Kremlin Conspiracy*, as well as W.T. Tyler's *The Man Who Lost the War*.

In some ways the idea of the rogue agent goes back to the individualism of the spy hero of the 1960s, but now the hero has rejected the organisation which has trained him, and relies upon his own network of friends and contacts to outwit the bureaucracy on both sides. The rogue agent perhaps relates indirectly to the popular 1970s notion that the CIA was a 'rogue elephant' out of control and no longer representative of the best aspirations of American democracy – if such were the case, the individual was surely justified in striking out alone. The development of the rogue protagonist in the spy novel is also very firmly in the tradition of the maverick private eyes of Chandler and Hammett.

In the novels in which the maverick appears, he sometimes gives voice to the importance of the human element in intelligence, or humint – as opposed to the increasing employment of technology in espionage. The technological changes had started in the 1960s when the importance of overhead photography grew, with a corresponding growth in electronic intelligence collected by the National Security Agency. The huge increase in the amount of information collected by these technical systems posed a problem in their correlation and analysis, which could only be solved by the further use of technological means, computers and electronic data processing. Despite the increase in technology in espionage, the human agent is still essential in providing information which cannot be obtained by technical means. In the 1970s, there was a campaign, successful by the end of the decade, for a revival in the use of humint both in the field and in the analysis of data.

There are a number of novels that deal exclusively with the analyst spy hero. The adoption of the analyst is a further stage in the development of the spy hero, and shows that at least some writers were trying to escape from the restrictive conventions of the sensational approach. Authors have dealt with the new hero in different ways. For example, James Grady in his *Six Days of the Condor* and Robert Littell in his *The Amateur* put the analyst into the field, an understandable device in a traditionally action-packed genre, since otherwise the action of the story would be seriously confined.

Will Perry had a different way of handling the problem of the analyst spy hero, as we can see in his 1978 novel *The Kremlin Watcher*. Though Perry is British, his book is not only set in America, but, like Fleming's work, potentially catalytic for the development of US spy fiction. As we have already seen in the case of Aarons's work, the fictional agent in the field can be contemptuous of the desk-bound analyst. Perry develops this theme in a different way.

In The *Kremlin Watcher* the plot involves a race for the truth. There is a battle between two principals purportedly representing the political attitudes of the State Department and the CIA. State's Kremlinologist, Leo Farel, and the CIA station chief on the spot, Frank Dober, act out their bitter rivalry. At one point, Farel explains to a friend the advantages of his own particular approach:

> 'The lonely life has its advantages, Bruno. When one does all one's own research, one can combine it all in one's mind and reach conclusions immediately, unlike staff or team work, when you need to put all your heads together and pool what you've got to make the right connections. Apart from a part-time file clerk, I run a one-man operation.'
>
> 'I'm surprised you don't use computers more.'
>
> 'They have their limitations – and their dangers. In my opinion, they're best used to sift and assemble the evidence once you know what facts you are looking for. You know yourself, Bruno, how easy the clues are to miss. A slight divergence from the past Soviet pronouncements, a shift in emphasis in Chinese statements, a hint between the lines of

some obscure journal: For that work, you need the best computer of all – the human computer!'[18]

When it comes to the presentation, to the President, of the evidence which will determine his policy, there occurs a revealing conversation. Dober asks the director of the CIA what evidence Farel has for his case. The director replies, voicing all the prejudices against the analyst: 'Nothing you need worry about. All analytical stuff – nothing hard like what you've got. How can they match what you've found out on the spot in Warsaw with what he digs up a couple of thousand miles away in New York? It doesn't make sense.'[19]

This novel is subtly different from its sensational counterpart – instead of just stating a prejudice as we saw with Sam Durell, the author airs the difference between the two methods of assessing information, and gives them equal representation in the two characters of the novel. Rather then reinforcing prejudices, Perry seeks to explain them.

Since the intelligence debate of the mid-1970s, readers of spy fiction have become more discerning, and more critical of the methods of the CIA. The spy fiction writers themselves are also better informed about the activities of the intelligence community. There is an opportunity for new sophistication in the construction of the stories, in the development of the characters, in the behaviour and function of the spy hero, and in the different settings for the plots. In the words of American spy fiction novelist Paul Henissart:

> Today's spy stories undoubtedly require a high degree of realism and precision. Readers to whom they are addressed are better informed than in the past, a fact which an author should look upon with satisfaction: it is no challenge to write for the uninformed.[20]

There is indeed evidence of a new sophistication in some of the novels by W. T. Tyler. This author makes no claim to have worked for an intelligence agency, and yet critics have praised him for being one of the more authentic writers in the field. Andy Reddish, the central figure in Tyler's 1982 novel *Rogue's March*, is a far cry from the cold war spy hero. Unlike Bond, he is no fantasy figure – he is acting out a role not unrecognisable as that of the CIA intelligence officer stationed abroad. Reddish, moreover, is very much a victim and not a mover of events. The depiction of this character proves that it is artistically possible to have an ordinary man, complete with ordinary human weaknesses, as a spy hero. Joseph Hosey, an ex-CIA employee who reviewed spy fiction, drew attention to the nature of Tyler's latter-day authenticity as evidenced in *Rogue's March*:

> Apart from a few necessary safe houses, encrypted cables, ambiguous phone calls, and casual sexual relationships, the day-to-day machinery of the usual fictional intelligence operation is not to be found here. But the atmosphere of doubt, anxiety, caution, and unexpected conflict in which real intelligence operations are in fact conducted has seldom been so well portrayed.[21]

If further proof were needed of the new trend, it might be found in the reflections of a particularly talented recent author, David Ignatius. This author worked in the Middle East for three years while writing for the *Wall Street Journal*. His first novel, published in 1987, was called *Agents of Innocence* and discoursed on the relationship between the CIA and the Palestine Liberation Organisation in the Middle East.

Reflecting on his novel in a letter written in 1989, the author says it 'parallels the real history of the Middle East during the 1970s, and the CIA–PLO relationship is similar to one that really existed. But the characters are imaginary.' He goes on to say:

> As a writer and a reporter I try to penetrate to the heart of the way that the world works, and to describe what I see in the simplest and most direct way. That is what spies are supposed to do, so there is a neat fit. This is, for me, a world painted in shades of gray, rather than black and white, and spy fiction is the fiction of the grays.

Ignatius's beliefs are suggestive of the fact that spy fiction has changed in the last few years, and that, instead of providing a platform for preaching ideologies and reaffirming political prejudices, it can now be informative and entertaining without sacrificing political truths, however unpleasant they may be. Finally, it is worth noting Ignatius's conviction that a novel may provide a creative outlet which can explain the facts which journalists sometimes omit:

> I think a journalist turns to fiction to express things that don't
> fit in a newspaper or magazine story. The purpose is to tell
> the truth, in an entertaining way. I don't see how someone
> whose purpose was primarily political could write a satisfac-
> tory novel.[22]

Another modern author, Alan Furst, has gone so far as to distinguish his work from that of the traditional spy novelist. He says: 'I
don't actually write what I call "spy novels" – I write historical
novels about intelligence services.'[23] Two novels of Furst's, *Shadow
Trade* and *Night Soldiers*, respectively published in 1984 and 1988,
do confirm at least a new direction in American spy fiction, if not
the emergence of a new genre of historical intelligence novel. Thus
Shadow Trade is the story of Guyer, an ex-CIA officer who sets up
his own private business in clandestine operations. It gives us
an insight into how secret intelligence agencies operate, and the
dangerous lengths to which they will go to achieve results. Far from
being about the exploits of a sensational hero, it is an exploration of
the endless manipulations that occur within and between secret
services.

Furst's other novel, *Night Soldiers* is quite different from his first
work. It blends the historical novel with the espionage story. It is
set mainly in Europe between the wars, and the author evokes a
vivid and historically-accurate picture of the locations he describes.
Its authenticity derives, however, from the author's grasp of political
complexity. We are told the story of a young and inexperienced
Bulgarian – Khristo Stoianev – and of how he is recruited into the
NKVD and brought to Moscow in the 1930s, to be trained in the
arts of espionage. His first experience comes with his involvement
in the Spanish Civil War. He is quickly disillusioned and we follow
his fate. This novel engages the sympathy of the reader with the
hero in order to present a view of events which is different from
Hemingway's, yet is free of Western clichés.[1]

Robert Littell, who has written quite a few novels with an espionage theme, overcomes the problem of genre cliché in his own ways,
for example by substituting humour for sensationalism as a means
of sustaining entertainment. He displays versatility rather than
reliance on stock plots and characters. In 1973 in *The Defection of
A. J. Lewinter*, he dealt with the problem of evaluating a defector.
In *The Amateur*, 1981, he used an analyst spy hero. This hero,
Charles Heller, blackmails his superiors in the CIA to train him so
that he can take his revenge upon the terrorists who murdered his

girlfriend – one of the more constant themes in Littell's novels is recognisably modern, the conflict between the individual and a secret organisation.

In his 1990 novel *The Once and Future Spy*, Littell perhaps had an opportunity to tackle a post-cold war theme. But he declines the opportunity. Instead, he deals with the issues of rivalry and control within the intelligence service, and raises the question of who is to control the organisation if control cannot be achieved from the outside – themes that reflect the debate over Congressional oversight of the intelligence community in the late 1970s and at the time of the Iran–Contra controversy. At the same time there is within *The Once and Future Spy* a parallel story of the last few days of America's patriotic spy of the Revolutionary War, Nathan Hale, with whom our hero identifies. Like Alan Furst, Littell seeks to accommodate a contemporary story with history.

The critical response to Littell is not only favourable, but indicative of the fact that higher intellectual ground is now being claimed for the contemporary US secret intelligence novel. A reviewer in Britain's *Sunday Times* remarked of *The Once and Future Spy*: 'the interweaving of past and present is handled with delicacy and conviction'.[25] Another writer and critic of spy fiction, James Melville, praises the same novel in a telling vein:

> This is espionage writing of a high order, involving perceptive insights into obsessive behaviour and the morality of patriotism, a plot with several breathtaking twists in its tail, and a cast of characters many of whom are almost loony enough to resemble people we have all met. Robert Littell offers not only a cracking good story but also food for thought.[26]

The modern expectation is that the spy novel should be not just 'entertaining', but thoughtful and informative as well.

I have tried to show that in recent American spy fiction, espionage is given a more serious treatment than in the past. The books still offer entertainment, but they do not sacrifice political sense in achieving it. The quality of the writing has improved, and it is no longer standard practice to over-sensationalise in spy fiction. The improved quality is surely in evidence in those novels I have mentioned, *Agents of Innocence* by David Ignatius, and *Shadow Trade* and *Night Soldiers*, by Alan Furst. One might argue that the American spy novel has reached a new standard of maturity. For this reason, spy fiction could become a valuable source for political and cultural history in future years, especially in view of current political developments. In this context, it is significant that US spy fiction writers are ambitious for the future of their genre. Alan Furst spoke for a number of authors and critics when he said:

> I'd like to see an evolution into complexity, with demands of good fiction elevating the form. I'd like to see British and American novels less instinctively prone to condemning their national services, not so quick to fall back on 'betrayal' and 'conspiracy' etc. as literary devices – that's much too easy and fairly dishonest. The future depends on the form improving, but I believe it will.[27]

It is possible that the American spy novel, having bobbed for so long in the wake of its British counterpart, may at last be about to forge ahead. In Britain, some spy novels are already out of date. Len Deighton's *Hook, Line and Sinker*, just published, suffers from time-warp perhaps in an unlucky way, as it is part of a long-running trilogy that has stood still conceptually regardless of the speed of political change. More seriously, British writers seem to find diffi- culty in breaking out of certain familiar themes, such as that of the mole. With the end of the cold war, some British spy novelists may be unable to adapt their fiction. It could well be that American spy writers will take over from their British counterparts as exponents of the art of realistic and mature spy fiction.

Some critics may be tempted to proclaim the death of the spy novel – Alan Furst, as we have seen, prefers not to be known as a spy novelist. The argument here would be that the spy novel may be one of the first casualties of the end of the cold war. What we are more likely to see, however, is the not unwelcome demise of the cold war spy novel. As le Carré recently commented on the publication of *The Russia House*, the spy story was not invented by the cold war, and will not be finished off by the ending of it:

> On the contrary, this is a new springtime for espionage writ- ing. Spying will take a more benign form in the future, but we haven't deloused the earth quite yet. We haven't got rid of the mutual suspicion and hostility between the powers. We are still poised to destroy each other. For a writer it is a great opportunity. I feel as if I've been given a whole new pack of cards to play with . . .[28]

The conscious irony in these words is all too clear. There are still all too many themes and political problems to inspire the spy novelist. As long as the authors perceive the spy novel as the right medium in which to work them out sensibly, spy fiction will continue to flourish and mature in America.

Novels mentioned in the text

Aarons, Edward S. *Assignment to Disaster* (New York: Fawcett, 1955; London: Fawcett, 1956). *Assignment: School for spies* (New York: Fawcett, 1966).

Buckley, William F. *Stained Glass* (New York: Doubleday, 1978; London: Penguin, 1979). *Who's On First* (New York: Doubleday, 1980; London: Allen Lane, 1980).

Fleming, Ian. *Casino Royale* (London: Cape, 1954; New York: Macmillan, 1954).

Furst, Alan. *Shadow Trade* (New York: Delacorte 1983; London: Quartet, 1984). *Night Soldiers* (London: Bodley Head, 1988; Boston, Mass. Houghton-Mifflin, 1988).

Garfield, Brian. *Hopscotch* (New York: Evans, 1975; London: Macmillan, 1975).

Grady, James. *Six Days of the Condor* (New York: W.W. Norton, 1975).

Hunt, E. Howard. *The Berlin Ending* (New York: Putnam, 1973). *The Hargrave Deception* (New York: Stein & Day, 1980). *The Kremlin Conspiracy* (New York: Stein & Day, 1985).

Ignatius, David. *Agents of Innocence* (New York: W. W. Norton, 1987; London: W.H. Allen, 1988).

Le Carré, John. *The Russia House* (London: Hodder & Stoughton, 1989; New York: Knopf, 1989).

Littell, Robert. *The Defection of A. J. Lewinter* (Boston, Mass. Houghton-Mifflin, 1973; London: Hodder & Stoughton, 1973). *The Amateur* (New York: Simon & Schuster, 1981; London: Jonathan Cape, 1981). *The Once and Future Spy* (London: Faber, 1990; New York: Bantam Doubleday Dell, 1990).

McCarry, Charles. *The Miernik Dossier* (New York: Saturday Review Press, 1973; London: Hutchinson, 1975).

Tyler, W. T. *The Man Who Lost the War* (New York: Dial, 1980). *Rogue's March* (New York: Harper & Row, 1982).

Notes

1. Malcolm Bradbury, *The Modern American Novel* (Oxford: Oxford Univ. Press, 1983), p. 7.

2. Cf. Edward W. Bennett's observation that until 'a few years ago . . . sometimes fiction gave a better idea of what espionage was like than purportedly true stories': Bennett, 'Intelligence and history from the other side of the hill'. *Journal of Modern History*, 60 (June 1988), 312.
3. Quotation from the introduction to *The Philby Conspiracy* by Bruce Page, David Leitch and Phillip Knightley (New York: Ballantine, 1981), p. 7.
4. Allen Dulles, *Great Spy Stories* (New York: Harper & Row, 1969), p. xi.
5. Yet later Bond adventures, perhaps prophetically, found him battling against international crime syndicates, such as SPECTRE – the Special Executive for Counter-intelligence, Terrorism, Revenge and Extortion.
6. Quotation from an article by Richard Middleton, *Daily Mail*, 13 Aug. 1990, p. 5.
7. Ronald J. Ambrosetti, 'A Study of the spy genre in recent popular literature' (Bowling Green State University Ph.D. dissertation, 1973), p. 14.
8. Quoted in Bruce Merry, *Anatomy of the Spy Thriller* (Dublin: Gill & Macmillan, 1977), p. 47.
9. See Victor Marchetti, *The Rope Dancer* (New York: Grosset & Dunlap, 1971).
10. Merry, *Anatomy of the Spy Thriller*, p. 5.
11. Edward S. Aarons, *Assignment: School for spies* (New York: Fawcett, 1966), p. 10.
12. E. Howard Hunt, *Undercover: Memoirs of an American secret agent* (New York: Berkeley, 1974), p. 133.
13. Another aspect of the spy novel which Hunt could have developed (and without being censored by the CIA) was the exploration of the moral ambiguities of espionage. He did eventually attempt to do this, but not until his later novels written in the late 1970s and early 1980s, in which he shied away from the cold war conflict and developed other themes such as terrorism.
14. Letter from S.J. Hamrick to the author, 30 Oct. 1984.
15. Douglas S. Blaufarb's review of *The Secret Lovers* by Charles McCarry, in *Periscope*, III, No. 3, (1977), 6. *Periscope* is the quarterly journal of the Association of Former Intelligence Officers (AFIO).
16. See William F. Buckley *Who's On First* (New York: Doubleday; London: Allen Lane, 1980), which describes the competition between the superpowers to put the first satellite into orbit. Also see Charles McCarry's *The Tears of Autumn* (New York: Saturday Review Press; London: Hutchinson, 1975), in which he offers an explanation for the assassination of President Kennedy.
17. John Atkins, *The British Spy Novel* (London: John Calder, 1984), p. 119.
18. Will Perry, *The Kremlin Watcher*, (New York: Dodd Mead, 1978), p. 34.
19. *ibid.*, p. 114.
20. Paul Henissart, 'Of spies and stories', *The Writer* (May 1978), 16.
21. Joseph F. Hosey, review of *Rogue's March* by W. T. Tyler, *FILS (Foreign Intelligence Literary Scene)* I (Dec. 1982), 8.
22. All the quotations are from a letter from David Ignatius to the author dated 23 Jan. 1989.

23. Letter from Alan Furst to the author dated 20 Dec. 1988.
24. NKVD is the acronym for the Russian security service, which from 1934 to 1946 was called the Narodnyi Komissariat Vnutrennikh Del. Ernest Hemingway's novel *For Whom the Bell Tolls*, based on his own experiences in the Spanish Civil War, appeared in 1940.
25. Marcel Berlins, review of *The Once and Future Spy*, by Robert Littell, *Sunday Times* Book Section (1 July 1990)p. 7.
26. James Melville, review of *The Once and Future Spy* by Robert Littell, *Ham and High*, (29 June 1990), 99.
27. Letter from Alan Furst to the author dated 20 Dec. 1988.
28. Quoted from *Spy Fiction: A connoisseur's guide*, by Donald McCormick and Katy Fletcher, (Oxford: Facts On File 1990), p. 11.

A guide to further study

The aim in this guide is to suggest some sources of knowledge and inspiration for would-be students of intelligence history who are as yet beginners in the field. Some of the suggestions may also be of assistance to teachers in schools and higher institutions of learning who are seeking to introduce their students to the intelligence history field. Wherever possible, recommendations of easily accessible items are made, but unpublished doctoral dissertations or obscure articles are included if they are the best or an indispensable source on a particular topic. Reference librarians can advise on how to borrow these items or obtain photocopies of them.

Those who would like more specialised guidance will find that this is readily available elsewhere: perusal of the notes to Chapter 1 will yield details about specialist bibliographies, other works of reference and journals which are helpful to students already versed in the rudiments of intelligence history.

The Historical Background

In the cases of both Canada and the United States, the main *institutional* developments in the history of secret intelligence took place within the last hundred years. In the case of the United States, however, secret intelligence played an important if often impromptu role from the time of the American Revolution on. In 1821 James Fenimore Cooper published his novel *The Spy: or, A Tale of Neutral Ground*. This is justly celebrated as a work of *fiction* that heralded the arrival of a new nation on the literary stage. But, based on the experiences of the US counter-intelligence agent Enoch Crosby and written under the inspiration of the statesman John Jay, the novel bears the stamp of authenticity. It conveys the atmosphere of those perilous times when George Washington spent a substantial portion of his budget on secret agents (though not, as Cooper's plot reveals, on their pensions). Available as it is in modern editions, *The Spy* would be an agreeable starting point for the enquiring reader.

Edward F. Sayle, formerly curator of historical intelligence at the Central Intelligence Agency, explored the possibilities of writing a verifiable account of secret activities in the Revolutionary War in his article 'The historical underpinnings of the US intelligence community', which appeared in the very first issue of the *International Journal of Intelligence and Counterintelligence* (spring, 1986), 1–27. In 1990 Stephen Knott added extensively to our knowledge of the same subject in his Boston College doctoral dissertation, 'Lifting the veil: the roots of American covert activity'. This is a long-overdue examination not only of Washington's Secret Service, but of the Federalists' analysis of the constitutional dimensions of secret intelligence, and of congressional provision of funds in the early national period. Plans are afoot to publish Knott's well-written thesis, which should become more readily available to the general reader fairly soon.

Once America had won its independence, *foreign* intelligence became both technically possible and a regular feature of presidential activities. To understand foreign intelligence one must, of course, be acquainted with its context, foreign policy. Walter LaFeber has written a lively survey of US foreign policy in which he draws on a wide range of literature and shows a sensitivity to intelligence matters: *The American Age: United States foreign policy at home and abroad since 1750* (New York: W.W. Norton, 1989).

Nathan Miller, *Spying for America: The Hidden History of US Intelligence* (New York: Paragon House, 1989) is an overview of the history of American espionage from George Washington's day to the 1980s. It is entertainingly written, and balanced in its judgements on a wide range of controversial issues; its endnotes supply helpful guidance on further reading. Charles D. Ameringer, in *US Foreign Intelligence: The secret side of American history* (Lexington, Mass.: D.C. Heath Lexington Books, 1990), covers the same period. He has some especially interesting things to say about the role of covert operations in achieving American expansionist objectives in the nineteenth century, and writes with authority on US clandestine activities in Central America from the days of President Theodore Roosevelt's acquisition of the Panamanian Canal Zone to the more recent interventions by the CIA. Though it contains some inaccuracies, it is entertainingly written, well-researched, and remarkably balanced in its judgements on a wide range of controversial issues. It is particularly helpful on the history of nineteenth-century espionage, a subject on which there is a scarcity of reliable literature.

Miller believes that the nineteenth century was the age of the 'amateur' in American espionage, and perhaps the dilettantish reputation of secret intelligence accounts for its generally poor treatment by historians. Yet there is some noteworthy scholarship on some topics. Anna K. Nelson is instructive on President James K. Polk's secret operations in Mexico in her article 'Mission to Mexico: Moses Y. Beach, Secret Agent', *New York Historical Society Quarterly*, 59 (July 1975), 226–45, and Knott's work, mentioned above, enlightens us further on Polk's political motives. When it comes to the Civil War, however, the literature on secret intelligence operations is, like the operations themselves, extensive but bordering on incompetence. One exception is Harriet Chappell Owsley's scholarly article, 'Henry Shelton Sanford and federal surveillance abroad, 1861–1865', *Mississippi Valley Historical Review*, 48 (Sept. 1961), 211–28. Two works that reward examination in the absence of more serious scholarship are Harnett T. Kane, *Spies for the Blue and Gray* (Garden City, NY: Hanover House, 1954) and John Bakeless *Spies of the Confederacy* (Philadelphia, Pa: Lippincott, 1970).

One of the most controversial secret operations in American history was the Pinkerton detective agency's penetration, in the 1870s, of the so-called Molly Maguires. The allegation that the Mollies (if they really existed) conducted a terrorist campaign (or was it provoked by the Pinkertons themselves?) against Pennsylvanian coal capitalists in defence of the rights of Irish-Americans (or of trade unionists? or of the working class?) resulted in several executions in the wake of an unfair trial. All this helped to ensure that American *foreign* espionage would not, in future years, be entrusted to a private corporation like the Pinkerton agency – though the agency's founder, the Glasgow-born Allan Pinkerton, had originally moved to Chicago from Canada in the expectation of flourishing in a police-free society. Sir Arthur Conan Doyle's last novel, *The Valley of Fear*, first published in 1914, deals with the Molly-Maguire episode. It reeks of prejudice against the Mollies and is surely Sherlock Holmes's worst adventure. A more critical view of private detection from a Pinkerton veteran's perspective is supplied in *The Red Harvest* (first published in 1929), one of Dashiell Hammett's finest novels. The 1970 film *The Molly Maguires* (Paramount) starring Richard Harris, Samantha Eggar, and Sean

Connery, the Edinburgh-born actor celebrated for his portrayal of James Bond, is even-handed in its treatment. The standard book remains Wayne G. Broehl, *The Molly Maguires* (Cambridge, Mass.: Harvard Univ. Press, 1964).

In 1893, when President Grover Cleveland and a group of US capitalists conspired in a covert operation to overthrow the queen of Hawaii with a view to the archipelago's annexation, Senator George F. Hoar of Massachusetts secured passage of an amendment restraining the executive's powers. Hoar's protestations foreshadowed what became, in the twentieth century, an important constitutional debate. Henry M. Wriston placed the Hoar Amendment in its historical and constitutional context in his book *Executive Agents in American Foreign Relations* (Baltimore, Md.: Johns Hopkins Univ. Press, 1929).

The War of 1898

To understand the significance of the 1898 war for the intelligence services of North America, one needs some appreciation of Canadian foreign relations. In light of Graeme Mount's expertise on covert activities within Canada, the sensible choice of a sympathetic text is the book he co-authored with Edelgard E. Mahant, *An Introduction to Canadian American Relations* (2nd ed. Toronto: Nelson, 1989). The relevance of another of Mount's publications is evident from its title: 'Friendly liberator or predatory aggressor? Some Canadian impressions of the US during the Spanish–American War'. *North/South: Canadian Review of Latin American and Caribbean Studies*, 22 (1986), 59–70, Norman Penlington *Canada and Imperialism, 1896–1899* (Toronto: Univ. of Toronto Press, 1965) examines Canadian attitudes towards both American and British imperialism at the end of the nineteenth century.

A chapter in Rhodri Jeffreys-Jones's *American Espionage: From Secret Service to CIA* (New York: Free Press, 1977) discusses the Montreal spy ring within the context of the development of United States espionage. G.J.A. O'Toole, in his book *The Spanish War: An American epic* (New York: W.W. Norton, 1984), presents a thorough account of the war as a whole, and of related intelligence activities world-wide. P.E. McGinty's two-volume 1983 Georgetown University doctoral dissertation, 'Intelligence and the Spanish American War', remains unpublished.

Graeme Mount is almost alone in his efforts to discover the historical antecedents of Canada's espionage establishment. There is, however, a growing literature on Canadian intelligence during and after the Second World War. One of the least unreliable treatments of the key Allied spymaster code-named 'Intrepid' is H. Montgomery Hyde, *The Quiet Canadian: The secret service story of Sir William Stephenson* (London: Hamish Hamilton, 1962). On Canadian counter-intelligence, see Reg Whitaker, 'Origins of the Canadian government's internal security system, 1946–1952', *Canadian Historical Review*, 65 (June 1984), 154–83.

United States Secret Intelligence up to 1941

Developments in the United States between 1898 and American entry into the war in 1941 are now attracting serious attention from intelligence historians, though several inadequacies remain. There is no authoritative work on the United States Secret Service, though James Bamford is working on one. For an overview of the history of military intelligence, we still have to rely on narrowly focussed institutional narratives: Marc B. Powe, *Emergence of the War Department Intelligence Agency 1885–1918* (Manhattan, Kas.: Military Affairs, 1975) and Bruce B. Bidwell, *History of the Military Intelligence Division, Department of the Army General Staff, 1775–1941* (Frederick, Md: Univ. Publications of America, 1986). But there does exist a fine study of the counter-insurgency dimension of military intelligence, a subject that was important both in the Theodore Roosevelt administration and subsequently – Brian M. Linn, *The US Army and Counterinsurgency in the Philippine War, 1899–1902* (Chapel Hill, NC: Univ. of North Carolina Press, 1989).

Jeffrey Dorwart has addressed the history of naval intelligence in two scholarly volumes, *The Office of Naval Intelligence: The birth of America's first intelligence agency 1865–1918* (Annapolis, Md: Naval Institute Press, 1979) and *Conflict of Duty: The navy's intelligence dilemma, 1919–1945* (Annapolis, Md: Naval Institute Press, 1983). Dorwart supplies an institutional narrative, details the bureaucratic struggles within naval intelligence, and examines the threat that the ONI posed to civil liberties at home. Because of these emphases, his coverage of tactical and strategic intelligence is relatively light.

The First World War produced an intensification of intelligence activity in both Europe and North America. There is no good overview written from the American standpoint, though Miller's *Spying for America* is worth consulting and Jeffreys-Jones's *American Espionage* describes the State Department's intelligence system. Barbara W. Tuchman's *The Zimmerman Telegram* (London:

Constable, 1959) is about Germany's secret inducements to Mexico to enter the war by attacking the USA from the rear in 1917, about the exposure of the plot by the British and American secret services, and about the affair's role in provoking a United States declaration of war against Germany. The book is a readable and scholarly account of one of the most important events in intelligence history.

Wartime hysteria permitted and encouraged the intelligence services to endanger civil liberties in the name of national security. In both Canada (which was already at war) and the United States (which was not), local authorities permitted British intelligence to move ruthlessly against Indian revolutionaries acting under encouragement from Germany – the story is told in L.P. Mathur's *Indian Revolutionary Movement in the United States of America* (Delhi: S. Chand, 1970). On FBI anti-left activities in the Red Scare of 1919–20 as well as subsequently, see Richard G. Powers, *Secrecy and Power: The Life of J. Edgar Hoover* (New York: Free Press, 1986). As Dorwart indicates, naval intelligence was implicated in domestic transgressions in the 1920s. The same can be said of military intelligence, as Joan M. Jensen shows in her essay 'All pink sisters: the War Department and the feminist movement in the 1920s', in Lois Scharf and Joan Jensen, eds., *Decades of Discontent: The women's movement, 1920–1940* (Westport, Conn.: Greenwood, 1983).

Spy scares and films about them helped to prepare the American public for the Second World War and, it seems evident from an article by Stephen Vaughn, contributed to the emergence of a well-known actor and politician: 'Spies, national security, and "The inertia projector": the secret service films of Ronald Reagan'. *American Quarterly*, 39 (1987), 355–80. In 1941, Warner issued a remake of *The Maltese Falcon*, based on Hammett's 1931 spy thriller of the same title. With Humphrey Bogart as Sam Spade and John Huston as scriptwriter, this production launched the *film noir*, a genre whose greys and shadows seemed suited to the moral relativisms of the world of espionage. Though both Bogart and Huston were later to demonstrate their own unambiguous morality by fighting McCarthyism's secret blacklists in Hollywood, Bogart helped to portray the moral ambivalences of war in a further film, *Casablanca* (Warner, 1943). It is here that he woos his girl (Ingrid Bergman) with the immortal line 'Here's looking at you, kid' – stealing her, in the process, from a hero of the German underground resistance.

Both Jeffreys-Jones (*American Espionage*) and Miller (*Spying for America*) qualify the view, much favoured by some members of the

post-1940s intelligence community, that United States intelligence
was fatally weakened by the 1930s, and that this accounts for America's being caught by surprise by the Japanese attack on Pearl
Harbor in 1941. In her book *Pearl Harbor: Warning and decision*
(Stanford, Calif.: Stanford Univ. Press, 1962), Roberta Wohlstetter
analyses the weaknesses in the US intelligence system, concluding
that incoming information was mismanaged and poorly analysed.
One scholar who disagrees with her view is David Kahn, the author
of *The Codebreakers: The story of secret writing* (New York: Macmillan, 1967). Kahn's view that incoming information on Japan was
insufficiently extensive appears in his essay, 'The United States
views Germany and Japan in 1941', in Ernest R. May, ed., *Knowing
One's Enemies: Intelligence assessment before the two world Wars*
(Princeton, NJ: Princeton Univ. Press, 1985).

The Second World War and the OSS

Rather confusingly, the two best general works on the OSS are
both by men called Smith. Richard Harris Smith's book appeared
before archival materials became widely available on the subject.
It is nevertheless critical and well informed, as well as a readable
and in places amusing introduction to its subject matter: *OSS:
The secret history of America's first central intelligence agency*
(Berkeley, Calif.: Univ. of California Press, 1972). Bradley F. Smith,
The Shadow Warriors: OSS and the origins of CIA (London: André
Deutch, 1983) is a formidable work of scholarship that utilises newly
available archival materials and takes a sceptical view of the motives
and bureaucratic tactics of OSS officials.

An important specialist study on the OSS is Barry M. Katz,
*Foreign Intelligence: Research and analysis in the Office of Stra-
tegic Services, 1942–1945* (Cambridge, Mass.: Harvard Univ. Press,
1989). Katz is less interested in how R and A functioned as a
component of the intelligence community than in R and A personnel as exemplars of the American scholarly community. But his
book advances our knowledge of the vital analytical component of
the intelligence community and demonstrates further how vast is
the quantity of primary material now at the disposal of the historian
of wartime intelligence.

There is a shortage of overviews of American secret intelligence
in the Second World War, as well as of certain aspects of it, notably
military and naval intelligence. Historians are, however, writing
books on special topics which will be building blocks for future
works by generalists. Two examples of illuminating studies are

Ronald Lewin, *The American Magic: Codes, ciphers and the defeat of Japan* (Harmondsworth: Penguin, 1983) and Leslie B. Rout and John N. Bratzel, *The Shadow War: German Espionage and United States counterespionage in Latin America during World War II* (Frederick, Md: Univ. Publications of America, 1986).

One of the most recent and most accessible introductions to the Tyler Kent story is *The Man who was M* (Oxford: Blackwell, 1984) by Anthony Masters. If possible this should be supplemented by Hayden Peake's article, 'The putative spy' in the American intelligence magazine *FILS*, 5 (March–April 1986), 1, 7–8 (May–June 1986), 3–5, and by 'Roosevelt and prewar commitments to Churchill: the Tyler Kent affair', *Diplomatic History*, 5 (fall 1981), 291–311, by Warren Kimball and Bruce Bartlett. Richard Thurlow, *Fascism in Britain* (Oxford: Blackwell, 1987) is excellent on the British background, while *The Creation of the Anglo-American Alliance 1937–41: A study in competitive cooperation* (London: Europa, 1981) by David Reynolds gives the wider American political dimension. At the time of going to press, Ray Bearse and Anthony Read have produced a book whose interpretation of Kent as a right wing ideologue is fundamentally opposed toAndrew Lownie's judgement: *Conspirator: The untold story of Tyler Kent* (New York: Doubleday, 1991).

While the two Smiths' books on the OSS supply information on Operation Torch, it is helpful to turn to other works for guidance on the political and strategic context within which the operation took place. *Roosevelt: The soldier of freedom* (New York: Harcourt Brace Jovanovich, 1970) is a biography by James MacGregor Burns that contains many good insights. Briefer but more up-to-date is Frank Freidel, *Franklin D. Roosevelt: A rendezvous with destiny* (Boston: Little, Brown, 1990). Robert Dallek, *Franklin D. Roosevelt and Foreign Policy, 1932–1945* (New York: Oxford Univ. Press, 1979) helps to explain the domestic constraints on FDR's policymaking. For an official historian's account of Allied strategy making, see Maurice Matloff's essay, 'Allied strategy in Europe, 1939–1945', in Peter Paret, ed., *Makers of Modern Strategy: From Machiavelli to the nuclear age* (Princeton, NJ: Princeton Univ. Press, 1986).

Reliable information on the activities of the OSS in Burma is hard to come by. Chapters 9 and 10 in R. Harris Smith's *OSS* are helpful, though they do not focus on the problem of the Burma Road itself. For a first-hand description of the physical dimensions of the military transport challenge, see Gerald Samson, *The Burma Road* (London: London China Society, 1946). Barbara Tuchman comments on the Chinese end of the operation in her *Stilwell and the American Experience in China 1911–1945* (London: MacDonald, 1981). Sources illustrative of the romanticisation of the US covert operation in Burma are more abundant. One is the novel by the American Tom T. Chamales, *Never So Few* (New York: Scribner, 1957). MGM's 1959 screen version of this novel features a general who wins the Medal of Honor putting everything right in the last reel, with Frank Sinatra, Gina Lollobrigida, Steve McQueen and Charles Bronson in starring roles.

The Modern North American Intelligence Community

The literature on the post-Second World War period is voluminous, with some first-class books available. A heavy concentration on the CIA has, however, led to the neglect of other intelligence agencies located in the State Department, the armed forces and elsewhere. There is no scholarly book on the Defense Intelligence Agency, or on the Drugs Enforcement Agency. There is, nevertheless, a thoughtful treatment of modern undercover police activities, including anti-drug operations: Gary Marx, *Undercover: Police surveillance in America* (Berkeley, Calif. Univ. of California Press, 1988). There is also a study of the National Security Agency: James Bamford, *The Puzzle Palace* (Boston, Mass.: Houghton-Mifflin, 1982). This book is soundly documented on the NSA's bureaucratic history and on some civil liberties issues, but the top-secret nature of the subject matter means that we are left in the dark about some of the strategic intelligence issues involved in high-technology international surveillance.

A detailed account of the evolution of the Central Intelligence Group and early CIA is to be found in the official history by Thomas Troy, *Donovan and the CIA: A history of the establishment of the Central Intelligence Agency* (Frederick, Md: Univ. Publications of America, 1981). Two general histories of the CIA deal with that institution's origins: John Ranelagh, *The Agency: The rise and decline of the CIA* (New York: Simon & Schuster, 1986) is detailed and written from a supportive standpoint, while Rhodri Jeffreys-Jones, *The CIA and American Democracy* (New Haven, Conn.: Yale Univ. Press) is more concise and discursive. The debate on the intentions of the Truman administration with regard to the CIA is by no means over: the University Presses of Edinburgh and Kansas will soon publish a book, Sallie Pisani's *The CIA and the Marshall Plan*, which will offer an economic explanation for the origins of the US intelligence community's expanded international role.

We are short of studies of British McCarthyism and of comparisons between it and its American counterpart or parent, but historians of both countries will find it instructive to read Bernard Porter, *Plots and Paranoia: A history of political espionage in Britain 1790–1988* (London: Unwin Hyman, 1989) and Mark Hollingsworth and Charles Tremayne, *The Economic League: The silent McCarthyism* (London: National Council for Civil Liberties, 1989). Similarly, the book by Richard M. Freeland, *The Truman Doctrine and the Origins of McCarthyism: Foreign policy, domestic politics, and internal security 1946–48* (New York: Schocken, 1974), with its idea that 'liberal' politicians may have contributed unintentionally to intolerant policies, might prove enlightening on the European as well as the American side of the Atlantic.

The study by Athan G. Theoharris, *Spying on Americans: Political surveillance from Hoover to the Huston Plan* (Philadelphia, Pa: Temple Univ. Press, 1978) bears comparison with its British counterpart by Porter. For expositions of more recent American legislative deliberations on security matters, see Loch K. Johnson, *A Season of Inquiry: The Senate intelligence investigation* (Lexington, Ky: Univ. Press of Kentucky, 1985) and *America's Secret Power: The CIA in a democratic society* (New York: Oxford Univ. Press, 1989).

The Canadian dimension to spy scandals and spy scares was important in America and Britain, as we can see from Karen Potter's essay, but it was also, of course, a problem 'on location'. On the scientific impact of Soviet espionage within Canada, see Paul DuFour, ' "Eggheads" and espionage: the Gouzenko affair in Canada', *Journal of Canadian Studies*, 16 (fall/winter 1981), 188–98. The growth of Canadian counter-intelligence in response to security threats eventually produced a reaction that mirrored comparable trends in other countries. The extensive literature discussing Canadian demands for oversight includes the article by C.E.S. Franks, a member of the McDonald Commission into wrongdoing by the Royal Canadian Mounted Police, 'Political control of security activities', *Queen's Quarterly*, 91 (autumn 1984), 565–77.

Both Canada and the United States have since the 1970s legislated to provide for legislative oversight of their security services. This legislation is described in chapter 7 of Richard Norton-Taylor's *In Defence of the Realm? The case for accountable security services* (London: Civil Liberties Trust, 1990). Two works are of special interest to students of the history of oversight attempts in the United States. Harry H. Ransom argues there was an inverse relationship between congressional enthusiasm for oversight and the intensity of the cold war: 'Secret intelligence in the United States, 1947–1982: the CIA's search for legitimacy', in Christopher M. Andrew and David Dilks, eds., *The Missing Dimension: Governments and intelligence communities in the twentieth century* (London: Macmillan, 1985). Frank J. Smist believes there are two types of congressional oversight committee, investigative and institutional, the one probing, the other responsible, and that the historical record indicates that it is unlikely that a successful blend of the two can be achieved: 'Congress oversees the United States intelligence community, 1947–1984' (Univ. of Oklahoma political science Ph.D. dissertation, 1988).

While the history of the Defense Intelligence Agency remains an underexplored subject, an overview of military intelligence may be obtained from the book edited by Gerald W. Hopple and Bruce W. Watson, *The Military Intelligence Community* (Boulder, Colo.: Westview, 1986). On the management style of the Secretary of Defense at the time of the DIA's creation, see James R. Roherty, *The Decisions of Robert S. McNamara* (Coral Gables, Fla: Univ. of Miami Press, 1970). Two books which help to put the DIA in its historical and institutional context are William R. Corson, *The Armies of Ignorance: The rise of the American intelligence empire* (New York: Dial, 1977) and Tyrus Fain *et al.*, *The Intelligence Community: History, organization, and issues* (New York: Bowker, 1977). Corson's book has the further merit of being unusually informative on the United States Secret Service. The role of the DIA with respect to strategic intelligence is considered in a perceptive work which must rate as one of the more constructive contributions made to the good of mankind by a scholar: Lawrence Freedman, *US Intelligence and the Soviet Strategic Threat* (London: Macmillan, 1977).

The significance of the composition of the CIA élite embraces the performance issue as well as the question of equal opportunity. Freedman's book is therefore helpful background reading, as is Walter Laqueur's *A World of Secrets: The uses and limits of intelligence* (New York: Basic, 1985). Two books which convey some of the popular assumptions about the CIA's leadership are David Wise and Thomas B. Ross, *The Invisible Government* (London: Jonathan Cape, 1964) and Stewart Alsop, *The Center* (New York: Harper & Row, 1968).

The problem for biographical quantifiers is not a scarcity of information, but incomplete and irregular runs of data. One large accessible source available from CIABASE, P.O. Box 5022, Herndon, Virginia is a four-megabyte IBM-compatible data base compiled by agency veteran Ralph McGehee. R. Harris Smith, *OSS* is informative on who moved on to the CIA from the OSS, and on the background of the individuals concerned. Robin W. Winks has supplied information on many individuals and detailed biographical studies of a few of them in his *Cloak and Gown: Scholars in the secret war, 1939–1961* (New York: Morrow, 1987).

By coincidence, Winks is also an authority on spy fiction, though his reflections on the subject appear in the context of a work mainly directed to detective stories: *Modus Operandi: An excursion into detective fiction* (Boston, Mass.: David R. Godine, 1982). Fenimore Cooper is no longer the only eminent United States fiction writer to have devoted a major novel to intelligence. In 1991 there appeared Norman Mailer's *Harlot's Ghost* (New York, Random House; London, Michael Joseph), a work that addresses, in relation to the CIA hierarchy, some of the questions aired in Robert Spears' essay. But there is still a distinct scarcity of critical works specifically devoted to the American spy-fiction genre. Christine Bold has begun to close the gap with her study, 'Secret negotiations: the spy figure in nineteenth-century American popular fiction', in Wesley K. Wark, ed., *Spy Fiction, Spy Films and Real Intelligence* (London: Frank Cass, 1991). Earle Davis in his article 'Howard Hunt and Peter Ward: CIA spy novels', *Kansas Quarterly*, 10 (fall 1978), 85–95, describes in detail the plots of the novels in the Ward series and their relation to E. Howard Hunt's experiences in the CIA. In his *Anatomy of the Spy Thriller* (Dublin: Gill & Macmillan, 1977) Bruce Merry offers a literary critique of the spy novel with emphasis on British examples, but with some American content too. Myron J. Smith in his *Cloak and Dagger Fiction: An annotated guide to spy thrillers* (Santa Barbara, Calif.: ABC Clio, 1982) supplies a helpful introduction, followed by plot synopses of many works, especially those by better-known authors – but he neither discusses nor mentions the geographic provenance of his writers. *Spy Fiction: A Connoisseur's Guide* (Oxford: Facts on File, 1990), by Donald McCormick and Katy Fletcher, lists and discusses the works of mainly British and American novelists, and in a final section contains essays on themes in spy fiction.

McCormick and Fletcher also have a chapter on the spy film. For an earlier discussion of screen portrayals of espionage, see

Leonard Rubenstein, *The Great Spy Films* (Secaucus, NJ: Citadel, 1979). Students and teachers who find it more convenient to view spy films on video have at their disposal a well-indexed compilation that describes various films (including some of those mentioned above) and indicates their geographic provenance. Edited by James J. Mulay *et al.*, it is called *Spies and Sleuths: Mystery, spy and suspense films in videocassette* (Evanston, Ill.: Cinebooks, 1988). Two works that will be a special inspiration to future generations of scholars are Wark's work cited above, and Larry Langman and David Ebner, comps., *Encyclopedia of American Spy Films* (New York: Garland, 1991). The thousand entries in the latter work span the entire history of American cinema.

Index

Aarons, Edward, 221, 225, 227, 238–9
Alexander, Tsar, 87
Arcadia Conference, 82, 88
Attlee, Clement, 63, 144, 150–1

'Bay of Pigs', 20–1, 136–7, 163, 183–6,
  210–11
Beard, Charles A., 4, 11, 23, 27, 78
Bedell Smith, General Walter, 25–6,
  138, 140, 209
Bird, Harry, 51
Bissell, Richard, 138, 184
Bonnilla Martel, Eusebio, 35–6, 38–9
Brzezinski, Zbigniew, 25
Buckley, William, 229, 238–9
Bullitt, William, 51, 64, 74
Bundy, McGeorge, 185
Bureau of the Budget, 171–2

Calligos, 68, 77
Carranza, Ramon, 35–7, 39, 41
Carroll, Lt-Gen. Joseph, 187, 189,
  191–3
Cervera, Admiral, 41
Chamberlain, Neville, 50, 61
Chennault, General Claire, 106
Church Committee, 26, 159, 162, 185,
  197–201, 213
Churchill, Winston S., 15, 49–50, 52,
  56, 59, 61, 67, 73, 79, 83, 99, 109,
  149
CIA, 5, 8, 10–11, 14, 16, 20–1, 25, 27–8,
  123–5, 132–42, 168, 172, 183, 186,
  196, 249–52
  and literature, 227–40
  origins of, 17–18, 123–42
  and recruitment, 202–17
CIA's historical office, 6–7
CIG (Central Intelligence Group), 124,
  130–3, 137–42, 164–5

COI (Co-Ordinator of Information),
  88–89, 104–5, 108
Colby, William, 203–5, 207
Congress of Vienna, 87
Corson, William, 163, 168, 198

Danischewski, Irene, 57
Darlan, Admiral Jean, 92–3, 97
Darling, Arthur, 7, 25
DCA (Defence Communications
  Agency), 173
Defence Reorganization Act (1958),
  170, 172–3, 189
Deighton, Len, 225, 237
DIA (Defence Intelligence Agency), 14,
  20, 158–201, 251
The 'Doctor', 54–6
Donovan, General William, 7, 16, 80,
  95, 99, 105, 108, 113, 115–16, 121,
  123–7
Driberg, Tom, 62
Dubosc, Juan, 35–9, 41
Dulles, Allen, 137–8, 160, 182–4, 198,
  208–9, 211–12, 216–17, 223, 239
Dulles, John Foster, 138, 209
Dunn, Jimmy, 54

Eberstadt, Ferdinard, 130, 135
Economic League, 144, 155
Eden, Anthony, 87, 99, 150
Eifler, Captain Carl, 103, 105–6, 109,
  118
Eisenhower, General, 91, 96
  President, 139, 171–2
El Alamein, Battle of, 97

FBI, 42–3, 50, 246
Fitzhugh Report, 159, 161
Fleming, Ian, 224–5, 227–9, 232, 238
Forrestal, James, 130, 135

Frankel, Rear Admiral Samuel, 187
Fuchs, Klaus, 147

Gangadharan, Mrs M. V., 68
Gates, Thomas, 173
Gaulle, General de, 85
Geyl, Pieter, 6, 24
Gilchrist, Sir Andrew, 114, 121
Giraud, General Henri, 89, 92, 95, 101
Goodfellow, Miles, 105
Gowen, Franklin, 57, 75
Graham, Major General Daniel, 161

Halifax, Lord, 57, 62, 71
Harvard University, 209, 212, 214
Helms, Richard, 213, 228
Hess, Rudolph, 54–5
Hillenkoetter, Roscoe C., 7
Hinsley, Sir Harry, 6, 8, 10
Hiss, Alger, 147
Hitler, Adolf, 85, 93, 97, 99
Hoover, Edgar, 43, 69, 187, 246
Houston, Larry, 133
Hull, Cordell, 51, 58, 64
Hunt, E. Howard, 21, 225, 227–9, 231, 238–9, 252
Hyatt, Clara, 64

Ignatius, David, 221, 234, 236, 238–9
Ilovaiskaya, Tatania Alexandrovna, 51, 65, 68–9
Inglis, Admiral Robert, 127

Janke, Kurt, 54
Johnson, Herschel, 53–7
Johnson, Colonel Louis, 109
Joint Chiefs of Staff, 89, 162, 164, 168, 169
Joint Intelligence Group, 168–70, 175, 179–80, 192
Jowitt, Viscount, 59, 76, 147
Joyce, William, 53, 60

Kennan, George, 4, 11, 23, 27
Kennedy, Joseph P., 53–4, 57, 58, 62–3, 65–7, 72, 74
Kent, Tyler, 15–16, 49–78, 248
Kent, William Paton, 50
King, Admiral Ernest, 106, 127
Kirkpatrick Jr, Lyman, 160, 172, 174–5, 197
Knight, Maxwell, 53, 56

Langer, Dr William, 3, 6, 10, 16, 23, 25, 27, 100, 119, 126
League of Nations, 81
Leahy, Admiral William, 95, 126
Le Carre, John, 221, 223, 225, 237–8
Liddell, Guy, 53, 55–6
Lindbergh, Charles A., 49
Littell, Robert, 232, 235–6, 238, 240
Long, Breckinridge, 55, 58, 65, 75

MacArthur, General Douglas, 103, 106, 119
McCarry, Charles, 230
McCarthy, Joseph, 144–7
McCone, John, 194, 211–12
Macfarlane, Ian Ross, 61–2
Mackie, Marjorie, 53
McNamara, Robert, 20, 159–60, 162, 164, 176–83, 185–99
Marchetti, Victor, 161, 226
Marks, John, 161
Marsalka, John, 68
Marshall, General, 83
May, Alan Nunn, 151
Metternich, Prince, 87
MI6, 91, 112
Miles, General Marion, 127
Military Intelligence Division (MID), 90
Miller, Joan, 53, 74
Molotov, Vyacheslav, 82
Montague, Ludwell Lee, 7, 25–6
Moore, Walton, 51
Mountbatten, Admiral Lord, 113, 117
Mosley, Sir Oswald, 56
Murphy, Robert D., 88, 92–4

National Intelligence Estimates, 164, 171, 175, 180–1, 194
National Security Act (1947), 135, 165, 168, 191
National Security Agency, 12, 14, 190, 231, 249
National Security Council, 174, 199
Newsam, Sir Frank, 64
Nicholson, Christabel, 56
Nixon, Richard, 161, 205, 213, 215

Office of Naval Intelligence, 10, 103, 106, 130, 245
OMPOS (Office for Management Planning and Organizational Studies), 177

OSD (Office of the Secretary of
 Defence), 159, 161, 164, 166,
 168–9, 173–4
OSO (Office of Special Operations), 169
OSS (Office of Strategic Services), 10,
 12, 14–17, 79, 88–140, 207, 247–8
 Research and Analysis Branch, 5, 90,
 122, 126
Owen, John Bryan, 62

Pearl Harbor, 10–11, 27, 76, 81, 104,
 164, 247
Penkovsky, Oleg, 171
Petain, Marshal Philippe, 92–3, 95–6
Phillips, Morgan, 154
Phillips, William, 107, 110, 113
Pike Committee, 159, 163, 198
Pipes, Richard, 213–15, 217
Polo, Luis y Bernabe, 34–5
Princeton University, 209, 212, 214

Quinn, Lt-Gen. William, 187

Raborn, Admiral William, 211–12
Ramsay, Archibald Maule, 52, 56, 59,
 61
Rascon, Count of, 38–9
Reagan, Ronald, 4, 122
Reorganisation Act (1958), 167–8, 170,
 189
Right Club, 52–3, 56–7
Roosevelt, Franklin D., 4, 15, 49–50,
 52, 54, 59, 61, 66–7, 72–3, 79–87,
 92, 96, 98–9, 107, 110, 123, 125
Ross, Charlie, 128, 130, 141

Sagasta, Praxedes, 40
Sledgehammer, Operation, 83–4
Slim, Sir William, 102, 120
Smith, Gerald, 63
SOE (Special Operations Executive),
 112, 114, 117
Solis, Pedro Arias y, 32
Souers, Admiral Sidney, 26, 124–5,
 127–42
State Department, 50, 110–11
Stilwell, General Joseph 102, 104–6
Stokes, Richard, 61, 64
Straker, Mrs, 69
Strong, General George, 127

Taylor, General Maxwell, 184–5
Torch, Operation, 16, 79–101
Torroja, Joaquin, 32, 35
Treaty of Versailles, 81
Troy, Thomas, F., 7, 99, 249
Truman, Harry, 123–42, 144, 150–1,
 164
Turner, Admiral Stansfield, 25, 210,
 214, 217

USIB (United States Intelligence
 Board), 171, 175, 179–83, 188, 194

Vandenburg, Hoyt S., 7, 134–5
Vansittart, Lord, 144–7, 156

Welles, Sumner, 52, 111
Wingo, Otis T., 61
Winks, Robin, 5, 13, 24
Wolkoff, Admiral Nikolai, 52
Wolkoff, Anna, 52–3, 56–7, 59–60, 71

Yale University, 208–9, 214, 217